D1824784

The ArtScroll Series®

Rabbi Nosson Scherman / Rabbi Meir Zlotowitz

General Editors

SHOAH

Published by

Mesorah Publications, ltd

In conjunction with

ARTSCROLL
Jerusalem, ltd.

SHOAH

A Jewish perspective on tragedy in the context of the Holocaust

By **Rabbi Yoel Schwartz**
and **Rabbi Yitzchak Goldstein**

Translated by Shlomo Fox-Ashrei

FIRST EDITION
First Impression . . . July, 1990

Published and Distributed by
MESORAH PUBLICATIONS, Ltd.
Brooklyn, New York 11232

Distributed in Israel by
MESORAH MAFITZIM / J. GROSSMAN
Rechov Harav Uziel 117
Jerusalem, Israel

Distributed in Europe by
J. LEHMANN HEBREW BOOKSELLERS
20 Cambridge Terrace
Gateshead, Tyne and Wear
England NE8 1RP

Distributed in Australia & New Zealand by
GOLD'S BOOK & GIFT CO.
36 William Street
Balaclava 3183, Vic., Australia

Distributed in South Africa by
KOLLEL BOOKSHOP
22 Muller Street
Yeoville 2198
Johannesburg, South Africa

THE ARTSCROLL SERIES®
SHOAH
© *Copyright 1990, by* MESORAH PUBLICATIONS, Ltd.
4401 Second Avenue / Brooklyn, N.Y. 11232 / (718) 921-9000

ALL RIGHTS RESERVED.

No part of this book may be reproduced
in any form *without* **written** *permission from the copyright holder,*
except by a reviewer who wishes to quote brief passages in connection with a review
written for inclusion in magazines or newspapers.

THE RIGHTS OF THE COPYRIGHT HOLDER WILL BE STRICTLY ENFORCED.

ISBN
0-89906-402-7 (hard cover)
0-89906-403-5 (paperback)

Typography by Compuscribe at ArtScroll Studios, Ltd.

Printed in the United States of America by Noble Book Press
Bound by Sefercraft, Quality Bookbinders, Ltd. Brooklyn, N.Y.

Publisher's Preface

It is not possible adequately to describe the trauma, the horror, the mystery of the Holocaust. "What has Hashem done to us?" Many great men have attempted to find its causes, to ascertain its lessons. Even more great men have bowed their heads in silent acceptance of a Divine judgment beyond their comprehension. One might well say that every tragedy; personal or communal, may seem equally incomprehensible to its victims. But isn't there an obligation on believers in Divine Providence, people who believe in the principle of reward and punishment, to delve into the meaning of events and attempt to discern their purpose? To at least learn how to accept misfortune?

The authors of this thoughtful, inspiring book said yes. Distinguished scholars and thinkers both, they delved into a very broad range of sources, from Talmudic to contemporary times. They read, sifted, contemplated, analyzed and compiled a work that has enlightened and comforted many thousands of people in its original Hebrew edition. And it has spurred readers to strive for understanding and elevation in their own lives, for although the title and primary subject of the book is the Shoah, it applies equally to all the myriad trials that bedevil people throughout life. It is our privilege, therefore, to present the public with this English edition, which has been translated with minor changes from the Hebrew.

We are grateful to the authors, Rabbi Yoel Schwartz and Rabbi Yitzchak Goldstein; to the translator, Shlomo Fox-Ashrei; to the editor, David Fohrman; and to Mrs. Shifra Slater, for their efforts in producing this book. On behalf of the authors we express gratitude to Rabbi David S. Ribner and Rabbi Moshe Solo for generously providing access to their Holocaust library. Mrs. Judi Dick read and commented on the manuscript, and Mrs. Faigie Weinbaum proofread, both with their customary diligence and skill.

It is our sincere hope that this book will help many people and that the Jewish people will merit the end of all holocaust and tragedy, speedily in our time.

Rabbi Meir Zlotowitz, Rabbi Nosson Scherman

ᵉᵍ Table of Contents

SHOAH

Introduction

Remember ancient days.
Understand the years of each generation.
(*Devarim* 32:7)

T IS OUR TRADITION to respond to the changes in our long history with introspection. After the expulsion of the Jews from Spain (1492), R' Yosef Ya'avetz wrote *Or HaChaim*, and R' Yehudah Ibn Virga wrote *Shevet Yehudah*. After the pogroms of *Tach v'Tat* (1648-9), R' Nosson Nota Hanover wrote *Yeven Metzulah*.

Our generation has suffered a terrible tragedy — the murder of a third of the Jewish people. Certainly nothing is more natural than to turn to our traditional response — looking again at ourselves, our deeds and misdeeds, our faith and our world.

Such a response is the theme of this work.

IT IS NOT EASY TO ANALYZE history on a Torah basis. This difficulty is expressed in the following passage from Responsa *Lev*

Analyzing *Avraham*, by R' Avraham Weinfeld (sec. 129):

History Our Torah is a Torah of life: it encompasses all the days of our life, from birth until our final moment, setting forth the *mitzvos* whereby one may attain life in this world and the next. All the positive commandments and prohibitions are explained and detailed in the Babylonian and Jerusalem Talmuds, the *Sifra*, *Sifrei*, *Mechilta*, and other Tannaitic and Amoraic works. These works are in turn illuminated by the commentaries of the *Geonim*, *Savoraim*, and *Rishonim*, whose opinions and rulings were codified in the *Shulchan Aruch* and its commentaries. These Codes are followed by the more recent sages, the Torah authorities whose words guide our lives today. In their teachings we find solutions to new questions that arise in our day-to-day life. Inferences are drawn from given principles and answers arrived at in accordance with the rules of halachic interpretation and decision-making.

Sometimes complicated questions arise for which it is difficult to find an explicit precedent in the Talmud and *Poskim*. It is in these cases that we must put our questions before the great Torah scholars of our time. In approaching the issue, these sages bring the full breadth and depth of their experience to bear, so that they may isolate an underlying principle in the Torah which matches the situation, and render a decision.

However, there are times when Hashem presents us with a reality which is difficult to judge solely in the light of clear-cut *halachah*. In searching the words of *Chazal* and *Rishonim* one cannot find precedents or principles which accurately match the given reality. [The difficulty results] because the purpose of *halachah* is to guide conduct: to teach what is forbidden and what is permitted, when a person is obligated to perform a certain action and when he is exempt. The solutions to problems outside this realm do not always have a clear halachic basis. In situations of this kind, only a true prophet could assess with certainty the exact nature of the reality, and what its outcome will be. Even the greatest Torah scholar, however, when faced with this type of problem, has only one course open to him: to fulfill the dictum of *Chazal* "Teach yourself to say, 'I don't know' " *(Derech Eretz Zuta,* ch. 3; *Berachos* 4a).

The word "teach" here is instructive, for to know one's limits requires much learning. The "I don't know" is the product of prolonged toil and study, weighing and balancing evidence and proofs, until one finally concludes that none of them can lead to a clear-cut halachic ruling. At this point, the ultimate knowledge is to know that one simply does not know.

Consider for example the recent events in Europe — the annihilation of six million of our fellow Jews: among them innocent children, as well as outstanding individuals of great saintliness. The great question persists: Why did Hashem do these things to His people? What brought about His wrath? We, who affirm the reality of Providence, try to find explanations in the Torah; but after all the answers have been proposed again and again, it remains crystal clear that none of our great Torah leaders can stand up and declare: 'I know the reason for this tragedy.' Indeed, all of us believe "He is righteous and just," and everything He did was fair and just. But, understand? — we cannot! We do not understand the ways of Hashem. His ways are hidden from us, for "My ways are not your ways, and My thoughts are not your thoughts." Knowledge of Divine rationale is beyond human grasp. Just as we cannot know His essence, so is it impossible to comprehend His ways. . .

Although a full understanding of the Divine scheme is beyond us, we may nonetheless learn much from studying the Holocaust. It is in this spirit that we approach an analysis of the Holocaust.

IN RECENT TIMES an effort has been made to understand the existence of the Jewish People on a purely secular basis.

Is "Shoah" the Right Word?

Paralleling this is an effort to see the remarkable chain of Jewish history, with its almost self-evident Divine roots, as if it were no more than the history of one of the ancient nations, in which religion is only one of many relevant aspects. These presumptions have also influenced some contemporary views of the Holocaust.

The Holocaust, it is claimed, was not a religious persecution per se; nor did Jews sacrifice themselves in the normal sense of *Kiddush Hashem*, i.e. in giving up one's life for one's faith. Here, secular Jews were persecuted by gentiles who did not act out of religious conviction. Nevertheless, as we shall see later (Chapter 6), the attempt to "secularize" the Holocaust is truly ill founded. On an inner level, the "secular" persecution of the Jew was directed most pointedly against his Jewishness, against the moral goodness which the Nazis perceived as symbolized by the Jew.

The *gaon*, R' Yitzchak Hutner זצ"ל, in a *mussar* talk said:

> Is the term *Shoah* acceptable? The answer is clearly that it is not. The word *Shoah* in Hebrew, like "Holocaust" in English, implies an isolated catastrophe, unrelated to anything before or after it, such as an earthquake or tidal wave. As we have seen, this approach is far from the Torah view of Jewish history. The *churban* of European Jewry is an integral part of our history and we dare not isolate and deprive it of the monumental significance it has for us. (*The Jewish Observer*, October 1977)

Without question, R' Hutner's point is valid. We use the term *Shoah* in this book only for the sake of convenience and brevity. Though the dimensions of this most recent destruction exceed all those that preceded it, both in the sheer number of Jews murdered and in the degree of sadism of the murderers, our use of the word "Holocaust" is not intended to disconnect this tragedy from the unity of Jewish history. On the contrary, we shall seek to highlight and emphasize the elements which the Holocaust shares with earlier catastrophes. The Holocaust is unique only in its magnitude; in essence it remains an integral part of our two thousand-year exile.

The Holocaust showed that the Jew cannot escape his Jewishness. Even those whose parents or grandparents had assimilated long ago were murdered for being Jewish. "That which you believe can never be. You say: 'We shall be like the nations . . .' But with a strong hand and with an outstretched arm and with wrath poured out shall I rule over you" (*Yechezkel* 20:32-33). Not only did assimilation fail to save the individual from the collective fate of the Jewish people, but it was assimilation itself that was a main cause of the ruthless anti-Semitism that led to the Holocaust.

The Holocaust was not a one-time occurrence in our history. It was the nadir of a long, frightful process of murder and persecution that has befallen us during our lengthy years of exile. The Holocaust befell a generation in which the majority of Jews denied the uniqueness of the Jewish People and its history. Perhaps it was for this reason that it was the Holocaust itself that demonstrated this uniqueness in the most searing manner.

How much longer will we close our eyes to the Divine voice that reveals itself to us through our history? Truly, we cannot spell out the reasons why these terrible sufferings were decreed upon Hashem's people, for the ways of Hashem are hidden from humankind. But one simply cannot deny the basic fact that Hashem did indeed afflict us. To view Jewish history as a chain of chance occurrences is untenable; it flies in the face of rational historic interpretation. Is it mere coincidence that only the Jewish People has been persecuted so unceasingly, and nonetheless has outlived all the peoples that have persecuted it?

The Holocaust has once again placed before us — the next generation — an ancient challenge: to be Jews. Our evasive pretension that we are better than the previous generation — that a Holocaust of this nature could not have happened to us, God forbid, is pointless. We are not qualitatively different from the six million; we as well share their fate. We are one people, and thus, the challenge remains ours.

1

Contemplating History – Facing Tragedy

Remember ancient days.
Understand the years of each generation.
(*Devarim* 32:7)

I have cut off nations, their towers are desolated.
I have destroyed their streets, so that none pass by.
Their cities lie deserted, without inhabitants,
with none to settle them.
I said: Only fear Me; accept My rebuke.
(*Tzephaniah* 3:6-7)

*R*AMBAM WRITES:
It is a positive *mitzvah* of the Torah to cry out and to sound the trumpets upon any disaster that befalls a community, as it is written: "Because of the enemy that besieges you, you shall sound the trumpets" (*Bamidbar* 10:9). This refers to anything that oppresses you: drought, pestilence, locusts,

and other natural disasters — upon all these, you must cry out and sound the trumpets. This response to tragedy is one of the steps to repentance (teshuvah), for when [the people] cry out, they come to understand that it is their misdeeds that have brought the tragedy upon them, as it is written: "Your sins have caused these [evils], and your misdeeds prevented the good from reaching you" (Yirmiyahu 5:25). After internalizing this [realization] the people may set about to correct their wrong ways.

But when a community does not cry out and does not sound the trumpets, but rather feels: "This thing that has befallen us is in the natural way of the world; this trouble is only a chance occurrence," they act cruelly and become more attached to their evil deeds. Thus, the tragedy will bring more tragedies. Hence, the Torah writes: "If you walk with Me haphazardly, so shall I walk with you, wrathfully and haphazardly" (Vayikra 26:27-28). That is: When I bring trouble upon you so that you may search your deeds, if you instead ascribe its cause to chance, I shall put upon you the full wrath of that "chance" (Hilchos Taanios 1:1-3).

The Torah commands us to contemplate the troubles that befall our nation and through them, to be brought to teshuvah, for "this response is one of the steps to teshuvah." If this command to search our ways mandates our response to disasters such as drought or locusts, then undoubtedly it must dictate our reaction to the recent annihilation of a third of the Jewish People.

This mitzvah of contemplation is a fundamental one; it would seem that it is not only one of the 613 commandments but a foundation of them all. Indeed, one of Rambam's Thirteen Principles of Faith is:

He, Exalted is He, knows the deeds of men and is not indifferent to them, in contrast to those who say that Hashem created, and then abandoned the world, leaving it to function solely by its own natural laws. Rather, as it is written (Yirmiyahu 32:19): "Hashem is great in thought and masterful in action; He sees all the ways of mankind" (Rambam, Perush HaMishnayos, Introduction to Perek Chelek, thirteenth principle).

Rambam teaches that Hashem not only knows our deeds, but is intimately involved in our affairs as well: "He, exalted is He, rewards those who fulfill the Torah, and punishes those who violate it" (ibid., eleventh principle). Contemplating the events that happen to us, whether happy or otherwise, means contemplating the way Hashem involves Himself (*hashgachah*) in the world, and this strengthens our faith in Him.

Internalizing Knowledge

THE SAGES TEACH that in matters of faith, abstract knowledge alone is not enough. It is insufficient to acquire intellectual awareness which is divorced from practical life and feeling. Rather, one must breathe faith into everyday life, fulfilling the verse: "The *tzaddik* lives by his faith" (*Chabbakuk* 2:4). The Torah writes: "You shall know today *and put it into your heart* that Hashem is God in the heavens above and on the earth beneath; there is no other" (*Devarim* 4:39). It is not enough to "know today." One must also "put it into your heart" — one's intellectual knowledge must influence one's emotions as well. Likewise, it is not enough to know that Hashem is God "in the heavens above," and in *that* realm "there is no other." One must internalize that Hashem is God "on the earth beneath" too. Even in our everyday lives there is no other besides Him, for He alone controls all His creations and causes every event.

It is all too easy to ignore the significance of events which happen around us. Often, we fail to stop to think how Hashem's supervision of His creation finds practical expression in the world around us. This complacency, however, drains the lifeblood of faith and pushes belief into a neglected corner, as if it were set apart from practical life. What results is not only a misguided approach to a particular *mitzvah*, it is a weakness in faith itself. "A person has no part in the Torah of Moshe Rabbeinu until he believes that all our affairs and occurrences are miracles, and nothing happens through the natural way of the world" (*Ramban*, end of *Parashas Bo*). *Ramban* does not speak simply of "affairs and occurrences," but of "all our affairs and occurrences" — the events that make up our concrete, personal experience.

Certainly, Divine Providence is not obvious on a superficial level. One must work a lifetime before he merits to become intimately aware of it. But even if it is difficult to perceive every detail of the Divine plan, one may at least contemplate the major principles of *hashgachah* — the significance of great historical events and their overall trends. In this way he can achieve at least a general, albeit superficial, comprehension of the workings of *hashgachah*.

As *Ramban* points out, even the neutral, seemingly meaningless events of life must not be viewed as part of a "natural" chain of events; we must sanctify them by perceiving their Divine significance. How much more so then, does this apply to the events of the Holocaust. If one ignores this terrible outburst of evil in the world, he relegates it to the category of a natural, secular event; untouched by the hand of God. After all (*Eichah* 3:38), "From the mouth of the Supreme One, the evils and the good do not come forth," but only the good. "Everything the Merciful One does, He does for the good" (*Berachos* 60b). If one neglects to contemplate how even the seemingly evil in life is ultimately directed towards good, he leaves it, as it were, as an independent force that is not under Divine control, God forbid.

We thus have a special obligation to seek out the righteousness of a harsh decree, to try to discover something of the Divine meaning of evil occurrences. "A person is obligated to recite a blessing for the bad just as he recites a blessing for the good" (*Berachos* 54a). According to a number of the authorities who list the 613 *mitzvos,* one of them is:

> To seek out the righteousness of a harsh decree when tragedy occurs, whether it affects one's body, children, or property, as it is said: "You shall know with your heart that just as a man punishes his son, so Hashem your God punishes you" (*Devarim* 8:5). One must fix this in his heart, bow his head and remain silent, as it is written: "And Aharon remained silent" (*Vayikra* 10:3). One should not consider oneself more righteous than God. Nor should one say, "this happened by chance," for then Hashem will act towards him with "wrathful chance" (*Vayikra* 26:28). Rather, let him search his deeds

and return in *teshuvah* (repentance). This is an essential part of the *mitzvah*: "You shall love Hashem" (*Devarim* 6:5), for it is written, "with all your strength." — *Chazal* interpret this to mean (*Berachos, loc. cit.*): "with every measure that He measures out to you, whether good [things] or suffering" (*Sefer Charedim, Minyan Hamitzvos* 1:31).

An especially great obligation rests upon us to contemplate the Divine decree of the Holocaust, for there is no greater desecration of Hashem's Name (*chillul Hashem*) than to ignore its significance. The author remembers an incident in which he and a group of students from Yeshivas D'var Yerushalayim went to visit a non-religious kibbutz of the Shomer Hatza'ir movement. During our tour of the kibbutz school, we noticed that the teachers used the Holocaust to undermine faith and to reinforce anti-religious viewpoints. Questions and doubts of this sort generally stem from ignorance, but this in no way lessens our responsibility to correct false ideas and to help bring Jews closer to Hashem. The *chillul Hashem* is not limited only to those who have never been exposed to Torah values. Many observant Jews are confused about the topic also. Clearly then, we are obligated to deal with the Holocaust and grapple with its implications.

R' Tzvi Markovitch, *shlita,* writes:

> In the world-space of every Jew are suspended serious questions which accumulated during the "time of rebuke." What we went through during the period of the Holocaust strikes at our basic outlook on life. It shakes sanctified values and spiritual holdings which had seemed unassailable. Mighty world personalities were shaken and new questions arose — terrible, bleeding problems which force every Jew, and the Jewish nation as a whole, to re-examine our ways in life and our place in the world.
>
> And these severe problems demand solutions. They demand them with utmost urgency. They cry out to us with a basic, primal call, terrible and frightening. The solutions are shrouded in mystery like the secrets of Creation. Infinite chasms split open at our feet, with no spark of light to illuminate their void. Our fate has stunned us, placing us suddenly in front of a sealed wall. And to this day we have yet

to see the effort made to study and understand these events. Books that appear on the Holocaust give us merely the *narrative*, the events themselves. It is true, of course, that in this, they perform a great service: They allow us all to drink from the bitter cup of sorrow. The lamentation is taken up throughout the world, it reaches the far corners of the earth, alarms and shocks every far-off person, everyone with a trace of a Jewish heart and spark of a Jewish soul. Perhaps a weak echo even reaches those errant sons who contaminate their souls and cultivate alien vineyards. But, nonetheless, we have a fundamental obligation to attempt to understand the meaning of this terrible Holocaust . . .

In everything that happened, the feeling is one of confusion; a palpable perplexity which finds obvious expression. What has happened to us, that we have joined together in a conspiracy of silence? Why do we ignore and evade the study of this subject? After all, the problems weigh upon us like heavy mountains; the unanswered questions of our time secretly drain the vitality of our hearts. Great danger lurks here: a vacuum could be formed, God forbid, in the recesses of our personality, a conceptual and spiritual vacuum. Who knows what might fill it — what might develop from these abysmal problems if our spirits and hearts do not muster the enlightenment to absorb them? Why, then, have we formed a conspiracy of silence, evading discussion and thought?

Perhaps there is only one explanation: We are afraid. The tragedy is too enormous for man's feelings and powers of expression. It exceeds human comprehension, and its causes lie beyond the periphery of our understanding (*Binesivos Ha'emunah*, pp. 130, 132).

OUR OBLIGATION TO FACE the event of the Holocaust squarely derives from another source as well: "Remember what Amalek did

A Modern Amalek to you" (*Devarim* 25:17).

Some say that any nation which tries to annihilate the Jewish People represents Amalek. *Yalkut Me'am Lo'ez* (*Devarim*, part 3, p. 977) writes: " 'In every generation they rise up against us to destroy us' (*Pesach Haggadah*) — this refers to Amalek, who each time is embodied in a different nation." This explains why we are commanded to perpetuate our enmity only towards Amalek, and not towards other enemies of the Jewish People. For all other enemies are included in this *mitzvah*. This same idea is reiterated by the *gaon* R' Moshe Soleveitchik, the son of R' Chaim of Brisk, who infers from the wording of *Rambam* that according to Torah law anyone who plots to destroy the Jewish People is included in Amalek.[1]

The Gaon of Vilna (*HaGra*) is said to have considered the Germans in particular to be a nation with the possible status of Amalek (*safek Amalekim*). It is told of R' Yosef Chaim Sonnenfeld, that for this reason he avoided taking part in the official reception for the Kaiser when the German leader visited Jerusalem in 1899 (*Mara De'Ara De'Yisrael*, part 1, p. 200).

But, even if we may have reservations about categorizing the Germans as Amalekites in a *halachic* sense, their actions have epitomized evil in our generation. As such, we remain morally obliged to remember these deeds.

Sefer Hachinuch (mitzvah 603) states:

> One of the roots of this *mitzvah* (to remember the deeds of Amalek) is to impress upon our hearts that those who attack Israel are hated by the Holy One, Blessed is He. And the greater their evil and their damage, the greater will be their downfall and the evil of their punishment, as we find in the case of Amalek. Because they did great evil to Israel, being the first to harm them, Hashem, Blessed is He, commanded us to destroy their memory from the earth and to uproot their every trace.

In his analysis of the *mitzvah*, *Sefer Hachinuch* emphasizes the memory of the iniquity of Amalek. Others stress the weakness in Israel that led to the success of Amalek. *Sefer Charedim (Mitzvos Lo Sa'aseh Hateluyos Be'eretz Yisrael*, ch. 2) writes that the *mitzvah* is to remember that Amalek attacked because Israel was negligent in observing the Torah. Kabbalistic and chassidic works emphasize this point more sharply, saying that the *mitzvah* is to

---

1. (See *Ish Ha'emunah*, pp. 101-2. The inference is from *Hilchos Melachim* 5:5, where *Rambam* does not say of Amalek that "their memory has already been eradicated," as he writes in the previous *halachah* concerning the Seven Canaanite Nations.)

remember the Amalek that dwells within each one of us, and causes the external Amalek to appear.

All these interpretations apply to the study of the Holocaust as well. It is a *mitzvah* to remember the deeds of every enemy of Israel, and to impress upon our hearts that those enemies are hated by the Holy One, Blessed is He. Likewise, it is a *mitzvah* to think about our wrongdoings which lead to the success of the modern Amalek, and to wage war against the Amalek within ourselves. One cannot honestly perform this *mitzvah* in our day without contemplating the Holocaust.

2
Historical Analysis: A Jewish Approach

Remember ancient days.
Understand the years of each generation.
(*Devarim* 32:7)

It is impossible to write history
without prophetic power (*nevuah*)
or Divine inspiration (*ruach hakodesh*).
(Attributed to the *Chazon Ish*
in *Pe'er Hador*, part 3, p. 118, note)

ASHEM IS KNOWN in His world in two different ways: through nature and through history. In each, His presence is both revealed and concealed.

Seen from one angle, the laws of nature hide the Divine will embodied in creation. "He commanded and they were created,

Revelation in History and He established them forever and ever. He issued a decree that will not change" (*Tehillim* 148:5-6). It appears as if the only arrangement was "He commanded and they were created": A fixed natural order was established and can nevermore be violated; nature has an independent existence, cut off from the Divine command. But this is not true. We find in the blessing preceding the *Shema*: "In His goodness He constantly renews every day the work of Creation, as it is written (*Tehillim* 136:7), 'He makes great lights.' " "You made the heavens, the heavens of the heavens, and all their hosts, the earth and everything on it, the seas and everything in them, *and You animate all of them*" (*Nechemiah* 9:6). You made and *You keep alive*. The will of the Creator continues to vitalize the entire Creation as it daily renews the work of Creation. The statement "He issued a decree that will not change" does not indicate a natural order independent of the Creator, but the ongoing will of the God of the world, the Life of the universe.

The fixed laws of nature conceal the Divine; but more than nature conceals, it reveals. The unity of creation, the precise harmony among its disparate parts, its exalted beauty and the incomprehensible wisdom reflected therein — all proclaim the glory of God. "The heavens tell the splendor of God, and the sky proclaims the work of His hands" (*Tehillim* 19:2). All the created beings sing the praises of the King of the world, and thus, contemplating nature and its laws is "the readiest way to confirm the existence [of the Creator], and a well-paved road to knowing His truthfulness" (*Chovos Halevavos, Shaar Habechinah*).

The presence of Divine will within history — in the deeds and happenings of man — is more obvious than it is within nature, yet at the same time is more veiled. History does not follow fixed laws, at least none that are apparent to the observer. Paradoxically, Divine Providence over mankind operates through the principle of free will: Man is free to choose good or evil, and this choice is an entirely unfettered one. Yet, nonetheless, in history we find direct Divine conduct of the world, following no regular pattern, and undisguised by a veil of natural law. The Divine will is renewed every day — not a constant renewal of the same fixed order of Creation, but a new creation each day. "We must believe that all our affairs and occurrences are miracles. None of them are the natural way of the world" (*Ramban, Perush HaTorah*, end of *Parashas Bo*).

HASHEM CREATED THE universe in such a way that every force is counterbalanced by another. For every moment that we glimpse

Approaching the Enigma

Hashem's hand, there is a corresponding concealment of Divine Providence. The greater the revelation, the more subtle it in fact appears, and thus, the greater the concealment. If history is not governed by regular laws, the Divine influence is enveloped in the mask of randomness, of blind chance and coincidental combinations of circumstances. It is true that historical events are determined by man's free choice, but the connection between his choices and the events is not always apparent. A righteous person suffers a painful fate, and a wicked person enjoys prosperity. Providence hides Itself behind a veil of economic, social and political "laws" which seem to govern human events, just as natural laws govern physical occurrences. Corresponding to the revelation inherent in history, then, exists even greater concealment, simultaneously involving both fixed law and blind chance.

How is man to approach the puzzle?

Essentially, he must segregate. Man's work is to salvage the precious from the dross, to find the sparks which reveal the light of Hashem's hidden presence. Man must draw inferences from the obvious to the hidden; from the times when Hashem's face is revealed we must extrapolate to the times when His presence is concealed. "By means of the great and famous miracles, man comes to give thanks for the hidden miracles, which are the foundation of the entire Torah" (Ramban, loc. cit.).

By the very fact of his mortality, man cannot achieve complete understanding of history nor complete understanding of its significance. All the same, he has not only the right, but the obligation to contemplate the ways of Divine Providence (hashgachah), to try to give Divine significance to seemingly chance events. Such is man's task in life. As we established earlier, we cannot, nor are we required to, interpret events to perfection, but we must nonetheless endeavor to learn from the events we experience, and we cannot excuse ourselves with the claim that this is beyond our capability.

The task is not easy. If it is difficult to comprehend that which we personally experience, it is nearly impossible to grasp the full significance of events that we have only heard or read about. One can never be quite sure what is fact and what is simply the product of imagination. The *Chazon Ish* writes:

> Studying history greatly aids the development of the sage: He firmly anchors his wisdom on knowledge of the past. However, since men are fond of being original and of telling the public things they have not yet heard, history books accumulate many falsehoods. Indeed, people by nature do not hate inaccuracy; many love and court it. Hence the sage must carefully sift through the stories he reads, accepting truth and discarding falsehoods (*Emunah Uvitachon* 1:8).

Even if we could know clearly the truth of what actually transpired, accurate historical interpretation is still difficult. We have no clear way to gauge the relative weight of events, to understand what was central and what was marginal, what were causes and what were merely effects. Historical research is not an exact science, and provides us only with speculations, some more reasonable than others; but there is no way to be completely sure that these estimates are correct.

Hence, if it is difficult to analyze physical events, how much more difficult is it to understand the spiritual causes which lie at the core of history. Consider the deeds related in the books of *Yehoshua, Shoftim, Shmuel,* and *Melachim*. Undoubtedly if it were up to us to relate the history of these periods, our analysis could never penetrate to the chain of spiritual cause and effect spelled out in these writings. Who could determine the specific moral failings which caused a given war or famine? Even now, with the prophetic works in our hands, historians still doubt the reality of spiritual causes, and try to find various natural causes for the events related in *Tanach*. The sins described in *Tanach* were not apparent to everyone; only true prophets perceived them. The masses of these generations believed they were faithfully observing the Torah, as Yeshayahu states:

> They seek Me day by day, and they desire knowledge of My ways, like a nation that has done righteousness and has not

abandoned its God. They ask for righteous judgments, they desire closeness to God. "Why have we fasted and You did not see, afflicted our souls and You do not know?" (*Yeshayahu* 58:2-3).

The spiritual significance of men's deeds lies hidden, often imperceptible to the human eye:

> There are single merits that outweigh a number of sins, as it is said, ". . .because a good thing was found in him" (*I Melachim* 14:13), and there are single sins that outweigh a number of merits, as it is said, "Sinning once, destroys much good" (*Koheles* 9:18). These can only be weighed by the judgment of God Who understands all souls. It is He Who knows how the merits are weighed against the sins (*Rambam, Hilchos Teshuvah* 3:2).

The *gaon* R' Eliahu Dessler writes:

> *Megillas Esther* is the record of events that took place during a period of nine years, from the third to the twelfth year of Achashverosh's reign. Neither we nor greater men than ourselves would have perceived that all these happenings form one unified story. Only Mordechai, aided by his level of Divine inspiration (*ruach hakodesh*) — for not all levels of *ruach hakodesh* are equal — knew that all these happenings were integrally connected (*Michtav Me'Eliyahu*, part 1, p. 76).

Understanding History — the Tools

EVIDENTLY, IF THE BURDEN of interpretation rested solely upon us, understanding history would be impossible. But we do not have to rely on our unaided intelligence. The Torah gives us guidance for every problem, and by studying it and the words of Torah sages, we can acquire more accurate viewpoints upon past and current events.

R' Yitzchak Hutner writes:

> . . . Since Israel and the Torah are one, it follows that just as one can teach Torah in a halachically unacceptable way, so can one teach history in a halachically unacceptable way.

Everyone who learns *Gemara* knows the difference between studying a tractate which *Rashi* commented on, and studying one of those tractates that have no *Rashi*. Without *Rashi* we are like blind men walking through a marketplace: guaranteed to stumble and sure to fall. Imagine then, how one can even begin to speak about Jewish history, in which every period is like a complex and entangled *Gemara* passage . . . all this without any "commentary of *Rashi*"! How great is the danger, how many the pitfalls! We have already stated that to misrepresent a period of Jewish history is tantamount to presenting an interpretation of part of the Torah in a way which is contradictory to *halachah*. Israel and the Torah are one.

It is for this reason that the yeshivah world has generally refrained from the study of history; in a similar way, it has refrained from the study of the Jerusalem Talmud, since without the commentaries of the *Rishonim* we are at a loss. And it is not because of indifference to history as the *Maskilim* have said about the Yeshivah world; it is precisely because of our great respect for Jewish history that we have avoided delving into it, for we fear error. One can readily see the many writings which give false impressions, deliberately or unintentionally, in this field.

But this principle, that Israel and the Torah are one, is a two-sided coin. One of the aspects has already been mentioned: the responsibility of teaching Jewish history. Another side, though, also exists: All who are intimately familiar with Torah and who sit permanently under its tents acquire thereby a special facility for understanding the history of the Jewish nation. This is true even if they do not enter into analytical discussions of historical events, and are not expert in the precise details of historical periods. All the same, the soul and spirit of the nation's history lives in their heart and illumines their inner being. There is a special sense which Torah scholars develop for sensing the life-pulse of the nation. (*Pachad Yitzchak* — Letters and Writings, pp. 162-3)

R' Hutner directs us to listen to the Torah sages. From another angle, the *gaon* R' Elchanan Wasserman writes of contemplating the Torah itself:

Since "His judgments are in the whole world" (*Tehillim* 105:7), and the judgments of Hashem follow the laws of the Torah, therefore, just as one must deeply understand the words of the Torah, so too must one contemplate world events. One must find their basis according to the judgments of the Torah.

However, one must not rely on his own understanding, for human reasoning cannot grasp the intentions of Hashem. Rather, one must listen to the received tradition of the Oral Torah. Thus, the verse [states,] "Ask your father and he will tell you; your elders, and they will say to you." (History) is like the stories recorded in the *Tanach*, whose significance cannot possibly be understood from the verses alone, but only with the help of *Chazal*'s explanations.

In order to decipher history, the Torah gives us a powerful key to understand the pivot around which the Divine conduct of the world revolves. This is referred to in the next verses: "When the Supreme One apportioned inheritances to the nations, when He separated the sons of man, He established the borders of the peoples according to the number of the Children of Israel. For His people is the portion of Hashem, Yaakov is the share of His inheritance." The meaning of this is as follows: It is evident that all beings were created to do the will of their Creator. Of all existing creatures, the central species is the human race; and within the human race, the central people is Israel, who are the portion of Hashem and are His servants. . . Thus the ultimate goal of all Creation is for Israel alone. . . Hence, all that occurs in the world is primarily for the sake of Israel: "I have cut off nations, their towers are desolated. I have destroyed their streets. . . I said: 'Just fear Me, learn the lesson'" (*Tzefaniah* 3:6-7). This teaches us that punishment comes upon the world only for the sake of Israel (*Yevamos* 61).

For example, let us take the national boundaries recently agreed upon after the last war. One must understand that before they were drawn up at Versailles, they had already been written and sealed by the Heavenly Court. The ramifications are intended only for the sake of Israel, either for its benefit or its punishment and chastisement, as it is written

(*Yeshayahu* 10:5), "Alas, Ashur, the rod of My wrath" (*Kovetz Maamarim*, pp. 81-82).

One might add parenthetically that this last paragraph is itself a cogent example of the concept R' Wasserman seeks to express. Here stands a Jew — in all respects, quite distant from worldly life — who declares as if it were a matter of obvious fact that the Treaty of Versailles, the peace treaty drawn up at the end of the First World War, was in the scheme of things intended mainly to affect Israel. At first sight, nothing could be more absurd. What connection could there be between the fate of the Jewish People and the reparations imposed upon Germany, or the redrawn borders of Austria and Hungary? Undoubtedly, every seemingly "enlightened" person who read these words of R' Wasserman at the time of their writing must have thought that they were the product of ivory tower naivete. But history itself has ripped to shreds the sophistication of alternate explanations. Today no reputable historian would deny that the onset of the Second World War — and by extension, the demise of European Jewry — had its roots in the Treaty of Versailles and the humiliation which that treaty imposed upon Germany. Even a cursory glance at the subsequent chain of events will reveal the life-and-death significance of these boundaries for Jews who later fled the sword. Indeed, one who immerses himself in Torah, though he is worlds away from the delicate calculations of politics, is included in those who "know the will of the Supreme One." "Delve into [the Torah] again and again, for everything is in it" (*Avos* 5:26).

We must emphasize again, that to completely understand the significance of the historical mosaic is not possible at all, even through Torah study and listening to the words of the sages. Such global comprehension is altogether beyond human capability. Even Moshe Rabbeinu asked Hashem as a special act of kindness: "Please let me know Your ways" (*Shemos* 33:13), meaning, as the *Gemara* in *Berachos* interprets it, "Why do righteous men sometimes suffer and the wicked enjoy a good life?" Indeed, the *Tannaim* (*Berachos* 7a) disagree about whether this secret was ever revealed to him. As we approach history from a Torah perspective, we must from the onset discard any thought of knowing that which is ultimately beyond human understanding.

Analyzing the Holocaust — the Difficulty

IN ADDITION TO THE difficulties inherent in the study of Jewish history in general, one encounters additional obstacles in seeking to approach the Holocaust. Let us explore them:

Lack of historical perspective: The staggering destruction of European Jewry is still too historically close for us to objectively analyze it. One does not comfort a mourner before his loved one is buried, nor does one soothe an antagonist while his pain still burns. Just as one who wishes to grasp a work of art must stand at a distance to see it as a whole, so too is it impossible to comprehend a historical process of magnitude until a number of generations have passed.

Lack of guidance: The destruction also touched the world of Torah scholarship: Although by amazing miracles, a number of Torah sages were saved and founded new centers of learning in Israel and in America, the fact remains that the majority of the greatest scholars and their students were murdered along with their communities. The destruction that befell the Jewish People also befell the Torah, and the Jewish People have as yet still not recovered from their loss. It is thus all the more difficult in our days to turn to the Torah and its sages for guidance.

Hester panim — The concealment of Divine Providence: It is clear that the period of the Holocaust was one of terrible *hester panim*. The Divine conduct of the world was *intentionally* hidden. Even as we view the Holocaust in retrospect, the veil remains firmly in place. Attempts to discover, even partially, the spiritual significance of the events of the Holocaust involve the annulment of this concealment — and this is not possible.

R' Elimelech Bar Shaul writes:

> When we read the Passages of Rebuke (*Tochachos*), we see a central theme: "I shall abandon them and I shall hide My face from them, and they shall be left to be devoured. Many evils and troubles will come upon them, and they shall say in

that day, 'Behold, it is because my God is not within me that these evils have come upon me.' But I shall certainly hide My face on that day" (*Devarim* 31:17-18). *Hester panim*, the concealing of Divine Providence, must be understood not only as a cause of punishment, but, more primarily, as an integral part of the punishment itself. The "many evils and troubles" are physical afflictions and the *hester panim* at their core is the essential spiritual affliction. The soul is tormented as it stands confronting a bewildering void, wanting to understand: "What is the purpose of these travails? Why and to what end was the suffering poured out precisely at this time, precisely in these dimensions? Where is God's attribute of *erech apayim*, "slow to anger?" Where has His lovingkindness and mercy gone to?"

This is not mere concealment, but something more: "I shall certainly hide. . ." — a double hiding, concealment within concealment. Closed and sealed, buried and invisible within it, the very existence of the veil is invisible. It is said in the name of the Baal Shem Tov: "When you see a wall in front of you, you suppose that it is concealing something; but when you don't see the barrier, it doesn't even occur to you that there is anything hidden at all." During the actual tribulation, the physical torments are perhaps greater, but when the storm dies down, the spiritual pain is undoubtedly greater; it is the torment of a mystery which none can solve, and to which the aching heart is unwilling to accept any solution. . . This situation did not merely accompany the Holocaust; it is of the essence of the Holocaust (*Maarechei Lev*, part 2, pp. 211-12).

It would seem that these and similar obstacles are what stood in the way of the leading sages of the last generation, who did not make the Holocaust a pivotal point of their ethical teachings, and referred to it only infrequently and in the presence of their closest associates. Their muted response came not from narrow-mindedness or indifference to the tragedy, but from objective difficulties which the Torah leaders approached warily. Sometimes the only correct reaction is that laid forth in the verse, "And Aharon was silent" (*Vayikra* 10:3) — to accept suffering with silence; with the knowledge and faith that all is for our good though we as mortals cannot truly understand. Previous generations, too, followed this course after the calamitous expulsion from Spain, and the massacres of *Tach v'Tat* 5408-9 (1648-49).

Still, to achieve the silence of "Aharon was silent," is a difficult task. Also, it should be clear to ourselves and to others that this silence does not express weakness of faith, but an acceptance of suffering with love. To clarify all this we are obliged to study the Holocaust. It is a bitter obligation; painful to heart and soul. But the honor of heaven demands it, and we can not shirk it.

IN THE PAGES that follow, our approach to the Holocaust is based unapologetically upon a foundation of trust in Hashem. We

Historical Investigation — an Objective Pursuit?

shall attempt to understand those aspects of history which can be grasped, while we shall leave other areas with a question mark, and admit our limitations as human beings.

There will be those, of course, who will object that a religious approach lacks the objectivity demanded of historical investigation. This assertion stems from a misunderstanding of the methodology of historical research. In truth there is not and cannot be such a thing as a truly objective historical investigation. One must of course be objective regarding the facts themselves, not twisting them to fit one's prejudices or leaving out those which one finds inconvenient. But when it comes to interpreting events, ordering and piecing them together to form an integral whole — this process depends essentially upon the world view of the historian. Every historical study is stamped with the distinctive mark of its author.

If the study of history implies the holding of a prior world view, then it is the historian whose world view is rooted in belief in God who conducts the most objective study of all. Like all historians, he makes assumptions; yet his assumptions are not based upon the vicissitudes of personal opinion, but were revealed by the Creator of the world, Who Himself directs history. Faith in Hashem and His Torah is not founded upon the events of the Holocaust and thus cannot be annulled by them either.

Faith in God is an issue which all historians must come to grips with, whether they reject the concept or accept it. The issue is so basic that it cannot be ignored; it is impossible to remain neutral. One can regard events as being caused by chance, or one can see them as having meaning, whether revealed to or hidden from us. There is no other option. The difference between these two outlooks is so significant that it is impossible to skirt the issue; one simply must decide. One who writes history and ignores the issue of Providence, despite his protests to the contrary, in essence has decided against it.

Hence, while other studies pride themselves on their supposed objectivity, this work openly declares the *a priori* axioms upon which it is based. It is objective, in the sense that it does not seek to imaginatively reconstruct history or forge facts; but the viewpoint of the study is determined from the outset: I believe with complete faith that the Creator, Blessed is He, created and guides all beings; that He alone caused, causes, and will cause every event. I believe that He knows the deeds of men and all their thoughts; and that He rewards those who keep, and punishes those who violate His *mitzvos*. Our approach will be in keeping with these axioms.

In the chapters that follow, we will not simply list the events of the Holocaust, but we shall attempt to understand the moral lessons implicit within them. We shall seek the revelation of Hashem's hand, and attempt to come to grips with *tzidduk hadin*, the reconciliation of Hashem's acts in connection with this awesome national tragedy.

3

The Rock of Justice

The Creator, His actions are perfect,
for all His ways are judgment.
He is a God of faith, and there is no injustice;
righteous and straight is He. (*Devarim* 32:4)

[Your] eyes are too pure to see evil,
You cannot look upon injustice.
Why do You gaze upon traitors,
why are You silent while the wicked one
swallows up one more righteous than him?
And You have made man like the fish of the sea,
like the crawling creatures over which no one rules.
All are caught up in the net. (*Chabbakuk* 1:13-15)

On the contrary, this is the way it should be, that one has
difficulty understanding Hashem, Blessed is He. This is fitting
and proper for Him; it is in accord with His greatness and
exaltedness. From the very fact of His greatness — that He is
exalted far above our minds — it certainly follows that it is
impossible for us to understand or grasp how Hashem, Blessed
is He, conducts the world. Therefore it is inevitable that we
should be puzzled by Him. If His conduct followed the rules of
our intelligence, then His mind would be like our mind.
(Reb Nachman of Breslav, *Likutei Moharan Tinyana*, § 62)

A.

On the Suffering of the Righteous

THE QUESTION IS not new. It is as ancient as man himself, and is destined to accompany him to the twilight of history. It is one of the eternal questions, rooted in the very existence of mankind. It applies not to a particular nation or society, nor is it connected with any one faith.

Why Do the Righteous Suffer? The question has been asked in every place and age — and the gates to the answer have been sealed.

> It is something which pains the heart and troubles the mind. From it alone many throughout the generations have been drawn to completely reject belief. It is the fact that we see in the world crooked judgment, the righteous suffering while the wicked enjoy a good life. People say: "Why do these men succeed in their ways, while that one and that one, who appear to be righteous, are destroyed?" This is the root of rebellion within every nation and tongue (*Ramban*, Introduction to Commentary on *Iyov*).

In addition to many chapters and verses scattered throughout *Tanach* (e.g., *Tehillim* ch. 73, *Chabbakuk* chs. 1 and 2), the entire Book of *Iyov* is devoted to clarifying this issue. *Iyov* is a complex book, and it is difficult to understand the answer it intends to convey. In its simplest sense, however, its conclusion is that man cannot fathom the depths of Divine justice. After all of Iyov's discussions and dialogues, Hashem appears from the whirlwind and asks him: "Where were you when I founded the world? Say, if you grasp understanding" (*Iyov* 38:4). Iyov finally concludes: "I spoke, but I do not understand; the things are hidden from me, and I do not know" (ibid. 42:3).

Superficially, it would seem that the reply only evades the question, for it freely admits that there is no solution. But in truth the reply tells us something else: that the question of why the righteous suffer itself is not tenable. Just as in mathematics one of the set of possible solutions is always that no solution exists, so too it is here. The solution cannot be found — not because we avoid answering nor because of our ignorance, but simply because one cannot give a human answer to a Divine question. As R' Nachman said in the passage quoted above,

> By the very fact of His greatness — that He is exalted far above our minds, it certainly follows that it is impossible for us to understand or grasp how Hashem, Blessed is He, conducts the world. Therefore it is inevitable that we should be puzzled by Him. If His conduct followed the rules of our intelligence, then His mind would be like our mind.

Rambam puts it this way:

> . . .The way He conducts His creatures is not the same way we conduct the things we control. . . The only aspect common to both is that they share the same terms ["providence, conduct, control"]. This is the intent of the entire Book of *Iyov*, i.e., to make clear this fundamental principle of faith. . . Do not make the mistake of imagining that His knowledge is like our knowledge, or His intent, providence, and control is similar to our intent, providence, and control. When one realizes this, it is easier for him to accept that which happens, and the events of life do not cause him to have doubts about whether Hashem knows or doesn't know, whether He cares for the world or has abandoned it (*Moreh Nevuchim*, part 3, ch. 23).

"R' YANAI SAYS: 'The contentment of the wicked and the sufferings of the righteous — both are beyond our grasp'" (*Avos*

An Answer From the Whirlwind

4:15). *Bartenura* explains: "We do not know why wicked people succeed and the righteous are weighed down with sufferings." Rabbeinu Yonah comments on the same *mishnah*: "A truth of life is that our knowledge does not extend to this. . . we know in truth that there is an answer to the question, but we are not capable of understanding it."

Perhaps in our day it is easier to admit the limitations of our minds, for modern science has reached the conclusion that even the material universe cannot be fully understood by human intelligence. The most basic laws of particle physics are rationally incomprehensible. If we cannot decipher the actions of created things, certainly we are incapable of understanding the ultimate meaning of the actions of the Creator Himself.

According to *Ramban*, this is essentially the answer which God gave to Iyov, when He appeared from amidst the whirlwind. *Ramban* writes:

> See the great moral principle which the Holy One, Blessed is He, taught Iyov. He revealed to him His wondrous deeds and allowed him to know the works of God, showing Iyov the limits of his knowledge; for he did not know the secrets of the heavens and the earth, of the animals, the birds or the sea and its creatures. . . By this He conveyed to Iyov that although one cannot know all these things, he can nevertheless see Hashem's benevolent Providence over His creatures, and the order which permeates the world. All this is bestowed upon [non-human] creatures, even though they have neither merit nor guilt. Why, then, should one not realize in general that the judgments of God regarding mankind are hidden, and their secret lies closed and sealed along with the creation of man himself? Given one's limitations, why should one not assume that God's actions are righteous, since he sees His mercy and benevolent guidance of all the lower creatures? Why then entertain doubt about the King's actions which have already been done? (*Kisvei HaRamban*, ed. by R' Chaim Dov Chavel, part 2, *Shaar Hagemul*, p. 280).

Viktor Frankl — a Jewish, but non-observant psychologist — draws the following analogy:

> After a while I proceeded to another question, this time addressing myself to the whole group. The question was whether an ape that was being used to develop poliomyelitis serum — and for this reason punctured [by hypodermic needles] again and again — would ever be able to grasp the meaning of its suffering. Unanimously, the group replied that

of course it would not; for with its limited intelligence it could not enter into the world of man, i.e., the only world in which its suffering would be understandable. Then I pushed forward with the following question: "And what about man? Are you sure that the human world is a terminal point in the evolution of the cosmos? Is it not conceivable that there is still another dimension possible, a world beyond man's world; a world in which the question of and ultimate meaning of human suffering would find an answer?" (Viktor Frankl, *Man's Search for Meaning*, p. 186).

The author of *Esh Kodesh* frames the thought in a Torah perspective (p. 139):

> If we cannot understand even one blade of grass that Hashem made, and even less can we understand the soul, and even less an angel, and even less the mind of Hashem, Blessed is He, how can we seek with our minds to understand what He knows and understands?

FOR ALL ITS INHERENT incomprehensibility, we do find in *Tanach*, in *Chazal*, and in the writings of the *Rishonim*, a number

Seeking the Rationale of Divine Judgment

of approaches to the question of human suffering. The prophets and sages did not seek to reveal the essence of the Divine secret, for "As the heavens are high above the earth, so are My ways high above your ways and My thoughts high above your thoughts" (*Yeshayahu* 55:9). Nevertheless, they sought to bring the ways of Hashem as close as possible to our perception, allowing us to glimpse the fraction which we are capable of understanding. Our reason accepts the fact that we are dealing with things beyond our comprehension, but our heart demands palpably to grasp at least a faint shadow of an explanation. Thus, the author of *Chovos Halevavos* writes in *Shaar Habitachon*, Chapter 4:

> "The hidden things are for Hashem our God, and the revealed things, for us and our children" (*Devarim* 29:28). And the wise [King Shlomo] said similarly: "If you see that they oppress the poor and rob justice and righteousness in the

state, do not wonder; for high above high is the Watchman, and [His agents are] high above them" (*Koheles* 5:7). Moreover, the Torah says: "The Creator, His actions are perfect, for all His ways are judgment" (*Devarim* 32:4). Nevertheless, I saw fit to deal with this matter enough to provide a small measure of satisfaction. . .

Ramban writes that the *mitzvah* of knowing and loving Hashem requires us to seek the rationale of Divine judgment.

One might ask: "There are hidden matters in [the Heavenly] judgment; one must believe in His righteousness because He is the true Judge, Blessed and Exalted is He. Why, then, ought one study the reasons and the secrets that we have alluded to? Why not simply trust in the assurance that is given in the end — that with Him there is no forgetfulness nor injustice, but all His actions are just?"

Such a question can come only from those who reject wisdom, for the studies we mentioned can help us to be wise; knowing God, Blessed is He, through His way and His deeds. In addition we, more than others, shall believe and trust in Him, about both the known and the unknown; for we shall deduce the unexplained from that which is explained. Thus we shall know the justice of the verdict and the rightness of the judgment.

And in fact this is the duty of every created being who serves [his Creator] with love and fear — to investigate His intentions, to reveal the justness of the judgment and the truthfulness of the verdict to the fullest extent of his ability. These are some of the ways of the sages which we have explained, so that one's doubts will be resolved regarding this matter. The verdicts of one's Creator will be shown to be truthful. One justifies that which he recognizes and knows, and acknowledges the righteousness of the judgment of that which is hidden from him. It is all the more true that the explanation of the secret we alluded to [*gilgul*] will remove all doubts from one's mind and one will have no further skeptical claims. If he wishes to stop his investigations (of God's ways) here, he is permitted to do so, for it supplies adequate explanation of the entire conduct of created beings (*Kisvei HaRamban, loc. cit.*, p. 281).

WHAT ARE THESE "partial answers which calm the heart?"

Essentially, they all point in one direction: Man questions

Seeing With Mortal Eyes because of his limited knowledge. To him, the world seems to contradict the laws of justice and morality, for he sees with finite, mortal eyes. Only from the Divine viewpoint, which embraces the full sweep of history, is it possible to understand the true meaning of evil in the world. Only from this vantage point does evil assume its proper place in the order of the universe. Morality and justice remain steadfast, for: "The judgments of Hashem are truth; they are right [when seen] all together" (*Tehillim* 19:10). They must be seen "all together" in order to be understood as "right."

If man's life is only a link in a chain of *gilgulim*, and if all the life of this world does not match an hour of eternal life in the world to come, it follows that the data which man needs to analyze the righteousness of suffering is only partially visible to him; in his short life he sees merely the tip of an iceberg jutting up from a vast sea.

The *Chafetz Chaim* writes:

> Many ask: "Why is this man poor and that one rich? For we often find that the poor man does just as many good deeds as the rich man, and sometimes even more."
>
> Our questioner is like a traveler who visited a synagogue and saw that the *gabbai* who called people to the Torah chose a *Kohen* and a Levite who sat on the south side. The third man he chose from the east, the fourth from the west, and the fifth and sixth from the north side. The guest was surprised. "Why did you choose those men from the south side?" he asked. "There were more important ones on the east. And why did you choose the third one from the east? You could have called someone from the south." Thus he went on, asking about all those who were chosen. . .
>
> A man answered the guest: "Your Honor visits for one *Shabbos*, and you wish to understand the order of those chosen? If you were here for a few consecutive weeks, you would understand that the order followed by the *gabbai* is correct. The first *Shabbos* of this month he honored the *Kohen* and the Levite who sit at the east, so this time he called those on the south. He called the man from the east for the

third *aliyah* because last *Shabbos* he gave that *aliyah* to someone from the north side. It is this way for all the *aliyos*. He skips the people who have recently had a turn and calls others instead."

So it is in the matter of wealth. A person comes into this world for a few moments — for how many are the days of one's life? — and he demands answers to all his questions. Why is one man poor and the other rich? If he had lived for a few centuries he would have seen that many years ago this poor man was rich, and this rich one, poor. At that time each went through his trials — one the trials of wealth, and the other the trials of poverty — and now their fate is reversed. But as things are, man's life is very short; he cannot see the world and its affairs in all their breadth and scope. We are like guests who travel from place to place; it is not ours to question the conduct of the King of kings, the Holy One, Blessed is He. One should instead walk simply with Him and trust that everything He does is for the good (*Chafetz Chaim on the Torah*, pp. 136-7).

WE ARE NOT JUST incapable of perceiving the context in which to judge good and evil. The very concepts themselves elude us.

Perspectives on Good and Evil

An example is death, which most men consider their most ill-fated moment. In an objective sense, however, this notion is not at all beyond question. *Chazal* comment upon the verse, "God saw all that He had made, and behold, it was very good" (*Bereishis* 1:31), that " 'very good' refers to death" (*Bereishis Rabbah, parashah* 9). *Matnos Kehunah* explains: "...for it separates one from this tenuous world and brings one to a permanent world..." We find the thought expressed in Rabbeinu Yonah's *Shaarei Teshuvah* (2:21) as well:

> Whoever has been endowed by Hashem, Blessed is He, with intelligence, should impress upon himself that Hashem sent him into this world to observe His *mitzvos*. He should not pay attention to anything except fulfilling this mission. At the End of Days, if he has faithfully done what he was sent to do, he will return with rejoicing, and with eternal joy upon him.

Because of our necessarily subjective viewpoint, we are not capable of looking upon death as it really is — a transition to another life, to the only existence really worthy of the name "life." Yes, we intellectually understand that the soul is eternal and that this world is only a hallway leading to an eternal palace. But this knowledge does not thoroughly permeate the human heart — enmeshed, as it were, in the vanities of this "hallway." Material reward and punishment are very tangible concepts; we can see them with our eyes and feel them with our senses. But eternal bliss or rebuke escape the senses; they are as yet only abstract concepts. Our senses deceive us. The true reality is the spiritual one, of which the material world is only a pale reflection. "An hour of satisfaction in the World to Come is better than all the life of this world" (*Avos* 4:17). Material gratification shrinks to insignificant dimensions when measured against the reward and punishment of the World to Come. And the reverse also holds true: It would be better to suffer the sufferings of Iyov (Job) one's whole life long than to be sentenced to *Gehinnom* (*Ramban*, Introduction to *Iyov*).

If such is the case regarding death, that "worst of fates," how much more is it true that the other supposed "evils" of this world are not truly evil at all. The Prophet Yeshayahu (45:7) declares that Hashem *fashions light and creates darkness, makes peace and creates evil. Radak* explains that *create* in this context means *decree;* thus, God decrees that there be darkness and evil. These negative situations are not "fashioned," because they are nothing more than the absence of light, the concealment of Hashem's Presence. Thus, evil does not exist as an actual reality; ultimately, it is illusory.

Some merit to see beyond the illusion. *Chazal* spoke positively of the phenomenon of suffering (*yisurim*). They saw it principally as atonement for sin, a substitute for harsher sufferings in the World to Come.

The *Gemara* relates that a Sage named Ibdan once received a terrible punishment for a certain minor sin: "At that moment Ibdan was struck with *tzaraas* (leprosy). Two of his sons were drowned, and the brides of his other two sons rejected their marriages."

R' Nachman bar Yitzchak's response to these multiple tragedies, however, is instructive: "Blessed is the Merciful One, Who punished Ibdan in this world" (*Yevamos 105*). All the *yisurim* of this world are of no weight compared to punishment in the World of Eternity.

Elsewhere, the *Gemara* says:

> R' Elazar bar Tzaddok said: "To what may the *tzaddikim* of this world be compared? To a tree [whose roots and trunk] are rooted entirely in pure soil but whose branches hang over into a place of impurity. If the branches are cut off, the tree is left standing entirely in a pure area. Thus the Holy One, Blessed is He, brings *yisurim* upon the *tzaddikim* in this world so that they will inherit the World to Come, as it is said, 'Your beginning will be small, but your end will be very great' (*Iyov 8:7*).
>
> "And to what may the wicked be compared in this world? To a tree [whose roots and trunk] are rooted in impure soil, but whose branches hang over into a place of purity. If the branches are cut off, it is left standing entirely in a place of impurity. Thus the Holy One, Blessed is He, bestows good things upon the wicked in this world, so that they may be sent to the lowest level of *Gehinnom*, as it is said (*Mishlei 14:12*), 'There is a straight road in front of a man, and its end is the way of death' " (*Kiddushin 40b*).

"There is no righteous man on earth who does good and does not sin" (*Koheles 7:20*). Perfection eludes even the most saintly man. If the greater measure of one's deeds are *mitzvos*, a minority are sins. His misdeeds are the branches that hang over impure soil, into the world of vanities and physical indulgence. The function of *yisurim* is to pare the "branches that hang over into a place of impurity" — to distance the *tzaddik* from his baser nature and to break his lingering attachment to materialism. Thus, all *yisurim* contain a fractional element of death, for like death they serve to separate one from the shackles of the material world. Indeed, the process effects not merely an atonement of sins, but an essential refinement and purification as well.

In short, if we claim that righteous people experience evil, or that wicked people receive good, we already make an assumption that we know what is truly good and what is evil. Yet, all of us occasionally experience an event which we immediately consider "good," but in the end it turns out to have been harmful. Likewise, that which we consider disastrous sometimes turns out to be our greatest fortune. If even on the mundane level, we mistake good for evil, we cannot expect our judgment to be more accurate when assessing the totality of life or its sufferings.

AS WE EXAMINE our faculty of judgment, we find it lacking in other ways as well. Not only do we inaccurately distinguish good

A Matter of Intent

and evil, we also fail to perceive who is righteous and who is wicked. We have previously quoted *Rambam* who states in *Hilchos Teshuvah* that the ability to judge the relative weight of sins and *mitzvos* lies solely in the hands of God. There are single merits that outweigh a number of sins, and single sins that outweigh a number of merits. The relative importance of deeds depends not only upon the objective status of the deeds themselves, but also — and perhaps mainly — on the intentions of the doer. Thus, *Chazal* said of the *mitzvah* of honoring one's father and mother: "There is a son who feeds his father the finest fattened fowl and yet the deed drives [the son] to an early death [for he does so begrudgingly]; and there is a son who makes his father toil at the grindstone, and yet this brings [the son] to inherit the World to Come" *(Kiddushin 31a)*. An act is unalterably affected by the intention that accompanies it.

Ultimately this intent is known only to Him Who examines the heart, for "Man sees the eyes, but Hashem sees the heart" *(I Shmuel 16:7)*. A man who appears to be a *tzaddik*, careful of *every mitzvah* whether minor or major, may in truth be of insignificant spiritual stature if his deeds stem from habit and do not express faith. Another person, one of a group of ignorant men, may earn tremendous spiritual reward by doing the few *mitzvos* he has knowledge of, for he does them with true intent and a pure heart.

IF WE EXAMINE our emotions honestly, we will in all likelihood find that the problem of "the suffering of the righteous" troubles us

Intuitive Standards

much more than the problem of the wicked escaping punishment. No doubt there are many reasons for this, but perhaps one of the main ones is that we are afraid of suffering ourselves, and we lack objectivity in our evaluation of righteousness and wickedness. We tend to judge ourselves leniently, underestimating the seriousness of our own misdeeds. Though we claim in the prayer of *vidui* (confession) that "We are not so arrogant and stiffnecked as to claim that we are *tzaddikim* and have not sinned," in the depths of our hearts we believe that, all the same, our sins are not all that consequential. A glance at the Torah, however, will prove that this outlook is unfounded. Seemingly minor sins are met with quite severe punishments, for man's every action is of incalculable significance.

"Whoever says that the Holy One, Blessed is He, compromises — such a person's life will be compromised" (*Bava Kamma* 50a). *Nefesh Hachaim* (shaar 1, ch. 12) comments:

> At first sight this seems strange. After all, even a kind man is willing to compromise with others. [All the more so Hashem, Who is the source of all kindness.] But the answer lies in that which we wrote above. [The evils that Hashem brings on man] are not a form of vengeance, God forbid. Rather, "Evil pursues sinners"(*Mishlei* 13:21). The sin itself is its own punishment. For at the time of Creation, Hashem, Blessed is His name, established the whole order of the functioning of the worlds in such a way that everything depends upon that which is aroused by the deeds of man, whether good or, God forbid, evil. All man's deeds and circumstances automatically make an impression and are recorded, each one at its source and root [in the upper worlds]. Thus [the wrongdoer] necessarily receives his verdict through those very forces of impurity which he strengthened by his deeds, in accord with the nature and severity of the spiritual damage done. It is only in this way that the damage to the universe and to the person's soul is rectified. . . This is why the idea of "compromise" is not applicable here.

According to *Kuzari*, *Ramban*, and other *Rishonim*, the sin of the Golden Calf was a "minor" defect in the worship of Hashem. It did not actually represent idol-worship. Nevertheless, destruction was almost decreed upon the whole Jewish People because of it, and to this day every disaster that befalls us contains an element of punishment for that sin. So it is with the sin of the spies, who were sent to search out the Land of Israel. The commentators are hard put to explain the way in which the spies failed in their mission. And yet, because of it an entire generation was condemned to die in the wilderness. Similarly, the sin of Moshe and Aharon at the Waters of Strife (*Bamidbar* ch. 20) is enshrouded in mystery. Most of the commentators write that it is a classic example of the dictum: "the Holy One, Blessed is He, is strict to a hairsbreadth with *tzaddikim*." Nevertheless, the punishment — denial of Moshe to enter the Land of Israel — was extremely severe. An even more striking example is that of King David and Batsheva (*II Shmuel* chs. 11-12). *Chazal* comment: "Whoever claims that David sinned is mistaken." David's actual wrongdoing was exceedingly minute. Yet, he suffered a terrible punishment for the infraction he committed. We are led to conclude that our intuitive standard for measuring the justness of punishment is quite far from the Torah's criteria.

THERE IS ANOTHER factor involved in the issue of seemingly unwarranted suffering. One may be judged not only for his own

Collective Responsibility acts, but also for those of others. A *tzaddik* who scrupulously fulfills the entire Torah may also be punished — for his responsibility extends beyond himself to the entire Jewish People. Indeed, *Chazal* comment upon the verse, "One man will stumble against another," (*Vayikra* 26:37) that "one man [will stumble] by the sin of another. This teaches that all Israel are responsible for each other" (*Shevuos* 39a).

"Whoever could have protested effectively against [the sins of] his wife and children and fails to do so — is punished on their account; against the people of his city — is punished for the people of his city; against the entire world — is punished for the entire world" (*Shabbos* 54b). The *Gemara* there goes on to explain that this applies even to "those who have fulfilled the entire Torah from *alef* through *tav* ."

It is written in *Tanna Devei Eliahu* (ch. 11):

> If you ask: "Those seventy thousand who were killed at Giv'at Binyamin (in the incident of the *pilegesh* — *Shoftim* chs. 19-20) — why were they killed?" The answer is that the Great Sanhedrin which succeeded Moshe, Yehoshua, and Pinchas ben Elazar should have gone and tied iron ropes around their waists, rolled up their clothes above their ankles, and traveled throughout the cities of Israel. They should have gone one day to Lachish, and another day to Beit El, one day to Chevron, and another to Yerushalayim, and so on to all the places of Israel — and they should have taught Israel proper conduct *(derech eretz)* for a year or two or three until Israel had settled in their land. . . .But they didn't. Instead, when Israel entered their land each man went into his own vineyard or field with his wine and said, "Peace is upon me," so as not to have too much hard work. . . That is why in Giv'at Binyamin, where the people did not occupy themselves with Torah and with *derech eretz*, they gathered instead to go to war, and seventy thousand of them were killed. And who killed all these? No one but the Great Sanhedrin which succeeded Moshe, Yehoshua, and Pinchas ben Elazar.

God applies His attribute of uncompromising justice (*midas hadin*) more strictly to *tzaddikim* than to ordinary people. As the *Gemara* says, the Holy One, Blessed is He, is strict with them to a hairsbreadth. Precisely because of their closeness to the Holy One, are they required to serve Him to perfection, and even the smallest infraction detracts from this perfection. In a similar way, the Jewish People are judged more exactingly than other nations. "You alone have I truly known among all the families of the earth; therefore I charge you with all your sins" (*Amos* 3:2). The righteous are closer to God, and thus they bear greater responsibility: "*Tzaddikim* are punished for the sin of the generation." (*Shabbos* 33b.) Thus, it is not surprising that the Jewish People have throughout history suffered more than any nation. For, as a "nation of leaders," they bear the responsibility of all mankind.

B.

The Suffering of the Righteous Within the Context of the Holocaust

I F THE QUESTION OF why *tzaddikim* suffer is indeed "the root of rebellion within every nation and tongue," then the question as applied within the context of the Holocaust is one of the main roots for dissension from faith within our generation. Who among us has not encountered one version or another of the query? In nearly every debate between religious and secular the question is raised: "Where was God during the Holocaust?"

The truth is that this is not the same question when asked by someone who survived the horrors of the Holocaust and someone who did not. Let us admit frankly: There are people whose suffering during the Holocaust caused them to lose faith in their Creator. A very few of these did not actually suffer, but their pain at the sufferings of their fellow Jews was nonetheless sufficient to shatter the foundations of their belief. Many others sanctified the great Name by dying in various ways, and their faith was not shaken even while inside the horrible gas chambers. As for those who lost their faith — we cannot condemn them; the Mishnah in *Avos* warns us, "Do not judge your fellow man until you reach his situation."

We were not there; the only ones who can serve as our guides are those who themselves experienced the agony. If Jews in the shadow of the furnace doors cried out, "Hear, O Israel: Hashem is our God, Hashem is One" — how can we, who know nothing of their experience, complacently question Hashem's whereabouts during the Holocaust?

The vast majority of people, however — both those who were there and those who were not — do not and did not make their decision about faith based on factors solely related to the

Holocaust. Of those who survived the Holocaust and "stopped believing" as a result of it, some were religious only in name, belonging to observant families or traditional social groups. With the great disruption and dissolution of the social frameworks that had supported these people's observance, they naturally ceased to keep the *mitzvos*. Others were children when the Holocaust raged, and their faith had not sufficiently matured — not all of them, of course, but many. As for those who did not experience those events, their perception upon life and religion was almost without exception not formed initially by the Holocaust.

All this is not intended to diminish the seriousness of the question nor the sincerity of those who ask it. We seek merely to put the issue in perspective. Our point is that the question of how God allowed the Holocaust is not the determining factor in most peoples's faith. Rather, their faith determines how they approach this question.

THE PERSON OF genuine faith also questions the Holocaust. His question, however, is not an act of investigation, for he does not

Posing the Query truly seek a rational answer — this, he knows with profound certainty, he shall never possess. He does not address the question to himself, but to his Creator. He asks, for he cannot remain silent. In questioning, he pours out his heart before his gracious and merciful Father; and seeks to draw closer to Him.

The question "Why do the righteous suffer?" must be directed to Hashem, for we are not dealing here with an intellectual issue, but with one that transcends reason. Just as the truly faithful person tells his Creator of his material sorrows, so does he place before Him his spiritual torments, any injustice as it appears to his human perception. He knows that all his sorrows are for the good, but the simple fact is that he suffers, and he opens his heart to his Father in heaven. *Ramban* states:

> That which the prophets say about this matter, and their outcries on this subject (the success of the wicked and the suffering of the righteous) are only like the utterances of a sick person who is in pain from his disease. He expresses its

severity by screaming about the fierceness of the suffering and pain: How can he be in such a state, and how can he have such great pain? In other words, the prophets express amazement before Hashem and say to Him: "Master of the universe, why do You employ this attribute, allowing us to pass our days in distress, while those wicked ones who stretched out their hand against Your holy place enjoy peace and contentment in the world?" [They ask this] even though they know that the measure is true and the verdict is just (*Kisvei HaRamban, loc. cit.*, p. 275).

A great man of faith of the previous generation was the *Admor* of Piastchene, author of *Chovas Hatalmidim*. He was killed in the Holocaust, after living through the first years of its horrors. His talks during this terrible period were miraculously saved and have been transcribed in a book entitled *Esh Kodesh*. In it, he cries out:

> In truth it is a wonder how the world continues to exist after so many screams like these. At the death of the Ten Martyrs it is said that the angels cried out: "Is this Torah and is this its reward?" A Heavenly Voice answered: "If I hear another sound, I shall turn the earth into water." And now innocent children — pure angels, and great and holy men of Israel — are killed and slaughtered only because they are Jews. They, who are greater than angels, fill the whole space of the world with screams like those, yet the earth is not turned into water; it goes on existing as if, God forbid, He is not concerned.
>
> The *Gemara* says (*Berachos* 32) that since the day the *Beis Hamikdash* was destroyed, an iron wall separates Israel from their Father in heaven. Why does the wall have to be iron? Because the prayers of Israel have the power to demolish [stone] walls. Hence an iron wall is necessary. But against screams like those, how can even an iron wall stand? It is beyond comprehension. And we are not alone in our prayers, for surely our forefathers, too, all the prophets and prophetesses, the righteous men and women of ages past, have no rest in our time of trouble. Surely they clamor in all of *Gan Eden* over the greatness of our sorrow. What comfort can they take in the fact that, no matter what happens, the Jewish People as a whole will survive — for even if one single

Jew is, God forbid, in danger we are obligated to desecrate *Shabbos* to save his life? (*Esh Kodesh*, p. 187)

This searing cry does not undermine faith, God forbid; it stems from, and is an expression of, living and breathing faith. It is a continuation of the outcries of Moshe Rabbeinu and Yeshayahu, Chabbakuk and Yirmiyahu. This is no accusation directed heavenward; it is only the intuitive scream of a torn heart, a prayer that the day will come when we will be able to understand the reason for our calamity. Precisely because the speaker's faith is so flamingly alive, the pain of the distancing of God's Divine Presence is all the more searing. When one hurts, one screams.

IN *TANACH*, IT IS Iyov who cries a bitter cry. Elifaz Hateimani and Iyov's other friends attempt to console him with proofs that

The Honest Outcry

Hashem acted justly. But at the end we find: "Hashem said to Elifaz Hateimani: 'My wrath is kindled against you and against your two friends, because you did not speak of Me correctly like My servant Iyov'" (*Iyov* 42:7). *Ralbag* explains: "They used arguments which they knew were false to justify Hashem, Blessed is He. But Iyov, though at first he did not arrive at the true understanding, said only what was right according to his thought."

The *Gemara* (*Yoma* 69b) relates:

> Why were they called the Men of the Great Assembly (*Anshei K'nesses Hagedolah*)? Because they returned the crown to its former [glory].
>
> Moshe came and said: "the great, mighty, and awesome God" (*Devarim 10:17*). Yirmiyahu said: "Idol worshipers are dancing in His Temple. Where is His awesomeness?" — [therefore] he omitted the word, "awesome." Daniel came and said: "Idol worshipers have enslaved His sons. Where is His might?" — [therefore] he omitted the word, "mighty." The Men of the Great Assembly came and said: "On the contrary, this is His might, that He suppresses His anger and is patient with the wicked; and this is His awesomeness, for were it not for His awesomeness, how could one nation continue to exist among seventy nations?" The *Gemara* then

asks: How could Yirmiyahu and Daniel rely on their own understanding to question the might and awesomeness of God which Moshe had declared? The answer is given in the name of R' Yitzchak bar R' Elazar: "Because they knew that the Holy One, Blessed is He, is truthful. They did not lie to Him."

Before the true God, one may speak only true words. Thus, honest outcry of pain is an expression of faith also. However, the complacent heart which declares, "I can no longer believe after the Holocaust," is another matter entirely. One must reject the practice, so widespread in post-Holocaust art and literature, of using the Holocaust as a post-facto justification for atheism.

ONE CANNOT DEBATE with someone who went through the Holocaust and had his faith shaken. His loss of belief is not an

The Sacrifice of Subjectivity

intellectual matter and thus cannot be remedied by an appeal to reason. It is his heart which has been injured, and the destruction of his faith is part of the overall destruction that befell the House of Israel. Some were physically wounded and others were spiritually wounded. The healthy soul by its very nature has faith in the Creator and His guidance of the world.

If psychological studies have found a higher incidence of mental illness among Holocaust survivors, it is not surprising that the spiritual illness of denial of God should strike under the same conditions of Nazi persecution. One does not try to convince a sick person he should not have become ill. The only solution is to heal him.

Neither can one reason with the one who did not experience the Holocaust, but uses it to deny the existence of God so that he may act as he pleases. All one can do is shake his self-assurance somewhat by asking if he believes himself the first one to discover the question of why the righteous suffer. One can only tell him that wiser and more brilliant men than he went through sufferings which he has never tasted, and continued to hold onto their faith — and not out of naivete. One can only recommend books on Jewish history to him, in which he will read of unimaginable disasters (perhaps on a relative scale no less terrible than the Holocaust) which befell the Jews, during which this wonderful and holy People walked into the flames with the *Shema* on their lips.

The present work, however, is not intended for either skeptic. We speak to those who seek the way of Hashem with honesty, and our goal is to help them deal with this difficult question.

The *Admor* of Piastchene writes:

> Sacrificing one's life (*mesirus nefesh*) with faith means that even at a time when Hashem's face is concealed one believes in Him — that everything from Him is for the good; that everything is just; that all *yisurim* (sufferings) are full of Hashem's love for Israel. Unfortunately, there are some — even among those who were complete believers — whose faith has been damaged. They question, "Why have You abandoned us? If You are punishing us in order to bring us closer to Torah and Your service — to the contrary, the Torah and everything holy is being destroyed. . ."
>
> If a Jew speaks this way as a form of prayer and entreaty, pouring out his heart in front of Hashem, this is good. But if, God forbid, he asks his question skeptically, if deep within his heart his faith is deficient, God forbid, then — may Hashem protect us.
>
> Faith is the foundation of everything. If, God forbid, one's faith is defective, then he is torn and is distanced from Him. . .
>
> And in truth what place is there for skepticism of Hashem's acts? It is true that *yisurim* like those we now suffer come only once in hundreds of years. But all the same, how could we presume to understand these deeds of Hashem, or claim that if we do not understand them we shall lose faith, God forbid? If we cannot understand even the blade of grass that Hashem makes, and even less can we understand the soul, and even less an angel, and even less the thought of Hashem, how can we seek with our minds to understand what He knows and understands?
>
> And why should one have his faith damaged more now by these *yisurim* than by all the *yisurim* that have come upon Israel in the past? When he read a verse, a *Gemara*, or a Midrash, and came to know of the sorrows of Israel from earliest times until now, was his faith damaged? So why has

he ceased to believe now? For those who claim that *yisurim* like these have never before come upon Israel are in error. During the destruction of the *Beis Hamikdash*, Beitar, and in other times, things like this occurred. (Note from a later period: Only the calamities that occurred up to the end of 5702/1942 have a precedent in history. But the grotesque torture and unnatural deaths that the murderers invented for us, the House of Israel, since the end of 5702/1942, to the best of my knowledge of *Chazal* and Jewish history, have no precedent. May Hashem have mercy upon us and save us from their hand speedily — 18 Kislev, 5703/1943.) Why, then, is one's spirit more sorely wounded by the *yisurim* of our time? Because affliction which one personally experiences affects him more. True, those who have lost their faith claim that they are shocked only because they see others so horribly tormented. And it is true that they worry and are grieved about the *yisurim* of other Jews. All the same, deep inside, the excessively strong reaction, even to the point of losing faith, and skeptically questioning heaven, God forbid, results from their fear lest they too, God forbid, reach the terrible fate that they have seen befall others.

This is the meaning of the point we made above — that one must sacrifice his life, that is, his personal subjectivity, to maintain his faith. Then he will believe with perfect faith that all occurs in justice and with the love of Hashem for Israel (*Esh Kodesh*, pp. 138-40).

C.

"Where Was God During the Holocaust?"

"HOW COULD GOD LET the Holocaust happen?"

Some answer using the dictum of *Chazal*: "Everything is in the hands of heaven except fear of heaven (*yiras shamayim*)." True, God is all-powerful. But Jew and non-Jew alike is given free will to choose good or evil, and God

The Holocaust and Free Will chooses not to interfere with this choice. Hence, Hitler and his associates were free to choose, and they chose evil — to murder to their hearts' content, and God did not interfere in that choice. Although Hashem allows evil to rage unchecked, this is only a necessary consequence of man's free will. Since this free will is man's greatest gift, it follows that the possibility of choosing evil is ultimately for man's greater good, as explained in *Ramchal's Derech Hashem*.

It would seem that this argument can be completely refuted. First of all, nowhere is it stated that free will includes the freedom to harm innocent people without provoking heavenly concern. It is true, on the one hand, that Rabbeinu Channanel states in his commentary to *Chaggigah* 5a that the verse, "Sometimes one is killed without judgment," (*Mishlei* 13:23) refers to "one who murders another." Similarly, the *Zohar* (*parashas Vayeshev*, p. 185) states that, because of the human ability to choose, it is better to fall into a pit full of snakes and scorpions than to fall into the hands of a human enemy, for the chance of being saved miraculously from snakes and scorpions is greater than the chance of being saved from men who seek one's death. But these statements are relative, not absolute: it is harder to be saved from a wicked person, for he is more dangerous. Thus, one must merit a greater degree of Divine intervention to be saved. Open miracles do not happen every day — nevertheless, it is clear that men are not completely free to murder without any heavenly reckoning.

It would also seem that this argument contradicts the essential message of *Tanach* — that all the events of history are directed from above — that the Holy One, Blessed is He, is the Master of wars, and the hearts of kings and princes are in His hand. The various exiles we have experienced were not the results of the wicked free will of Pharaoh or Nevuchadnetzar, but were the decrees of the King of all kings. Our enemies, in the final analyses, are only the rod of Hashem's wrath. Free will does exist, but the basic flow of Jewish history is not determined by its vicissitudes.

To argue that the Holocaust was solely caused by Hitler's free will comes dangerously close to asserting that "there is no justice and no judge," in world events. Both viewpoints remove God's Providence from our world. True, it is claimed that this absence of Divine intervention stems from God's will, not from inability or weakness; but in the final analysis it is a denial of Divine Providence. *Ramban*, in his Introduction to the Book of *Iyov*, notes two types of denial which result from the question of why the righteous suffer. The first denies that Hashem knows what is done in the world, and the second denies that He intervenes in events: "Due to the insignificance of man in comparison to His greatness and exaltedness, God does not take interest in [mankind]." Even though this second type of non-belief stems from awareness of His Exaltedness, it still is categorized as non-belief. Obviously, in our case, to excessively stress man's free will is not equivalent to a total denial of Divine Providence; but a trace of denial can still be detected here.[1]

ABOVE ALL, HOWEVER, it would seem that this claim cannot be applied to the Holocaust. One who studies the history of the

God Was There

Holocaust will see quite clearly that here was no mere concealment of Providence

---

1. This argument claims that free will precludes Divine intervention. This should not be confused with the concept that sometimes the Holy One, Blessed is He removes His supervision from a person and leaves him to the whims of chance. Such removal is a form of deliberate punishment, which itself is an aspect of Providence.

— no mere "natural chain of events," as it were. On the contrary, at every step of the way, one palpably sees the hand of Hashem dealing blows. Hitler's rise to power is a historical anomaly. Even with the benefit of forty years' hindsight, historians still regard it with an air of mystery. Lacking ability and desperately poor, mentally unstable and unfit for any kind of employment, a man who lived on the margins of society rose from the trash heaps to dominate half the civilized world. After being imprisoned with his cohorts following a failed coup attempt, he succeeded in winning an election by the plurality of his countrymen. From the jailhouse he ascended the throne. Is this a natural chain of events?

The entire progress of the Second World War was unnatural. The astonishing military success of the Germans, who conquered large, strong countries in a brief time, was unforeseen by the greatest military experts. The pact with Soviet Russia — a foremost enemy of Hitler from the beginning of his career — enabled him to smash Poland in a swift campaign. The pact was unexpected and unexplainable. Equally mysterious is Stalin's stubborn refusal to heed the warnings he received about an imminent German attack. As a result of this blind spot, an additional two million Jews fell under the Nazi regime. Indeed, the astounding successes of the Germans are matched in improbability only by the subsequent failures that led to the downfall of that regime — the miraculous reverse at Stalingrad being chief among them. Even with the benefits of hindsight, historians are hard-put to explain these events.

We must therefore conclude that God "was there" during the Holocaust; indeed, it was He Who brought it about. His hand intervened every step of the way, setting up both the factors which would catalyze the Holocaust, as well as those which would bring it to a sudden halt.

R' Dessler writes:

> The nature of miracles is such that the Holy One, Blessed is He, shows His control of world events openly, in such a way that anyone with a heart and mind realizes that this is no natural occurrence, but instead that the hand of Hashem has been revealed. Hence, just as miracles occur for our benefit in

this world, so too can they sometimes cause our suffering, when Hashem openly intervenes by helping our enemies. This is explicitly stated in the Torah: "Just as Hashem rejoices over you, to do good for you and to multiply you, so will He rejoice over you to destroy you and to annihilate you" (*Devarim* 28:63). The meaning of "rejoice" is to exceed all boundaries. In the positive sense, this is unlimited kindness (*chessed*). If He "rejoices" to destroy, however, it means that Hashem, Blessed is He, fulfills the will of our enemies without limit, doing miracles for them, God forbid.

We see this concretely in our generation. The ordinary way of the world is that those who excel in talent and ability — those who are best trained in the techniques of administering a state — become leaders, each one being given responsibility in the area in which he excels. But is it possible by natural means that a group of men totally unprepared and unqualified for leadership — men taken from the back kitchen of some cafe or bar, all of them unknown — should suddenly be found capable of rulership, and that all of them together should in fact govern whole countries? Yet this is exactly what we have witnessed in that wicked enemy and his cohorts, may their names be blotted out. For decades they were common men of the street, employed in small, insignificant work. Suddenly, all became leaders — leaders who distinguished themselves exceedingly in their ability to do evil. This is nothing other than direct Divine intervention (*hashgachah*), a miracle designed to punish us and open our eyes (*Michtav Me'Eliyahu*, Part 1, pp. 203-4).

Likewise, the Nazis' fanatical hatred of the Jews cannot be explained rationally. It is true that there had always been enemies of the Jews, but not in such extreme form. Historians have shown that Hitler regarded the war against the Jews as even more important than the campaigns waged on the battlefield. And if one man was possessed by madness, it remains altogether impossible to understand how an entire nation, one of the most cultured in Europe, took part in the systematic genocide of another nation. Without any rational basis, it devoted its most advanced scientific accomplishments to this purpose. Whole books have been written attempting to explain this astounding moral degeneracy of an entire nation, but in the end it remains a mystery.

> When, God forbid, they torture and torment us in ways that are of no benefit to the torturer and tormentor, but purely for the sake of tormenting us — this is a revelation of God's strict justice (*midas hadin*), which in no way disguises itself as a natural event (*Esh Kodesh*, p. 61).

One who tries to see the Holocaust as unaffected by Divine Providence will find himself confronted with difficulties no less great than "Why do the righteous suffer?" How can one divorce the anomalous historical events surrounding the Holocaust from the no less singular history of the Jewish People? Is it by chance or natural process that the Jewish People is tried again and again by political decree and calamity, by hatred that goes beyond reason or explanation; and yet again and again emerges hurt and wounded, but nevertheless enduring? How can one explain the hatred that appears against Israel in such disparate historical circumstances, and how can one explain the miracle of Israel's continued existence in spite of it all? How can one view the complete isolation of the Jews during the Holocaust without seeing it as the continuation of a permanent feature of their history? How can one explain how Jews who did not want their Jewishness, who even actively rejected it, failed to escape the fate of their people?

THESE AND OTHER QUESTIONS have no answer unless we see the Holocaust as an integral part of the history of the Jewish nation in exile. The saga of our people, aptly

Meta-History

defined by Dr. Yitzchak Breuer, as "meta-history" — a unified process spanning many historical eras — defies categorization as a chronological chain of random occurrences. One can no doubt find a political, social or economic explanation for every individual event in Jewish history. But, taken as a whole, the two-thousand-year chain of events — a chain which relentlessly duplicates itself despite the most disparate historical circumstances — totally refutes all normal historical analyses.

The very severity of persecution which the Jew has undergone throughout the ages is unparalleled in the history of any other people. The *Gemara* (*Kesubos* 66b) relates that Rabban Yochanan ben Zakkai, after the destruction of the *Beis Hamikdash,* saw a Jewish noblewoman gathering barley grains from the dung of Arabs' donkeys. The Sage declared: "Fortunate are you, O Israel! When you do the will of the Omnipresent, no nation or tongue has power over you. And when you do not do His will, He hands you over to a lowly nation — and not even to a lowly nation, but to the beasts of a lowly nation." The *Maharal* of Prague questions why Rabban Yochanan ben Zakkai used the term "fortunate" here, seemingly implying that Israel is fortunate even when not doing the will of their Creator. He answers that even the periods of Israel's decline do not conform to normal historical patterns. They, too, testify to Israel's special quality and chosen status: "Israel never has an intermediate position. Either they rule over all, or all rule over them" (*Netzach Yisrael*, ch. 14; also, see *Maharsha's Chiddushei Aggados* on *Kesubos* 66b). One can only understand the unique nature of Jewish history by recognizing the hand of Divine Providence that guides it.

IT IS NOT ONLY THE GENERAL TRENDS of Jewish history which point to the Divine hand within the Holocaust — the Torah itself

The Tochachah seems to warn of its impending occurrence. The sobering truth of these prophecies is itself the strongest affirmation that the Holocaust was not a product of blind political-historical processes.

In the Torah we find two passages of harsh rebuke, the *Tochachah* of *Vayikra* Chapter 26 and that of *Devarim* Chapter 28. Before the Jews even entered their land, they were warned of exile and persecution — and these warnings came true centuries afterwards. Nothing similar can be found in the history of any other nation. The classical commentators devote lengthy essays to interpreting the details of these terrible prophecies of wrath. They discuss whether all the prophecies have already been fulfilled in the destruction of the First and Second Temples, or in our long exile. But in every new period of persecution that befalls the Jewish People, new insights are revealed into the Passages of Rebuke, new interpretations taken directly from the tragic reality. In our age, too, these verses have again come alive.

The *Tochachah* describes ravishing hunger: "When I shatter the staff of bread for you, ten women will bake your bread in one oven, and they shall return your bread to you by weight" [for the loaves will break and crumble] (*Vayikra* 26:26). The verse calls to mind the distribution of bread in the concentration camps. Each group of prisoners (six, eight or more) received one loaf of bread, which they had to divide equally, without the aid of a knife; the intent was to cause arguments among the prisoners. There were thus many who received their bread "by weight." Another verse (ibid. v. 29) speaks of man driven by starvation to consume human flesh. According to survivors' accounts, this terrible curse, too, came true during the Holocaust.

The *Tochachah* also describes an all-consuming fear of pursuers: "As for those who remain, I shall bring fear into their hearts in the lands of their enemies. The sound of a rustling leaf will pursue them, and they will flee as if fleeing the sword, and they shall fall though none pursues" (ibid. v. 36). Holocaust survivors who fled into the forests or hid in other ways can testify how precisely this description fit their situation.

Many who experienced the Holocaust found their psychological strength outstripped by the horrors they witnessed. Nothing could more accurately describe their fate than the verse from the *Tochachah*: "You shall be driven insane from the visions which your eyes shall see" (*Devarim* 28:34). Even among those who survived, a significant number suffered mental illness as a result of their shattering experiences.

In describing the enemy, the Torah writes: "Hashem will bring upon you a nation from afar, from the end of the earth, as the eagle swoops down; a nation whose language you will not understand, a brazen-faced nation which will neither respect the old nor favor the young" (ibid. v. 49-50). The correlation to the Holocaust is chilling: a nation which neither favors the young nor respects the aged; one who attacks "as the eagle swoops down." It was indeed the Germans who perfected the technique of *blitzkrieg*, "lightning-war," and the most prominent symbol of both the Nazi party and the German army was, indeed, the eagle.

Perhaps the most unique aspect of the horrors of the Holocaust is that they transcended human powers of description; no pen nor tongue can express these sufferings as they actually were. This, too, is hinted at in the *Tochachah*, where it says: "Hashem will even raise up upon you all the sicknesses and all the plagues that are *not written in this book of the Torah*" (ibid. v. 61) — in its day of ultimate travail, Israel shall experience even those plagues that are impossible to write in a book.

Many of the great leaders of the Jewish People believe that the events of the Holocaust are to be seen as *chevlei Mashiach*, the birth pangs of the *Mashiach* (Messiah). The events of the period known as *chevlei Mashiach* are described in all their fearsome detail by the prophets and *Chazal*. Of this period Daniel says (12:1): "There will be a time of trouble such as never occurred from the beginning of nations until that time." It would seem that no words could better describe the period we are discussing. And in *Sanhedrin* 98b several *Amoraim* state: "May it come, and may I not see it" — that is, may *Mashiach* come, but may I not have to witness the terrible calamities of *chevlei Mashiach*.

It is possible to cite more and more details from the *Tochachah* which take on new significance when applied to the Holocaust. But the message is clear: the prophecies of the *Tochachah*, insofar as they foreshadow the Holocaust, indicate quite clearly that it was the hand of Hashem which dealt us this blow. We find the following verses in the Torah's introduction to the *Ha'azinu* song in the end of *Devarim*:

> My wrath will burn on that day and I shall abandon them. I shall conceal My face from them, and they will be [left] to be eaten; many evils and troubles will find them. And they will say on that day: "Behold, it is because my God is not within me that these evils have found me" ...and it shall be, when many evils and troubles find them, this song shall speak before them as a witness, for it

shall not be forgotten from the mouths of their descendants (Ibid. 31:17,21).

According to several commentators, this means that a time will come when, due to the great evils that befall them, the people will say that "my God is not within me," as if there were no justice and no judge. But, even in such a time, this song, in which all those troubles are foretold, remains the witness that God is the One Who brought the travails.

IT MIGHT BE CLAIMED that these prophecies and allusions are not specific, for they point to the Holocaust only in a general way,

Portentous Warnings

as part of the sorrows of exile or the birth-pangs of redemption. However, more specific warnings of future events are found in the words of *Chazal* and in the writings of more recent sages.

Upon the verse, "Do not allow, Hashem, the desires of the wicked; do not bring forth his schemes, which are arrogant" (*Tehillim* 140:9), *Chazal* commented that Yaakov said before the Holy One, Blessed is He: 'Master of the universe, do not allow Esav the desire of his heart.' [The words,] 'do not bring forth his schemes, which are arrogant,' refer to Germania which belongs to Edom [i.e., Esav]. If [their schemes] are realized, they will destroy the entire world (*Megillah* 6, according to the reading of *Gra* and *Yaavetz*; the version found in our *Gemara* reads: "Germamia.") The full implications of this fearful prophecy have been realized only in the 20th century.

It is said that the *Gra* considered the German people to have the status of *safek Amalek* — possible Amalekites. The only parallel in Jewish history to the attempted genocide of the Holocaust is the decree of an earlier Amalekite, Haman the Wicked, who attempted to annihilate the entire Jewish People in his day. A similar warning can be found in the biography of the *gaon* R' Yosef Chaim Sonnenfeld (*Mara De'Ara De'Yisrael*, part 1, p. 200):

> When the German Kaiser Wilhelm visited *Eretz Yisrael* in 5659 (1899), the whole Jerusalem community — leaders, scholars, and the masses — went out to greet him. They

wished to recite the blessing, ". . .Who gave of His glory to flesh and blood," and to fulfill the dictum of *Chazal* (*Berachos 58a*): "A person should run [to see] the kings of Israel; and not only the kings of Israel, but even the kings of the nations — for if he merits, he will see the difference between the kings of Israel and the kings of the nations."

While the excited preparations reached a peak, [R' Sonnenfeld] remained inside his home. His pure eyes saw into the distance, and he said simply: "That *Gemara* was not speaking about a king who descended from Amalek." (A footnote adds: "Rabbeinu — R' Sonnenfeld — was the only one who stayed home on that occasion. When he was asked about this, he quoted the words of the *Gra*, that the Germans are considered possible Amalekites.")

In the memoirs of R' Mazah (part 4, p. 154), a work written long before the Holocaust and published several years prior to it, we find a record of a talk given by the *Maggid* of Kelm:

The German will not persecute the Jew with ordinary, run-of-the-mill persecution. When he rises to power, he will not simply oppress Israel, but he will make the hatred of Israel into a kind of *Shulchan Aruch*, a Code of Law, heaven save us. My dear colleagues! Impress it upon your hearts. Because of the sin of the *Shulchan Aruch* of Geiger [founder of the Reform Movement in Germany], a new, German version of the *Shulchan Aruch* is going to arise against the Jewish People, and there — heaven save us — it will be written: "The only thing to do with even the best Jew is — kill him. The only thing to do with even the best Jew is — kill him." May Hashem save us!

These words were spoken more than sixty years before Hitler rose to power.

A similar statement is cited by R' Shlomo Wolbe, *shlita*, in the name of the *gaon* R' Yisrael Salanter. His words, too, were spoken decades before they became reality:

In return for the Reform "*Shulchan Aruch*" which permits intermarriage with gentiles, the day will come when the gentiles will write a "*Shulchan Aruch*" of their own which will forbid gentiles to marry Jews (*Bein Sheshes Le'Asor*, p. 78).

Of the Chafetz Chaim it is related:

> In the winter of 5690 (1930), one of the students from overseas came to receive a farewell blessing from him, for the student was preparing to leave the yeshivah and go to America. In the course of the conversation, the Chafetz Chaim began to murmur, as if to himself, saying: "Twelve million was only child's play. Only in another ten years will the thing really begin." He repeated these words two or three times, until the young man realized what was being said: The reference was to the twelve million people who had been killed or wounded in the First World War. The Chafetz Chaim appeared to foresee the coming war, which would exceed its predecessor in its number of victims and its cruelty. Almost exactly ten years later (5699 - 1939), the Second World War unleashed its full fury (Chafetz Chaim al HaTorah, p. 165).

Elsewhere it is told:

> In the year 5693 (1933), when the enemy of the Jews in Germany, may his name be wiped out, rose to power and took the reins of government in his hands, a prominent rav and rosh yeshivah asked the Chafetz Chaim: "What will be the fate of our brothers in Germany and Poland, now that Hitler has publicly declared that he aims to wipe out the name of Israel, God forbid?" The Chafetz Chaim answered that he would not succeed. Never has anyone succeeded in uprooting and destroying our whole people. . . for it is written: "If Esav comes upon one camp and smites it, the remaining camp will escape" (Bereishis 32:8).
>
> The questioner understood the danger was near, and went on to ask: "If, God forbid, the enemy succeeds in annihilating European Jewry, which constitutes the quantitative and qualitative majority of the Jewish People, which is the 'camp that will escape'?"
>
> The Chafetz Chaim replied: "This, too, is written explicitly in the words of the prophets: 'And in Mount Zion will be the refuge, and it will be holy' " (Ovadiah 1:17).
>
> The rav left the Chafetz Chaim, his hands trembling over the imminent destruction of European Jewry, and his heart sure that our Holy Land would be spared. And so it was (Ibid., pp.72-3).

The questioner in the incident was the *gaon* R' Yosef Shlomo Kahaneman, known as "the Rav of Ponevezh." Over the entrance to the Ponevezh Yeshivah, which he subsequently founded in Bnei Brak, is inscribed the verse which the Chafetz Chaim had quoted: "And in Mount Zion will be the refuge, and it will be holy."

R' Weissmandl, *zt'l*, in his work *Min Hameitzar*, tells (p. 42) of a discussion he had with his teacher, the *gaon* R' Shmuel David Ungar, *zt'l*, in 5691 (1931). R' Ungar had been offered the post of rav in Tirnau. He refused to accept the offer, despite entreaties from Tirnau, and he remained in his yeshivah at Nitra. When R' Weissmandl pressed him to reconsider, he answered: "My heart tells me that the time is near when there won't be a yeshivah anywhere except in Nitra, and I want to be there." Afterwards, he asked R' Weissmandl to promise that he would not tell anyone about these words of his. Only ten years later, when all the yeshivos of Slovakia were destroyed and only Nitra remained, did R' Weissmandl remember this prophetic moment with his rav.

That which we have cited from the Torah and the words of the sages throughout the generations seems to indicate that it was the hand of Hashem that dealt us this blow. No one can claim that the Torah leaders of the previous generation knew exactly what was going to happen. If they had known, they certainly would have acted differently. Even the Chofetz Chaim, who spoke of horrible events "in another ten years," only mentioned a further war. He spoke of it as a more terrible war than its predecessor, but called it only a war, not the complete annihilation of European Jewry. Nonetheless, the very fact that the Torah sages knew that something awful awaited the Jewish People places the events of 1939-1945 squarely within the Divine framework of the scheme of Jewish history.

D.

A Partial Reconciliation

WE HAVE ESTABLISHED that it was the hand of God that struck us, but we have not dealt with the central question: Why? How could it be? True, the intervention of Divine Providence in the Holocaust cannot be denied, but how can it be that God, Who is gracious and merciful, Who bestows His goodness even on those unworthy of it — how could He pass such a shattering verdict upon millions of people, many of them innocent children? In particular, how could He pass such a verdict upon the Jewish People, the nation whom He chose from among all the nations to be "the people who are close to Him" (*Tehillim* 148:14)? In this searing question, we find the plea "Why do the righteous suffer?" multiplied six million times or more.

We cannot hope to find a definitive answer. Just as human beings are incapable of understanding why the righteous suffer in general, so too we are unable to perceive clearly why the righteous suffered in the Holocaust. The question defies solution, for the ways of Hashem, by their very nature, transcend human comprehension. "If His conduct followed the rules of our intelligence," R' Nachman writes, "that would mean that His mind is like our mind." The "partial answers" to why the righteous suffer, detailed earlier, serve merely "to calm the heart" for they give us only a minimal glimpse into Hashem's conduct of the world. Nevertheless, we shall proceed to explore their application to the Holocaust.

As we set forth before, it is axiomatic that man's primary reward and punishment is in the World to Come, the world of eternity. The delights and travails of this world pale in comparison to their counterpart experiences in the world to come. It is difficult, extremely difficult, for material man to look upon the world in which he lives as transitory, as only a prelude to a real world. And it is many times more difficult to believe with concrete, palpable faith, with all one's heart and soul, that the horrors of Auschwitz and Treblinka are no more than a shadow of the pain of eternal punishment. Yet, these truths remain steadfast, despite the difficulty that man, entrenched in his subjectivity, encounters in realizing them.

WE ALSO MENTIONED the faith in reincarnation, according to which man's lifetime is only one link in a long chain, and hence

For Past Sins one cannot know who is really righteous and who is not. Though we do not have definite knowledge on this subject, it is worthwhile here to cite some instructive words from R' Chaim Israel Zimmerman's book *Tammim Pa'alo*, which is devoted entirely to *tzidduk hadin*, justifying the decree of the Holocaust.

> In order to understand everything we went through during those terrible years, the terrible and fearsome destruction in which one third of our nation was annihilated in cruel and strange forms of death, we find it necessary to quote the words of the *Arizal* (*Shaar Hakavanos*, p. 1) [note: In the work quoted the passage is related in the name of R' Moshe Cordovero, not the *Arizal* himself]:
>
> > One must know what *Chazal* said: "The mourning of the Holy One, Blessed is He, is sufficient for Him, and the mourning of Israel is sufficient for them" (*Sanhedrin 97*). This dictum may be understood by means of the following preface. Until the generation of the Flood and the generation of the Tower of Babel, the Holy One, Blessed is He, poured forth an abundance of holy souls, six hundred thousand holy souls, until the generation of the Flood sinned so badly that Hashem, Blessed is He, chose to destroy them, in order to reforge them in Noach and his sons, as we shall explain later. Likewise in the generation of the Tower of Babel there was an abundance of holy souls amounting to the all-inclusive [number of 600,000], until they became defective through the sin of the Tower, and the Holy One, Blessed is He, placed them under the supervision of

seventy angelic princes [one for each of the seventy nations], setting apart Israel [the seventy-first nation] for Himself, as it is written (*Devarim* 32:9), "The portion of Hashem is His people." When Israel entered the Land, they were 600,000 holy souls, generation after generation. But they became very defective through the sins of idol worship, murder, adultery, and the like. He sent them His prophets to rebuke them, to see if they would repent, so that He would not have to put into effect the purifying forces that would be necessary for their souls, such as war, famine, and so on. But when the sins grew greater and they did not want to repent, He saw in His wisdom that they would require an overall purification, because it was no longer sufficient to purify them through ordinary death and reincarnation. Their sins had become very great, as at the time of the Flood. Therefore the *Beis Hamikdash* was destroyed.

Now, you may ask: Those who worshiped idols had already died in an earlier generation; or those who killed the prophet Zechariah in the *Beis Hamikdash* would not receive their punishment, since they had already died [before the *Beis Hamikdash* was destroyed]. But this is really no objection. The Holy One, Blessed is He, killed them in order to bring them back in *gilgul* [i.e. reincarnation]. Those who had worshiped idols in an earlier generation, or those who killed Zechariah — those very same ones were brought back in *gilgul* in order to receive their punishment in the destruction of the *Mikdash*. Each one received the punishment corresponding to his sin. Some had derived only a little enjoyment from sinning; they were killed with a minimum of suffering, dying immediately. Some had derived much enjoyment [from their sins], had repeatedly indulged in illicit relations, and the like. A person of this kind would be stabbed and would live for several days, lacking everything and slowly starving, seeing his children slaughtered before his eyes, God forbid. All was in exact measure, to cleanse each one according to his sin. Those Jews who survived served as the smelting-furnace to reforge all those souls that had been killed. That is why, during the period of the Babylonian Exile and the period of the Second *Beis Hamikdash*, [the Jewish People] were fruitful and multiplied very much.

We must study these holy words very deeply, and they will enlighten our eyes with the light of pure faith. We see that a sinner has no hope or escape. Either he must do *teshuvah* (repent), or he must be purified through hard and bitter sufferings by being brought back in *gilgul*, in order to cleanse his sin. "And when the sins grew greater and they did not want to do *teshuvah*, He saw in His wisdom that they would require an overall purification, because it was no longer sufficient to purify them through ordinary death." Rather, it was necessary to bring them back in *gilgul* in order to purify them through violent deaths. It makes one's hair stand on end to think about these things, and to see the results and heavenly verdicts when people are stubborn and do not want to repent.

The second basic concept that enlightens us in these words of the *Arizal* is contained in the sentence: "That is why, during the period of the Babylonian Exile and the period of the Second *Beis Hamikdash*, [the Jewish People] were fruitful and multiplied very much." All those people were the very souls that had worshiped idols or killed Zechariah. They themselves returned in a different body to receive their punishment in the destruction of the *Beis Hamikdash*. How these words illuminate our own situation! And how interesting are these words of the *Arizal* in connection with statistics recorded in a number of sources regarding the population of the Jewish People before and after the Holocaust. The figures are very instructive:

About one hundred years ago, the total world Jewish population reached four and a half million. During those one hundred years our population was multiplied by four, so that at the outbreak of the war we had reached seventeen million, and perhaps even more. This despite the fact that the century was not characterized by excessive love of the Jews, and had its full share of evils, of assimilation, of spiritual and physical destruction. Now [after the Holocaust] we have decreased in number with a tremendous and fateful decrease. Once again we stand at the level where we stood about fifty years ago, at the beginning of the twentieth century — that is, at about eleven million souls.

We have contemplated the great increase of population during the last century, and the great and terrible destruction, in which we lost a third of our people. When we consider all this, the holy words of the *Arizal* regarding the matter of *chevlei Mashiach*, the birth pangs of *Mashiach*, shine and illumine like the pure cloudless sky. Everything we have gone through and all the good things that are destined to happen to us in the near future are revealed to us in a clear light. Let us remember these holy words and repeat them to ourselves and to our children. "Some had derived only a little enjoyment from sinning; they were killed with the minimum of suffering, dying immediately. Some had derived much enjoyment [from their sins], had repeatedly indulged in illicit relations, and the like. A person of this kind would be stabbed and would live for several days, lacking everything and slowly starving, seeing his children slaughtered before his eyes, God forbid. All was in exact measure, to cleanse each one according to his sin." All the violent and cruel deaths — all were in exact measure. Here there is no randomness, God forbid. All is according to a precise and just reckoning, and all is for the good of the sinner, in order to cleanse his sin (*Tammim Pa'alo*, pp. 31-32).

A similar idea is expressed in *Shomer Emunim*, by the *Admor* R' Aharon Roth.

It is true that the passage from *Shaar Hakavanos* cited by R' Zimmerman requires more clarification, as is usually the case with kabbalistic writings and their unique style. But the passage is sufficiently clear to give us the proper perspective. It may be that the real solution to the question of why the righteous suffer is not to be found in this area at all, but the very possibility that this was the meaning of what happened shows us the superficiality of our questions and answers. It highlights how far we are, not only from knowing who the righteous are, and what suffering is, but even from knowing ultimately with whose responsibility we are dealing.

There are other facts which limit our ability to question why the righteous suffered in the Holocaust. As we mentioned above, man is not capable of knowing who is truly righteous and who is not. Even if could discern who is a complete *tzaddik*, one who "fulfilled the entire Torah from *alef* through *tav*," one must realize that it is precisely upon this *tzaddik* that Hashem's attribute of strict justice is applied with particular stringency. Every Jew is responsible for the deeds of the people as a whole, and this responsibility grows in proportion to one's piety. "*Tzaddikim* are punished for the sins of the generation," and similarly, the Jewish People are punished for the sins of the world. All these concepts can be applied without reservation to the Holocaust. Many habitually raise the question how so many children, who undoubtedly were innocent of any sin, could have died. But these questioners forget that even children are included in the mutual responsibility expressed by the principle, "*tzaddikim* are punished for the sins of the generation." An example is *Chazal*'s statement (*Shabbos* 32b) that "for the [adults'] sin of [violating] vows, children die in childhood." And some say (ibid.) "for the sin of neglecting Torah study."

WE EMPHASIZED EARLIER that it is difficult to accurately evaluate the severity of the sins which we commit. Misdeeds which

The Illusion of Triviality seem at first glance to be only minor infractions are often referred to by the Torah, the Prophets, and *Chazal* as receiving very severe punishments. An example cited was the sin of the Golden Calf — a sin for which destruction was nearly decreed upon the entire Jewish People. Complete national annihilation — a punishment more severe than even the terrors of the Holocaust — was nearly leveled against us for an error which the commentaries tell us was almost negligible, and was committed by only a minority of the Jews. Our existence as a people was similarly threatened in the days of Mordechai and Esther. There too, *Chazal* tell us that the pending heavenly decree was a response for only a minor infraction.[1]

Then there are the times that national tragedy was not averted,

---

1. According to one opinion, the Jews "enjoyed the feast of that wicked one [Achashverosh]," and according to another, they were forcibly coerced to bow down to an image (*Megillah* 12a).

when the Jews fell as a result of their shortcomings. Here too, our misdeeds were often seemingly marginal. Concerning the destruction of the Second *Beis Hamikdash, Chazal* said:

> "Why was the first *Mikdash* destroyed? Because there were three sins in [that generation]: idol worship, illicit relations, and murder. . . But regarding the second *Mikdash*, we know with certainty that they occupied themselves with Torah, *mitzvos*, and acts of kindness. Why, then, was it destroyed? Because of groundless hatred among them" (*Yoma* 9b).

The destruction of the Second *Beis Hamikdash* was not an isolated event: in addition to the historically localized disaster that befell the Jewish People two thousand years ago, all the subsequent persecutions of the exile, including the Holocaust, are but the dark sequels to that fateful calamity. Few of us, however, would have imagined that groundless hatred was severe enough to bring about the millennia of suffering which we have experienced on its account. Indeed, we often underestimate our own cosmic significance. In doing so, however, we also fail to see the monumental consequences of our deeds.

R' Elimelech Bar Shaul writes:

> The Holocaust was horrible. All who wrote about it, saw it, and lived it usually add that there has never been anything comparable in the history of the Jewish People. Undoubtedly this is true. But painful though it may be, we must remember for the sake of the truth that the Holocaust in its terrible dimensions, and earlier calamities which did not reach such dimensions, were in general not completely unexpected.
>
> We find in a number of places in the Torah harsh words regarding religious and moral situations which may arise at given times. Sometimes a verse inserted in the middle of many others epitomizes the profundity of heavenly justice in a truly frightening way. For example, the Holy One, Blessed is He, said to Moshe: "Now release Me, and My wrath will burn against them and I shall destroy them, and I shall make *you* into a great nation" (*Shemos* 32:10). Although Moshe did not acquiesce — he exerted himself in prayer and the decree was not effected — the very suggestion, the very fact that such a

thought arose, provides us with terrifying insight: Israel sinned with the Golden Calf — their first sin after the giving of the Torah. In reaction to this, Hashem revealed to Moshe that He was willing to bring destruction upon this people which had sinned. From the only remaining branch, from Moshe himself, this great nation — the chosen and destined people — would sprout anew.

This is a terrifying concept, but it is written explicitly in the Torah. And the Torah is meant to teach us something in every generation. . .

We find the Passages of Rebuke (*Tochachah*) written explicitly, not once but in two major sections, in *Vayikra* and in *Devarim*. The *Tochachos* begin with an abundance of blessings, but their main message is a scroll of sufferings which threatens to result if we do not obey the words of the Torah. In the synagogue we read the preliminary blessings aloud in a tone of celebration, and the words are sweet and pleasant; the harsh sections, on the other hand, are read quickly and in an undertone. We look forward to their end and are happy to move on. But our fear of the letters, our recoiling from listening, does not change or soften this scroll of suffering at all. . ."You shall be lost among the nations, and the land of your enemies will consume you" (*Vayikra* 26:38). The only limitation is: "But this too: When they are in the land of their enemies I shall not become disgusted with them nor reject them to destroy them" (ibid. v. 44). Indeed, all terrible and fearsome things can happen; all can be included within the plan of Divine Providence regarding the fate of Israel — except "to destroy them," to eliminate them completely. Except for this, anything is possible within a given historical circumstance.

All this was "predictable"; we were warned from the beginning about it all. These things were written in the Torah so that we would know of the terrible possibilities, so that this awesome warning would be alive and fresh in our national consciousness. . . "These are the words of the covenant which Hashem commanded Moshe to make with *Bnei Yisrael* in the land of Moav, besides the covenant which He made with them at Chorev" (*Devarim* 28:69). These words were spoken and were made the basis of a covenant with us as we stood opposite the gates of our land. We accepted them for all generations, in all their profound significance.

The Holocaust was not unpredictable. Not the recent great Holocaust, and not earlier holocausts. This is what the great leaders of every generation perceived when they witnessed suffering befall Israel. Not one of these leaders failed to mention the *Tochachah* as he bewailed the fate of the Jews during the time of a harsh decree. So we find with R' Yitzchak Abarbanel in the books he wrote after the decrees of the Inquisition and the expulsion from Spain; and so we find with the book *Yaven Metzulah,* written after the calamities of *Tach v'Tat* 5408-09 (1648-9). And so it was with many books and lamentations which have survived through the ages and come down to us. . .

We read in the Torah: "*Bnei Yisrael* went up armed (*chamushim*) from the land of Egypt" (*Shemos* 13:18). *Chazal* comment [based on the similarity of *chamush*, "armed," and *chomesh*, "one-fifth"]: "One out of five went out, and four out of five died during the three days of darkness." When we read these words, we shudder in our souls. For only that fraction who merited to be redeemed, from whom we are descended, we rejoice and celebrate for all generations, commemorating the exodus from Egypt. . .

This comment of *Chazal* contains a deep lesson: all our generations have seen it, absorbed it, and made it part of their consciousness. Who went out from Egypt? Only a fraction went out. For scores of generations we have read these words and taken them literally; we believed them and took them into our awareness and our heart. We also knew that such terrible events were potentially very real, and could be transformed from potential to actual. How they might come, or when — these were the secrets of heaven, the profound mysteries of Divine justice. We could presume, however, that these tragic happenings were likely to come in the wake of severe deviations from the path of faith and *mitzvos*; at a time when God's attribute of "slow to anger" reached a certain point — and halted (*Maarechei Lev*, part 2, pp. 207-211).

The severity of the potential harshness of Divine justice is intimately connected with, and somewhat mitigated by, belief in the immortality of the soul. If death is not the cessation of existence, but only a transition to another life, then one can see even death itself as only a cleansing of sins, a painful but necessary phenomenon which allows life to continue in the World of Truth. The difficulty in understanding how such severe punishments could be given for such apparently small sins thus comes not only from a lack of awareness of the seriousness of our misdeeds, but also from an inability to fully internalize faith in eternal life.

OTHER FACTORS LIMIT our objective evaluation of the Holocaust as well. Just as no individual Jew is perfect, neither is any

Coming to Terms With Hindsight

generation flawless. Indeed, throughout our history, Jews have not hesitated to say in their prayers: "Because of our sins, we were exiled from our land"; "our forefathers sinned and are gone"; "we and our fathers have sinned." By contrast, however, our generation has tended to idealize the generation which perished in the Holocaust, picturing them as a completely pure generation to which it is impossible to attribute any sin. Although this response is understandable, it is nonetheless not completely objective.

Despite its limitations, this idealized view is in a certain way quite proper. As a nation, we still stand as a mourner whose dead lies unburied before him. Indeed, one whose heart still quakes with grief cannot be asked to look objectively upon his departed — it is only natural to remember the shining qualities and to quietly forget the shortcomings. Also, there is the feeling that enough violence has been done to this murdered generation; that to speak of their sins would only desecrate their names unnecessarily. Undoubtedly, when all is said and done, we must remember that the generation of the Holocaust was certainly no less righteous than our own.

THIS, OF COURSE, is all true. The generation of the Holocaust overflowed with Torah, *mitzvos*, and true Jewish life, many times

R' Huna's Wine

more so than our own. A very considerable portion of the six million were true God-fearing individuals; among them "cedars of Lebanon", giants of Torah and their disciples. Nevertheless, to accurately evaluate the Holocaust, we must see all aspects of the picture. *Chazal* relate that four hundred barrels of R' Huna's wine once turned to vinegar. The Sages told him: "Search your deeds." Rav Huna replied: "Do you suspect me [of committing sins]?" — to which the Sages in turn responded, "Do you suspect the Holy One, Blessed is He, of passing verdict without a trial?" (*Berachos* 5b).

To properly assess the Holocaust, we must be willing to see the generation which perished as it truly was; we must acknowledge their greatness without hiding their shortcomings. Indeed, to admit the failings of those who died is not to dishonor them, for we are quite cognizant that all who perished were pure in death. *Chazal* said that one who is martyred by gentiles — even if he was guilty of a crime deserving capital punishment — is nonetheless counted among "the servants of Hashem" (*Sanhedrin* 47a).[1]

The Holocaust struck both Jews who observed Torah and *mitzvos* and those who turned away from their faith. However, this does not contradict the possibility that the decree was passed on account of spiritual failings: "Man sees into the eyes, but Hashem sees into the heart," and there is no way of knowing who really is or is not a *tzaddik* in the view of Hashem. Second, "all Israel are held responsible for each other," and hence the sin of the individual is the sin of the entire people. A person may be punished for the fact that he did not protest the sins of his household or anyone else over whom he has influence. Third, "Once the Destroyer is given permission to destroy, he does not distinguish between righteous and wicked; what is more, he begins with the righteous" (*Bava Kamma* 60a). With the righteous, Hashem is exacting to a hairsbreadth, and their death atones for the sins of the generation.

No one can claim to know "the reason" for the Holocaust. The ultimate explanation for the obliteration of European Jewry is as

---

1. Likewise, the *Shulchan Aruch* rules that one does not mourn for a relative who rejected the Torah. Nonetheless, *Rama* cites an opinion that if such a person was martyred by gentiles, one indeed must mourn for him (*Yoreh De'ah* 340:5). [The *halachah* is cited here only to illustrate the point under discussion. A competent halachic authority should be consulted before inferring any practical ruling.]

incomprehensible as the devastation itself. Nevertheless, any event of this sort clearly includes a certain spiritual settling of accounts and cleansing of sins. Thus, we must not ignore the possible areas of our accountability.

Let us realize then, that a large portion of those holy ones who were sanctified by their deaths did not observe Torah and *mitzvos* while they were alive. In the countries of Western and Central Europe the great majority of Jews were completely cut off from their faith; many had been alienated from authentic Jewish life for several generations. According to a study by Dr. Yaakov Robinson (*"The Holocaust of European Jewry,"* published by Yad Vashem, p. 198), only one half of the Jewish population in Eastern Europe (excluding the Soviet Union) remained observant. Even in the strongholds of Torah — Poland, Lithuania, and neighboring countries — a process of secularization and consequent abandonment of Judaism was rapidly advancing. Although Polish Jewry, in particular, constituted a glorious aristocracy of Torah observance, an examination of the pre-war writings of the Chafetz Chaim yields a truly dismal spiritual portrait of even this country:

> At present, only the smallest number [of children] are sent to a proper Jewish school; the vast majority enter secular schools. There, not only do [the instructors] neglect to teach Torah law and faith, but their whole aim is to oppose our holy Law ("A Time to Act for Hashem," article published in the month of Adar, 5686/1926, cited in *The Chafetz Chaim on the Torah*, p. 311).
>
> The amount of religious decline which once occurred over the course of a decade now occurs every few months. Torah [observance] collapses day by day. The evil inclination is conducting a great and terrible rebellion against our King, the King of all kings, the Holy One, Blessed is He (Ibid., p. 312).
>
> In our day, all can see the shocking domination of Hashem's wrath over the world. Since the beginning of the terrible war [World War I], the consequences have been awful: killing, epidemics, and famine. The troubles, within and without, have not yet ceased. All kinds of strange diseases [have spread], until in our day almost the entire

Tochachah [Passages of Rebuke, *Vayikra* ch. 26 and *Devarim* ch. 28] has been fulfilled. . .

Now, all of us, the Jewish People, believe and say aloud every day that He alone has, will, and does cause all to transpire; that He is a God of faith, and that there is no injustice [in His deeds]. If so, we are obligated to contemplate why all this is happening to us in our day. Undoubtedly, it is from Hashem — for we have sinned against Him. We have not desired to walk in His ways and we have not listened to His Torah. The foundations of Torah have begun to crumble. Desecration of *Shabbos* has increased greatly in a number of places. . . also the prohibition of *niddah* has been seriously undermined. . . And another major matter, one of the main principles of our Law, is the education of the children in Torah and service of Hashem. . . This, too, has been greatly weakened, due to our many sins (Ibid., p. 297, from the article "Remember the Torah of Moshe," Nissan, 5685/ 1925).

TOWARDS THE END OF his life, the Chafetz Chaim also witnessed the awakening of European anti-Semitism which

Spiritual Decline heralded the Nazi rise to power. He drew a parallel between this phenomenon and the spiritual decline of the Jewish People:

> We contemplate in these times of ours the pressures of the dreadful period that dominates the world, and the terrible tragedies that multiply today in the world. A tremendous hatred has awakened against our brothers, *Bnei Yisrael,* in the many countries where they had been contentedly settled. The enemies of Israel oppress them from every side. In addition to these [sorrows] a terrible poverty has overcome the world, so that many thousands and ten-thousands of our brothers, *Bnei Yisrael,* are literally starving to death, and there is not a loaf of bread to still their hunger. There is hardly a single person or family who has not been affected by the dire situation of this terrible time. And all ask: Why has Hashem done this to us?
>
> But the truth is that *Chazal*, with their prophetic spirit, have already revealed all this to us. We find in *Shabbos* 32: "For

the sin of neglecting Torah study and desecration of *Shabbos*, war and plunder come upon the world." In addition to the neglect of Torah study on the part of the schools (*chadarim*), the observance of the holy *Shabbos*, which is a foundation of our Law, has also been greatly weakened.

Moreover, the dictum of *Chazal* is well known: "On what does the world stand? On the breath of the mouths of children studying Torah." But tens of thousands of Jewish children have been alienated from the schools where Torah is taught. Instead of the breath of Torah which they formerly breathed, today their mouths are full of nonsense and empty songs. The pillars upon which the world stands are being shaken, and the troubles of the time grow day by day (Ibid., pp. 314-5, from the article, "Education of Chidren," Elul, 5692/1932).

R' Zimmerman, writing in *Tammim Pa'alo*, echoes the Chafetz Chaim's words:

If one examines the younger generation in those countries — how their education alienated them from Torah and Judaism — [one will find that] in almost every family there was at least one who "died" spiritually. We have heard that in the last years before the war, newspapers were unabashedly distributed on *Shabbos* in the city of Warsaw, as the number of Jewish stores that remained open on *Shabbos* steadily increased. There were homes in which the son, the father, and the grandfather — three consecutive generations — had abandoned Hashem and the Jewish religion.

Great men traveled through Germany and — witnessing how the Jews there assimilated with the gentiles and imitated their deeds — came to the conclusion that inevitably, Germany would be destroyed. And we are the witnesses that it happened. In many orthodox and chassidic families, the children left the Torah while the parents remained silent, reacting with polite indifference.

Elsewhere R' Zimmerman writes:

Let us think to ourselves to what extent the new generation became increasingly distant from us; to what extent it moved away from us, separating as far as east is from west and the heavens are from the earth. In Poland, as in other countries, they departed from faith in Hashem; departed from the Torah; departed in all their deeds from the deeds of their fathers, and looked upon everything as foreign to them. They desecrated the Law, the sacred, and Judaism, and in doing so became liable for the four designated types of capital punishment. We find in the words of *Chazal* (*Kesubos* 30b): "If one committed a crime deserving the penalty of stoning [and the penalty was not executed by a court], he falls off a roof, or a wild animal kills him. If he deserved death by fire, he dies in a fire, or a snake bites him. If he deserved death by the sword, he is turned in to the [gentile] government [for a capital crime], or killed by bandits. If he deserved death by strangulation, he drowns in a river or dies of suffocation."

Of course, after the fact [one may not accuse], for those people are all holy and pure, having died sanctifying His name, Blessed is He. As it is said in Tractate *Sanhedrin*, if one dies a violent death his sin is atoned for even without *teshuvah* (repentance). . . Nevertheless we must show that we know, each one to himself, that it is we who sinned. . . that Hashem is the righteous One, and that there can be no legitimate question "Why?" (*Tammim Pa'alo*, pp. 25-29).

THERE IS A CERTAIN reluctance to probe the shortcomings of the generation which perished in the Holocaust, for fear of implying

One Is Not Only an Individual

that one sees only the sins of others, while holding himself to be blameless. No such suggestion is intended here. We must remember that the Holocaust struck equally at all Jews: those who kept the Torah and those who did not. One's own personal commitment to Torah observance cannot be grounds for complacency, for one is not only an individual, he is an inextricable part of the community as well. "All Israel are held responsible for one another," and thus the obligation to say, "We are guilty". . . "because of our sins. . ." devolves equally upon every Jew.

If assimilation was the blight of pre-war Jewish Europe, then it is no less our national ailment today. Likewise, the Torah community, as the potential educators of the generation, cannot hold itself blameless. Indeed, its responsibility is unique: R' Yisrael Salanter said that when Torah scholars speak slander in the Kovno *beis midrash*, its spiritual ramifications cause desecration of *Shabbos* in Paris. All Israel is as one person, and every act influences the entire people.

Assimilation, however, is only the most visible shortcoming which can be identified. Men commit numerous transgressions — many of them, all too commonly dismissed as trivial, are in fact quite severe. *Lashon hara* — unnecessarily speaking ill of another person (even if the information is true) — is considered by *Chazal* to be an evil equal in dimensions to the three most severe sins of the Torah: idol worship, murder, and adultery. Similarly, groundless hatred caused the destruction of the second *Beis Hamikdash*, as well as the consequent troubles of exile. R' Yehonassan Eybeschitz writes:

> There have been many historical junctures which we considered particularly ripe for the End of Days, but our hopes were dashed. This is for no other reason than that we did not do *teshuvah* (repent), for from the sole of our foot to the top of our head there is no pure spot. We are especially [guilty of] groundless hatred, deceptive talk, and disrespect of Torah. This is the very thing that destroyed the House of Hashem (the *Beis Hamikdash*) — as *Chazal* said, "for the sin of groundless hatred.". . .Therefore we must strengthen ourselves very much in this — and especially in the areas of false talk and deception. For (in these areas) the gentiles are careful, and the Accuser uses this to rouse judgment against Israel. As I have told you frequently: For every *mitzvah* which the gentiles hold to strictly, if we are not especially particular about that *mitzvah*, anger is aroused against Israel (*Ya'aros Devash*, *drush* 5).

Similarly, the *Zohar* (*Zohar Chadash* on *Rus*, p. 79), in its account of the seven levels of *Gehinnom*, includes *lashon hara* among those sins deserving particular discipline. If such offenses are of sufficient magnitude to be singled out in the next world, does it not follow that one may experience their ramifications in this fleeting world as well?

IT IS THUS CLEAR that there is no room to distinguish between those who keep Torah and *mitzvos* and those who do not. Many

The Observant Public

of the sins which we were — and are — liable for as a nation are common among the observant as well. On the contrary, perhaps the heavenly reckoning against the religious segment was more stringent on this account. A large part of the non-observant public was in the category of *tinok shenishbah* — the unwitting victims of second- or third-generation assimilation. Whereas their sins were more the products of ignorance than anything else, this cannot truly be said of the Torah-observant public. We note with a shudder that it was against the observant segment of the Jewish population that the Nazis plotted with particularly intense hatred. Similarly, the Jews of outstandingly religious Poland were harder hit than those of Germany or Hungary, where assimilation was much further advanced.

CHAZAL SAID REGARDING the *ben sorer u'moreh*, the archetypal rebellious son mentioned in *Devarim* 21:18-21, that the boy

The Rebellious Son

is condemned to death only because of his inevitable future. His present sins do not in themselves warrant the death penalty. Nonetheless, the Torah understood the psychological constructs of this personality in their infancy. Inevitably, the son would recklessly dispose of his father's property. He would seek his accustomed pleasures and, not finding them, would rob men in the crossroads. The Torah said: 'It is preferable that he should die innocent than that he should die guilty'" (*Sanhedrin* 72a).

IN SUMMARY, WE must recognize that any attempt to explain the ultimate "Why" of the Holocaust is bound to fail. The true and

An Elusive Rationale

complete rationale for the existence of evil, whether within the context of the Holocaust or of history in general, is altogether beyond human comprehension. Even when the Torah explicitly reveals that a certain punishment was given for a specific sin, the matter still lies beyond our grasp. We can no more comprehend why small children die for adults' neglect of Torah study, than we can understand why men are condemned to *Gehinnom* for pride. The true cause-and-effect process linking sin to punishment always eludes the most meticulous of human calculations.

NEVERTHELESS, IF WE can never know the ultimate meaning of tragedy, we may be assured that its occurrence is not arbitrary.

Acknowledging Shortcomings

The fact that we may never decipher the definitive rationale for suffering does not relieve us of an obligation to search our deeds when catastrophe indeed strikes. If one cannot acknowledge his failings, his response to tragedy can only be to question Divine justice all the more intensely. One who recognizes the weight of his deeds, however, confronts calamity by peering inward. He knows that to fulfill God's commands is to do His Will, and for this we merit eternal reward. To sin, however, is to rebel — and rebellion against one's Father, King and Creator is an act of unfathomable spiritual significance; hence, so are its ramifications.

Our fathers' fathers believed that earlier calamities were, among other things, a Divine punishment for our collective sins. We cannot help but draw the same essential conclusion regarding the Holocaust. It would indeed seem that the scope of the Holocaust and its horrors exceeded that of any earlier disasters. But can we escape the possibility that perhaps our spiritual decline was all the greater as well?

E.

In Conclusion

WE MUST REJECT the widespread but superficial approach that the central issue raised by the Holocaust is whether or not God acted justly, as if we are capable of passing judgment on Him. To fruitlessly probe the thoughts of Him Who transcends comprehension is to distract attention from our

Finding the Balance real task of self-examination. The time has come for man to turn his back upon the advice of the primeval serpent: "and you shall be like God." Let us not presume to discuss that which we cannot fathom.

On the other hand, we are obligated to deal with those matters that lie within the bounds of our understanding. To the extent he can, man is commanded to clarify for himself the general paths of Divine justice. We are commanded to study the words of the Torah and our sages until we can truly affirm: "The Creator, His actions are perfect, for all His ways are judgment" (*Devarim* 32:4). And if the heart still does not acquiesce and the intellect is not yet satisfied, our task is not yet complete. We must pour out our hearts before our Maker, and entreat Him to help destroy the barriers which prevent us from knowing His ways.

IN OUR QUEST TO know the ways of our Creator, let us not be like judges gazing upwards, but like schoolchildren whose hearts

A Perspective Defined desire only to understand. Let us not be guided by pride or haughtiness. Let us not pound our confessional fist on the chests of our sanctified brothers, but rather search within ourselves for the faults that characterize us no less than our predecessors. Even in this endeavor let us willingly admit uncertainty, and shun the pretense of absolute knowledge.

We are obligated to contemplate all that befalls us. In doing so, however, we must ponder, not accuse. The Chazon Ish writes the following concerning the Holocaust:

> We deny all our sins and lowliness, at a time when we are soiled with our sins and crimes, and are empty of Torah and stripped of *mitzvos*. Let us not strive for things which are beyond us! Let us search our ways and repent, for this is our obligation, as it is written (*Yeshayahu* 58:6): "This is the kind of fasting that I [Hashem] choose" (*Kovetz Igros Chazon Ish*, 1:97).

A similar feeling is expressed by R' Michal Dov Weissmandl, in the name of his teacher, the *gaon* R' Shmuel David Ungar:

> In our communities there is a fixed custom that the rav gives a talk in the *beis knesses* on the seventh of Adar [the anniversary of the passing of Moshe Rabbeinu]. . . Our teacher fell ill at that time. . . and he commanded that I should speak in his place. And, in the bitterness of my heart from all the news pouring in then about the military battles and the decrees in our country, I said what I said, in order to arouse mourning and weeping, to plead for mercy from heaven, saying, "Why are You doing this to Your servants?" Our teacher, may his merit defend us, heard about my talk and was upset with me. He said, "If I had known that you were going to speak like this, I would have fought against my illness and given the talk myself. What were you thinking? You see that this is a time of disaster such as has never been. Terrible verdicts are decreed upon us from heaven. The Master of Mercy has stretched out the cord of strict justice over us. We see that the *Tochechah* (rebuke and punishments) written in the Torah is being fulfilled in us, as it is written, "And if you do not listen to Me. . ." (*Vayikra 26:14*). We have no power except *teshuvah* (repentance) and good deeds with which to transform His strict justice. And if you want to ask from the Creator, Blessed is He, that which there is to ask of Him, turn your face to the wall and say *Tehillim* (Psalms). But when you turn your face to the people, ask what you have to ask from them: *teshuvah* and good deeds."

The question raised by the Holocaust is not, then, the issue of Divine justice, but the question of the meaning and significance of the Holocaust for man. The question is not "Where was God?" but "Where was man?" If we contemplate the events of history from this vantage point, we may discover that tangential questions fall away of their own accord. We are thus free to concentrate on the real issues.

4

"Why the Holocaust?" –
Searching for a Meaning

R' Yochanan said: "If you see a generation becoming fewer and fewer, expect him [*Mashiach*]."

R' Yochanan also said: "If you see a generation upon which numerous disasters pour like a river, expect him." (*Sanhedrin* 98a)

A.

Birth Pangs of Redemption

MANY GREAT TORAH leaders have viewed the Holocaust as *chevlei Mashiach*, the birth pangs which precede our final Redemption. R' Eliahu Lopian writes: "That which occurred twelve years ago, when the Nazis, may their name be blotted out, destroyed more than six million

Chevlei Mashiach   Jewish lives, was undoubtedly *chevlei Mashiach*" (*Lev Eliahu*, part 1, p. 77). Similarly, R' Isser Zalman Meltzer writes:

The Jewish People have seen during these years [in the words of the *Pesach Haggadah*] "blood, fire, and columns of smoke." Their blood was spilled like water by the enemy, who with terrible cruelty killed millions of our brothers. . . We must hope that it was "a time of trouble for Yaakov, and from it he will be saved."

The *chevlei Mashiach* are terrible. *Chazal* with their prophetic inspiration foresaw long ago the horrible disasters of the End of Days, so much so that they declared (*Sanhedrin* 98b): "May it [the time preceding the Redemption] come, and may I not see it [the terrible calamities]" (Introduction to *Even Ha'Ezel*, part 4).

We find this idea expressed by other *Gedolim* as well:

The *Admor* of Gur wrote of the Holocaust: "If the troubles become numerous, then these are *chevlei Mashiach!*"[1]

This subject is also discussed eloquently by R' Moshe Yonah Halevi Zweig (rav of Antwerp) in his introduction to *Ohel Moshe* (part 1):

Hashem founded the earth with wisdom, and no place is devoid of Him. He decided to dwell shrouded in mist, and no thought can comprehend Him at all. He does great, mighty, awesome wonders. Exceedingly deep are His thoughts, exalted are His ways. "And God saw that it was very good": This refers to suffering, for through it we reach the World to Come, the world which is wholly good. Thus, the paths of redemption are drenched in blood, and the sufferings of the generation of *Mashiach* are as great as the sufferings of the generation of persecution.

The face of the earth has not yet dried from the flood of fire which wiped out hundreds of thousands of Jews, the pride of the nation. Our eyes still pour forth tears for the modest girls and tender boys who, wrapped in their books, went up in flames; for the young men of Israel who were gathered into their world in sanctification of the Name, together with fathers and mothers; for the brides wrapped in their bridegrooms'

---

1. Letter dated "the first day of *parashas Bamidbar*, 5703/1943," printed in *Osef Michtavim Mikevod Kedushas Admor, shlita, Mi'gur*, August, 5707/1947, at the end of the book.

arms, stabbed with swords and bayonets, who became like the burnt ashes of the altar; for the *gaonim* of the earth, the cedars of Lebanon, crowned with the crown of Torah, whose butchered bodies were thrown to the animals of the field, while the beast blasphemes: "Who is over me in the heavens?"

But this, too: From this veil of confusion, this valley of terrifying vision — from this darkness of exile's night — from here the dawn of the End of Days begins to glimmer; the fulfillment of the vision of redemption.

And shimmering as sapphires are the words of *Chazal* (*Midrash Tehillim, mizmor* 20): "To what may this be compared? To a father and son who were walking down the road, and the son became tired. He said to his father: 'Where is the city?' The father replied: 'My son, keep this sign in mind: If you see a graveyard in front of you, know that the city is close to you.' Thus the Holy One, Blessed is He said to Israel: 'If you see that calamities are covering you, at that moment you will be redeemed.' "

In a famous pamphlet written before the Holocaust, R' Elchanan Wasserman declares that the upheavals destined to befall the Jewish People in our generation are those of *chevlei Mashiach:*

If we wish to grasp the essence of the events (which will occur) in our lifetime, we must seek verses and statements (of *Chazal*) regarding the period called *Ikvasa DeMeshicha* (lit: the heels, i.e. footsteps of *Mashiach*) — the transition between exile and redemption (*Ikvasa DeMeshicha*, p. 9).

In the Book of *Daniel*, Chapter 12, it is written that the troubles of those days (preceding *Mashiach*) will exceed anything that has befallen Israel since they became a nation; the disasters will exceed in scope even the destruction of the *Beis Hamikdash*. The same is stated in Chapter 30 of *Yirmeyahu*. *Chazal*, who foresaw the terrors of *Ikvasa DeMeshicha*, declared: "May it come, and may I not see it" (*Sanhedrin* 98a, and end of Tractate *Sotah*). In other words, "May *Mashiach* come, but may we not be witnesses to the circumstances of his coming." The *Gaon* of Vilna writes that the Redemption is called "birth," as it is written, "Zion trembled and also gave birth" (*Yeshayahu* 66:8). The

Hebrew people then will be born anew: just as the pains, the birth pangs, foretell the birth, and the closer the birth approaches the stronger the pains become, so too *chevlei Mashiach* will precede the Redemption. As the Redemption approaches, the birth pangs of *Mashiach* will daily become more severe (p. 10).

Just as the pains of pregnancy cannot be compared to those of childbirth, so too the disasters of exile cannot be compared to *chevlei Mashiach*. The disasters of exile follow a known sequence, hinted to in the opening of the *Parashah* of Exile (the beginning of *Parashas Vayishlach*). There it is stated: "The remaining camp shall escape" (*Bereishis* 32:8). While Jews were cruelly persecuted in one country, there was always another country which served as a refuge. At the time of the expulsion from Spain, the lands of Turkey, Poland, and Holland opened their gates to the refugees. But in the time of *chevlei Mashiach*, it will be different. Jews will be persecuted everywhere, with nowhere to rest; they will be expelled from every place, and no one will take them in (pp. 27-8).

Similar words are cited in the name of R' Israel Shapira, the *Admor* of Grodzinsk:

When they brought the people of the concentration camp — a crowd of several thousand — into the annihilation courtyard of Treblinka, the people turned to the *Admor* of Grodzinsk, R' Israel Shapira: "Rabbeinu, what do you say now?"

Then our holy Rabbi began to speak:

"Hear, my brothers and sisters, people of Hashem. Ours is not to question the deeds of the Holy One, Blessed is He. If it has been decreed that at this time we shall be sacrificial offerings. . . to be put upon the fire, fortunate are we who have merited this. As for *Chazal*'s statement, 'May it come, and may I not see it,' that only applies before one reaches the situation; but we, who have reached this level, must rejoice to have merited that our ashes, like the ashes of the Red Cow, will purify the entire Jewish People. We are obligated to see ourselves as fortunate that it is our lot to pave the way for the Redeemer who rapidly approaches. We must lovingly accept our *akeidah* — our being bound on the altar for the sanctification of His name. I now command you not to hesitate and not to weep as you go to the furnace — on the contrary, be happy, and sing *Ani Ma'amin* ["I Believe," the song of the Thirteen Principles of Faith]. Be like R' Akiva in his time, who left the world reciting *Shema Yisrael*, and whose soul departed with the word, *Echad* (One)."

The public fulfilled his holy command; and with the melody of *Ani Ma'amin* and the recitation of *Shema Yisrael*, they publicly sanctified the Divine Name (*Ani Ma'amin*, pp. 44-45).

Chevlei Mashiach — Punishment or Purification?

WHAT IS THE GOAL of the dreadful suffering which precedes our final redemption? Ultimately, the answer lies shrouded in mystery, as with all secrets of the Divine. Nonetheless, the sages of past generations have considered the issue.

R' Elchanan Wasserman, writing in the name of his teacher the Chafetz Chaim, argued that *chevlei Mashiach* come to purify the world of sins that accumulated throughout the generations. The *Admor* of Piastchene, in his work *Esh Kodesh*, took a different approach. He asked:

> Clearly, the aim of *chevlei Mashiach* is to cleanse our sins before the revelation which is the coming of *Mashiach*. But why does this generation of the coming of *Mashiach* have to suffer for all the past generations as well?

The *Admor* concludes that the birth pangs of *Mashiach*, like the pains of actual childbirth, are not actually punishments *per se*. Although the anguish which accompanies birth was a result of Adam's sin, the travail is not so much a punishment for this primal sin as a natural consequence of it. Similarly, the pains which herald the birth of our redemption are part of a comparable "natural process":

> It is impossible for anything to be born — i.e., that through it, new light should be drawn down and revealed — unless part of its own light becomes annulled. This conforms with the established principle that nothing can reveal the light of Hashem except through annulment of its own existence. . .

Chevlei Mashiach, as far as we can understand the concept, is something similar. The Redemption is a Divine revelation, by which Hashem will reveal some of His light and holiness. This revelation comes about through Israel, for the entire Redemption and its timing depend on Israel. Therefore, in order for Israel to merit that such great light should be revealed through them, some of their powers must be annulled — and this is *chevlei Mashiach* (*Esh Kodesh*, p. 106; for the source of this concept see *Maharal's Netzach Israel*, chs. 35 and 36).

ACCORDING TO EACH of these explanations of *chevlei Mashiach*, one thing remains clear: It is the purpose of these troubles to **False Hopes?** in some way prepare the world for Redemption. We may then ask, if the Holocaust was indeed *chevlei Mashiach* — a prelude to Redemption — where is the Redemption itself? It seems that there should be not only a bill of accounts, but also a receipt. How is it that we have not, as yet, witnessed the advent of *Mashiach*?

Yet another question pierces the heart: We are not, indeed, the first in Jewish history to see our catastrophes as *chevlei Mashiach*. Every generation has hoped that its sorrows heralded salvation. One need not make a careful study of our history to see that in all times of great trouble, Jews tried to predict the date of Redemption, and impostors posed as *Mashiach* as well. So it was after the expulsion from Spain, and so it was after the massacres of 5408-9 (1648-9). Indeed, the Chafetz Chaim and other great sages thought that the terrors of the First World War were *chevlei Mashiach*. In that time, not only were we not redeemed, but we suffered the Holocaust of the Second World War only two decades later. How the words of Yeshayahu strike home!:

> Hashem, in calamity they remembered You. They poured forth prayer when You chastised them. Like a pregnant woman whose time has come to give birth, she trembles and screams in her pangs — so have we been before You, Hashem. We became pregnant, we trembled, but it is as if we gave birth to wind! Salvations are not performed in the world — the enemies do not fall (*Yeshayahu* 26:16-18).

Rashi explains: We believed that our travails were the birth-pangs of destined Redemption, but we have only given birth to mere wind. . .

What if now, too, our suffering has been only "false labor?" Can it be that the sorrows of our era are not yet *chevlei Mashiach*, but only another link in the long chain of the sufferings of exile?

We can never know with finality; only in hindsight does history yield such clarity. Nonetheless, it would appear that there is basis to believe that the destruction of European Jewry was indeed part of the prologue to Redemption. Let us bear in mind that in important aspects, the Holocaust stands out as a unique event in Jewish history. First, there can be no denying that the sheer scope of the destruction of European Jewry outstrips that of any previous national calamity. Only to the Holocaust can the words of *Daniel* (12:1) truly be applied: "a time of trouble such as never has been, from the beginning of nations until that time." Similarly, as R' Elchanan Wasserman noted, the Holocaust stands alone in our history as the only calamity which almost completely precluded escape. No nation opened its doors as refuge: The persecuted had nowhere to flee. Let us quote a Jewish youth who in the midst of the Holocaust transcribed these words into his diary:

> This . . .question is whether our distress is part of the anguish which has afflicted the Jewish people since the exile, or whether this is different from all that has occurred in the past. I incline to the second answer, for I find it very hard to believe that what we are going through today is only a mere link in a long chain of suffering. I find it difficult to believe this primarily because of the effect that the restrictions and persecutions are having on me, but I know that it is very difficult to base the solution to a problem of such importance solely on personal feelings. Doubtless the Spanish persecutions or the Chmelnicki massacres in 1648, for example, or other periods of anguish also affected our people greatly, as they were happening. Possibly the impression made by those events was even greater than today's events make on me — this may be assumed from the appearance of false messiahs, etc. . . We should therefore compare our sufferings and theirs in order to find the difference between them.

First of all, we see that in former times the persecutions were always localized. In one place Jews were very badly treated, while in another they lived in peace and quiet. Secondly, and perhaps more important, is the official character of our oppression today, and the organization created solely to persecute us. This difference is really very obvious. Unlike the Spaniards, for instance, who gave our religion as their reason, the Germans are not even trying to justify their persecutions; it is enough that we are Jews. The fact that we were born Jews is sufficient to explain and justify everything.

To the first difference, we may add another; that today it is quite possible to destroy the entire people of Israel. . . (Diary of Moshe Plinker, may Hashem avenge his blood, a Jewish youth from Holland, published by Yad Vashem as *Young Moshe's Diary*, pp. 26-27).

These words were written at a time when the full scope of the German decrees were not yet known. In hindsight, it is indisputable that since the destruction of the *Beis Hamikdash*, nothing comparable to the Holocaust has occurred in the history of our people.

Moshe Plinker, too, concludes that the calamities of the Holocaust are *chevlei Mashiach* — and for this reason he expresses certainty that the war will end, not with victory for Germany or England, but with the complete Redemption. (See ibid., p. 21, and numerous other places throughout the diary.) But here we arrive again at our original question. The war has ended: "The harvest-time has past, the drying season is finished, and we have not been saved" (*Yirmeyahu* 8:20).

A Chance Juxtaposition? HOWEVER, IN RELATION to this point, too, there is a difference between the present time and the period that followed the expulsion from Spain or the pogroms of 5408-9 (1648-9). It is a fact that only a short time after the end of the great destruction of European Jewry, permission was given for every Jew to come and settle in the Holy Land, as a result of the establishment of a Jewish state in Israel. The opening of the Land of Israel to world Jewry not only occurred immediately after the Holocaust, but the Holocaust was a direct cause of this historic event. As the war ended and the concentration camps were revealed, a shocked world confronted the reality of the Nazi atrocities. It was only because of the intense public pressure to solve the problem of hundreds of thousands of Jewish refugees that the world community agreed to the establishment of Israel as a sovereign state. Two of the most unparalleled events in modern Jewish history — the Holocaust, and the opening of our land to unrestricted Jewish immigration — occurred side by side. Can the juxtaposition be mere chance?

IT IS CLEAR THAT the establishment of Israel as a state does not constitute our Redemption — we still wait and pray for the coming

A Jewish State of our *Mashiach*. The precise historical significance of the advent of the state, however, is the subject of a difference of opinions within our Torah leadership. Some see the establishment of a state within our homeland as the beginning of Redemption; others see it as the final stage of exile. We have dealt with this issue in detail in our work *Tzion Beis Chayeinu*, and a fuller discussion of the matter falls beyond the scope of our present discussion. Nevertheless, as we mentioned there, all agree that the period [of the founding of the state] was a time of Divine favor. R' Wolbe, *shlita*, in his work, *Bein Sheshes Le'Asor* (p. 145), quotes the Rav of Brisk, as saying: "The resolution of the United Nations to uphold the establishment of the state was a smile from Divine Providence, but those who held power over the state spoiled it." Avraham Kariv, in *Misod Chachamim*, elaborates this point in greater detail:

> It is astounding to what extent all the signs mentioned [by *Chazal*] — really every single one, both on the public and on the inner horizons of our people — have come together in this generation of ours. The ruling kingdoms confronted each other in two world wars, the likes of which history has never seen. They still continue to confront each other in peace, a sort of peace that balances upon weapons of annihilation which have the power to destroy the entire world. A torrent of

sorrows rages and swells, and the graveyard opens as wide as all the Jewish settlements of Europe — without doubt there can be no descent lower than that of the recent Holocaust. That was the final descent about which they spoke, those who knew the secrets of the future.

On the spiritual and moral levels, too — both in the world and among the Jewish People — we are in a time of crumbling foundations, an orphaning from every heritage, orphaned of every certainty. "Truth has stumbled in the street. . . and truth will be missing" (*Yeshayahu* 59:14). The concept of truth has ceased to be a basis of life between nations, or between man and man. *Chazal* also emphasized that in the crisis destined to overcome the world at the time of the great renewal, natural feelings of shame and modesty will disappear. This phenomenon is very marked in our time.

In short, wherever we look, the crisis which *Chazal* foresaw is upon us in all its force. By this alone, even if there were as yet no sign of redemption, we would be justified in listening for the footsteps of [Eliahu]. All the more so now, for in fact a new element has appeared. Nothing even remotely similar to it has been granted to any generation since the destruction of the Second Temple. Right next to the graveyard — right next to it in time — a state has in fact been revealed: a State of Israel on the territory of *Eretz Yisrael*. Undoubtedly, this is not yet the Redemption for which the generations of Israel have longed. But, after all, "This is the way of the redemption of Israel. At first gradually. . ."

But our Sages said: "the Holy One, Blessed is He, wanted to make Chizkiyahu the *Mashiach*, and to make Sancheriv — Gog and Magog." And why did this not happen through Chizkiyahu? "Because he didn't sing a song of praise [*shirah* — as *Bnei Yisrael* sang after crossing the sea, or as Devorah sang after the victory over Sisra]" (*Sanhedrin* 94a).

It is surprising indeed that such an apparently small matter prevented the redemption of Israel. However, *Chazal* said: "All dreams go according to the mouth": The realization of a dream is guided by the interpretation one gives it. The same applies to a meaningful historical event. The implications for the future contained in the event depend upon the interpretation given to it; that is, its future consequences depend upon what the generation seeks to derive from it. A small-minded outlook on events can make the gateways of the future shrink into common doorways.

In this way King Chizkiyahu marred his own chance to be *Mashiach*, and missed the opportune moment for Redemption. Why didn't he sing a song of praise? Because he did not properly appreciate the greatness of the event. As the *Tanach* relates, the entire mighty war camp of Sancheriv which encamped against Jerusalem was in one night transformed into a heap of corpses. An impenetrable siege melted away of its own accord, as if made of cobwebs. This miraculous end to Sancheriv's army contained an implication that the end had come to all conquerors and their war camps — that history was approaching its tremendous finale. But Chizkiyahu interpreted the event as significant only for its own time — *this time*, Jerusalem had been saved from the danger threatening her. And as he interpreted it, so it was. What Sancheriv had not managed to achieve, Nevuchadnetzar accomplished after him.

Likewise, there are grounds to assume that the establishment of the State of Israel and her attendant victories over her attackers constituted an exalted gateway into the future. But those who held power, as well as their contemporaries, saw the state only as a gateway into the community of nations, as a foothold by which to equate our existence with that of other peoples — as if the gentiles had already been redeemed and we simply had to catch up with them. The result is the situation in which we find ourselves today (*Misod Chachamim*, pp. 176-7).

According to this approach, our generation was witness to a time of Divine favor which was a potential gateway to the complete Redemption. Some believe that the opportunity has already been lost. Others, less pessimistic, hope that it is simply "the way of the redemption of Israel. At first gradually. . ." — that the spirit of *teshuvah* and purity will yet return to invigorate the Jewish people within their state. In either case, the practical implication is the same: We bear an awesome historic responsibility. We have it within our power to determine not only our own personal spiritual fate, but that of the whole Jewish People. If the moment of Divine favor at the time of the state's establishment was missed, still, *Eretz Yisrael* is in Jewish hands, and it is being settled by Jews from all over the world. This, in itself, is an historical opportunity of inestimable proportions. The time of Divine favor has not yet completely passed; it is still within our hands to shape the course of history.

DESPITE THE APPARENT promise of our historical opportunity, we must reiterate that one cannot hope to draw definitive

A Slice of Time conclusions from the events of such a short period of time. Although from an individual's perspective a period of a hundred years spans several long generations, the gaze of the Omnipresent encompasses eternity. In the Divine sweep of history, a thousand years are as a passing day.

We must remain aware that, as human beings, our historical vision is limited indeed. It is possible that the catastrophes of the last hundred years constitute only one long set of *chevlei Mashiach*; perhaps the final contractions and birth-pangs have not yet concluded. We must be careful not to minimize vast historical processes by reducing them to fit our petty scale of measurements. One cannot gauge history in decades. The world has anticipated Redemption from the six days of its creation — several tens of years more seems not long for it to wait.

IT SHOULD BE NOTED that some of our sages refused to comment on the significance of the Holocaust within our history.

The Guidelines of Speculation In contrast to those quoted above, it is said of the Chazon Ish that:

He refrained from expressing an opinion about the place of the Holocaust in the process of history and exile. When asked, he told a characteristic parable: A man going on a trip marks upon a map the stopping points he must pass through, and at each of these points he measures how far he has come and how far he must yet travel. It was not so, however, when we set out in exile. Although we knew that we must pass through many such stopping points, their number will not be known until the end (*Pe'er Hador*, part 3, p. 125).

Still it is possible that there is no fundamental disagreement between the *Chazon Ish* and those we quoted above — all of these views lead in essentially the same direction. We emphasized earlier that any speculation regarding the significance of the Holocaust, or other events of comparable magnitude, is undertaken with the full understanding that we shall never uncover their full meaning and import. Save through Divine inspiration, one can never know with certainty what is God's will or intent. This is true of the past and present, and is all the more true of the future. Indeed, the signs seem to indicate that the days of *Mashiach* draw near, but we are not prophets. *Rambam* writes concerning the Messianic era: "Regarding all these and similar matters, no one will know how it will be, until it in fact occurs" (*Hilchos Melachim* 12:2).

All this however, does not detract from the legitimacy of speculation upon the meaning of events. On the contrary, in given historical circumstances, it would appear that such speculation is incumbent. There is evidence in Kabbalistic literature that each period in which the sages of Israel indicated signs of redemption was truly a potential gateway into the Messianic Era. The fate of history, however, hinged upon the people: Had the Jews of those generations taken the sages' words to heart and prepared themselves for the great Day of Judgment, then it would have in fact occurred. As illustrated above, it would appear that in our era too, God's Providence smiles upon us — perhaps more so than at any other time over the last two millennia. We have been thrust into one of history's most significant moments. The opportunity is here — what will come of it, however, is in our hands.

B.

Search for Sins

EFORE ONE UNDERTAKES to seek the possible spiritual shortcomings which may have yielded the Holocaust, a fundamental question must be addressed: How is it possible for mortal man to pinpoint the spiritual causes and effects of history? We no longer have prophets, and even the sparks of prophetic inspiration — *ruach hakodesh* — are a rarity. Do we have any accurate standards by which to match meritorious action to reward, or sin to punishment? To select just one example: Some connect the Holocaust with the sin of rejecting Zionism; others, with the sin of accepting Zionism. How are we to determine the truth? How indeed are we to know what our God demands of us by His rebuke?

ALTHOUGH DIFFICULTIES REMAIN, it would appear that there are a number of criteria which can guide us in analyzing the causes

The Criteria of the Holocaust. First, it would seem that any wrongdoing which contributed to fostering the Holocaust would have to have been committed on the communal level. Such a sin could not be one of individuals, but must rather have been a national fault, a way of acting that characterized the whole Jewish People or at least a majority of them. If the punishment affected the entire nation as one, it follows that the community as a whole was the responsible agent.

Second, we must search for a sin which corresponds qualitatively as well as quantitatively to the punishment. The Torah teaches that the way of the Holy One is to respond in kind to the actions of his children, "measure for measure." Not only does punishment parallel sin, it is indeed its natural ramification: "He dug a pit and excavated it, and stumbled into the chasm he had created. . ." (*Tehillim* 7:16).

Another criterion of which we must remain aware: We must

guard against pounding the confessional fist on the chest of others. In our search for the wrongdoings which yielded the Holocaust, we ought to direct our focus primarily on the kinds of sins which are prevalent today. To attribute to those who died sins which we find ourselves innocent of today would only play into the hands of pretentious egoism. Our search for the causative faults of the Holocaust is not an academic one, for we concede from the start that we shall never truly know the answers. Instead, we seek only to locate the blemishes still within us, for our quest focuses primarily inward.

The *Gemara* teaches us:

> If one sees suffering come upon him, let him examine his deeds, for it is written: "Let us examine our ways and probe" (*Eichah* 3:40). If one searched and did not find [any wrongdoing], he should attribute it to neglect of Torah study (*Berachos* 5a).

Some interpret this to mean that if he "examined and did not find," then he can be sure that it was only neglect of Torah study which caused the sin to be hidden from him: Had he properly studied the Torah, it would have taught him where his fault lay, as well as the reason for his punishment. In our analysis of the Holocaust, we shall utilize the sources within *Chazal* and Torah as the primary foundations of our thought. It is true that if one wishes, one may find in the words of *Chazal* apparent evidence for nearly any idea he might wish to prove; indeed, many have so exploited the sayings of our Sages. This, however, does not preclude the possibility of a serious study of *Chazal*. One who studies the Torah with intellectual honesty and sincerity is assured of the fruits of his labor.

A final word of caution: Some of the Torah leadership seem to have vigorously opposed searching for the spiritual causes of the Holocaust. Strong words are cited in the name of R' Yitzchak Hutner:

> It should be needless to say at this point that since the *churban* of European Jewry was a *tochachah* phenomenon, an enactment of the admonishment and rebuke which *Klal*

Yisrael carries upon its shoulders as an integral part of being the *Am Hanivchar* — G-d's chosen ones — we have no right to interpret these events as any kind of *specific punishment for specific sins*. The *tochachah* is a built-in aspect of the character of *Klal Yisrael* until *Mashiach* comes and is visited upon *Klal Yisrael* at the Creator's will and for reasons known and comprehensible *only to Him*. One would have to be a prophet or a Talmudic Sage to claim knowledge of the specific reasons for what befell us; anyone on a lesser plane claiming to do so tramples in vain upon the bodies of the *kedoshim* who died *al kiddush Hashem* and misuses the power to interpret and understand Jewish history. *(The Jewish Observer*, October, 1977)*

Nevertheless, it would seem that the objection expressed above is only to a claim of indisputable knowledge of the will and intent of Hashem. The citations from sages concerning the Holocaust which are quoted in the following sections, however, do not claim certainty, but only suggest possible approaches to the catastrophe which befell us. They seek not to explain definitively, but only to draw lessons from the events, so that we may improve our ways and draw closer to the true service of Hashem.

C.

Assimilation and Decline

That which has come into your hearts shall never be,
that you say: "We shall be like the nations,
like the families of the lands, to serve wood and stone."
By My life, says Hashem, God, I swear that
with a strong hand and with an outstretched arm
and with wrath poured out, I shall rule over you.
(*Yechezkel* 20:32-33)

N THE PREVIOUS CHAPTER we quoted the words of the Chafetz Chaim, who at the end of his life connected the awakening of Nazi anti-Semitism in Europe to the spiritual decline of the Jewish People. In a similar vein, R' Yaakov Kanievsky, the Steipler, writes:

> We see this as the finger of God, for the rejection of Torah, may the Merciful One save us, first began in organized form in Ashkenaz [Germany], and from there disseminated to the other lands; likewise the decree to kill and destroy came from that wicked land (*Chayei Olam*, p. 37).

R' CHAIM OZER GRODZINSKY, too, connects the Holocaust with the fact that assimilation and the *Haskalah* (Enlightenment)

The Achiezer's Lament

movement began in Germany. In the Introduction to his responsa-work, *Achiezer* (part 3), published on the eve of World War II, he writes:[1]

> How terrible is the situation of our people. Never was there a time like this, even in the Middle Ages. The whole Diaspora is

---

1. The Introduction was written in Sivan, 5699/1939.

like one bonfire. Houses of study (*batei midrash*) and Torah scrolls are burned on every street-corner. New, cruel decrees are brought forth by our enemies, who seek to alienate us from our holy Law. Great and important Jewish communities are torn from their places, and the gates of countries are locked to them. They roam and wander upon the waves of the sea. Tens of thousands of families drift over the continent between swells of hatred that storm and drench them in full force. We are ridiculed, cursed, denounced, trampled. Even the light that had shone upon us from the east, from our desired Land, has been darkened by a heavy cloud, so that we do not know what each new day may bring. [The reference is to the bloody Arab riots of 5696-9/1936-9.] Numerous troubles surround us, killings, murders, expulsions, and wanderings. The whole Jewish People drowns in rivers of blood and a sea of tears, harassed and oppressed. Alas, what has become of us!

In the past — in medieval times and in the decrees of 5408 (1648) — our brothers *Bnei Yisrael* believed in Hashem; that the God of Israel would not ignore and abandon His people. Their faith gave them strength and courage to bear the oppressions of the arrogant. Not only did they endure their sufferings, but they went on to build great centers of Torah and tradition, as *Chazal* said: "Wherever they went into exile, the *Shechinah* (Divine Presence) traveled into exile with them."

But today, faith has weakened. In the western countries the Reform Movement has struck at the roots for several generations, and this has brought the masses to intermarriage and assimilation. And from there the evil has gone out now, to pursue them with wrath, to destroy them and expunge them from the earth — and they have caused the poison and hatred against our brothers, *Bnei Yisrael,* to spread to the other lands as well. Even in the eastern [European] countries, those who err — and those who cause others to err — have increased. The faithless have seized control of the land, luring the masses of the House of Israel away from the Torah's path. What is more, they have caused part of the people to publicly desecrate the holy things of the nation. Unable to withstand temptation, they opened gaping holes in the sanctity of *Shabbos*, the foundation of the whole Torah. At the

instigation of the many *Maskilim*, followers of the "Enlightenment," they polluted their souls by eating forbidden foods,
treifos and *neveilos*, though the Torah says: "You shall be a
holy people to Me, and you shall not eat meat torn (*treifah*)
from a live animal" (*Shemos* 22:30). Many gaps were also
torn in the purity of Jewish family life.

Despite all this, the people have not yet become conscious
of [the gravity of] what this is, and why they are so persecuted;
they have been struck with blindness. Every heart has melted
and every hand has become weak. There is no more strength
to bear the yoke of exile and the pressing calamities which
increase from moment to moment — fiercely, with mighty
anger, so that the curse of each day is worse than that of the
day before.

THE *GAON* R' ELIAHU ELIEZER DESSLER also draws a parallel
between the Holocaust and the assimilation and intermarriage

Emancipation and Holocaust

prevalent in pre-war Europe. In his characteristic way, he adds novel insight to the
discussion:

We are dumbfounded by the awful destruction that has
descended upon our generation, and we ask ourselves why
Hashem has done this to us. . . what is this great wrath? But let
us ponder: The entire period leading up to the Holocaust was
a time during which the servitude of exile was eased from the
Jewish People. Until a hundred and fifty years ago, *Klal
Yisrael* was a despised outcast among the nations of the earth.
Only in recent generations have the gentiles begun to lighten
our burden; giving us rights and legislating laws making us
equal to them. Thus began the era of "emancipation."
Moreover, in recent years they have begun to speak of *Eretz
Yisrael* and of the possibility of giving it to us as a place where
we can settle and be at rest. These are the same gentiles who
in the past ridiculed and despised us, who considered us the
most abject of the contemptible. And after all, they too believe
that *Eretz Yisrael* is a holy land. Even so, Hashem put it into
their hearts to consider granting it to us.

It is clear that the era of emancipation was given to us by
Hashem, Blessed is He, to serve as a time of preparation for

the coming of *Mashiach*. To this end, the yoke of exile was eased from upon us; for the task of preparing for *Mashiach* — the task of reaching the level [at which we may merit] redemption — requires a great spiritual effort on our part. A situation of incessant troubles and continual suppression is not fit to provide the motivation for the necessary spiritual ascent. Thus, this period of new illumination and the easing of our condition came so that we could use our advantages for purposes of *kedushah*, holiness. But we reversed the goal. Instead of perceiving the hint from above and preparing for the Redemption joyfully and with an expanded consciousness, we used the new situation to mix with the gentiles and imitate them. As a result, we were exposed to the danger which always comes when sanctification is not carried through to the end. . .

The process of assimilation had been progressing at an ever-quickening rate for a long time, and yet disaster has not overtaken us until now. This is because the Holy One, Blessed is He, delays His anger — He does not punish until we have reached the limit and there is no longer hope that kindness will lead to improvement. We see this regarding the First Temple, which stood for a long time [after the people had begun to sin], and the ten miracles [associated with the Temple services continued to take place daily], even after Menashe set up a graven image in the Sanctuary.

And if, after the terrible destruction, we find ourselves on the verge of a new era of Divine kindness, let us not repeat our foolishness. Let us recognize the hints from above and seize the period of illumination to return in complete *teshuvah* (*Michtav Me'Eliyahu*, part 4, pp. 124-5).

IT WOULD SEEM that if we were to choose one term to summarize the history of the European Jewish communities over

The Process of Assimilation

the past two hundred years, none could be more fitting than "assimilation." The process began in western Europe, with the "Enlightenment" (*Haskalah*) springing from Berlin, and the Reform Movement coming in its wake. The *Haskalah* and Reform movements led to the abandonment of Judaism through an epidemic of conversion and mixed marriages. In the end, there remained only a minority who followed the paths of their fathers, keeping the Torah and *mitzvos*.

In eastern Europe, the process began later, but by the period following World War One, it had gained its full force. Assimilation had progressed so steadily that even a non-observant scientist, on the eve of the Second World War, expressed the worry that for the first time in their history, the Jewish People stood in danger of extinction — this time not by enemies and attackers, but from the internal threat of intermarriage *(Milchemet HaYehudim Lekiyumam*, Jerusalem, 5700/1940).

Assimilation continues today. According to the estimate of Professor Robert Buckey (as publicized in the media in Av, 5743/1983), the Jewish population of the world today totals approximately ten million — there are less Jews existing today than were alive immediately after the Holocaust. Buckey's forecast for the future is even gloomier: in another seventeen years there will remain eight million, in twenty-five years, only six million. The chief cause of our dwindling numbers is intermarriage. In some countries the rate of mixed marriages within the Jewish community has reached sixty to seventy percent.

It strikes everywhere. There is an illusion that assimilation and intermarriage takes place only in the Diaspora. However, it is a fact that even in *Eretz Yisrael*, spiritual assimilation exists — even here assimilation threatens to transform the People of the Torah into a nation like all the others, with culture imported from Europe and America. No country where Jews have settled has remained unaffected.

It is clear, then, that intermarriage and assimilation is prevalent among us too, perhaps no less so than among the Jews of pre-war Europe. From the immensity of the punishment we must learn the severity of the crime. Many believe that they are far removed from intermarriage or assimilation, and that they are in no way accountable for this sin. However, "all Israel are held responsible for one another" — the entire people are judged as if one body.

Moreover, assimilation of the kind expressed in *Tehillim* 106:35, "and they mixed with the nations and imitated their deeds," is present to some degree in each of us. Even those who completely observe the Torah and the *mitzvos*, live in the Holy Land, and perhaps never in their lives come into contact with non-Jews, are nevertheless indirectly influenced by gentile customs and perspectives. One could even say that any deficiency in the completeness of Jewish life, even if it does not stem from gentile influence, detracts from the uniqueness of the Jewish People, and to that extent is subsumed under the general title of "assimilation."

If indeed, intermarriage and assimilation were responsible, in part, for the Holocaust, it must be remembered that observant Jews suffered at least as much as the non-observant — perhaps even more. This would seem to indicate that the observant, too, were not guiltless of assimilation.

PART OF THE UNIQUENESS of the Jewish People stems from the fact that the Torah of Israel, insofar as it places before its adherents

An Artificial Separation

all-encompassing requirements, cannot be compared to other religious systems. The Torah does not rest content with minimalistic rituals, but demands that all one's dealings be conducted according to the letter and spirit of the Law. Hence, the complete Jew is different from the non-Jew not only in his belief, but in his entire mode of living.

As both R' Yisrael Salanter and the Chassidic masters warn, the greatest potential mistake among those who observe Torah and *mitzvos* is to artificially separate between various aspects of Torah: between the *mitzvos* that relate to God — about which observant Jews are usually careful — and those precepts that relate to one's fellow man, many of which are all but ignored. Likewise, one cannot separate the practical performance of the physical *mitzvos* from an inner awareness of "the duties of the heart." To do so is to create a flaw within the singularity and uniqueness of the Jewish People. Truly, there can be no greater assimilation than this, for it strikes not just at the physical being of the nation, but at its very soul and the essence of its life. Perhaps the punishment for this spiritual type of assimilation on the part of those who bear the nation's banner and study its Torah is even greater than the punishment for the physical assimilation of individuals who are already half-severed limbs of the nation's body.

DO WE FIND EVIDENCE in the Torah and the words of our Sages that assimilation can cause such severe punishment? It would

The Obligations of the Chosen

seem that the answer is yes. At the opening of this chapter, we cited the words of the Prophet Yechezkel in answer to those who told him, "We shall be like the nations": "with a strong hand and with an outstretched arm and with wrath poured out, I shall rule over you." There is no evading the obligations which accompany the privileges of the chosenness of the Jewish People.

Ezra the Scribe, concerning the sin of intermarriage in his day, implores:

> Shall we again violate Your *mitzvos* and marry with these people of abominations? If so, You would become angry with us to the point of total destruction, leaving no remnant or refugee (*Ezra* 9:15).

And during that same period, the Prophet Malachi declared:

> Yehudah has committed treachery, and abomination has been done among Israel and in Jerusalem, for Yehudah has desecrated his own sanctity to Hashem, which He loved, by marrying the daughter of a foreign god. To the man who does this, Hashem will cut off his descendants from the tents of Yaakov and from those who present the meal-offering to Hashem, Lord of Hosts (*Malachi* 2:11-12).

If such extreme warnings are given about physically intermarrying among the other nations, can we expect the consequences of spiritual abandonment of Hashem's Torah to be less severe?

BEIS HALEVI WRITES IN *Parashas Shemos* that a direct connection exists between assimilation and anti-Semitism:

Assimilation and Anti-Semitism

We read in *Tehillim* 105 (1-2, 24-26): "Give thanks to Hashem, call upon His Name, make His deeds known to the peoples! Sing melodiously to Him. . . And He made His people very fruitful, and made them mightier than their enemies. [Then] He changed their hearts to hate His people, to plot against His servants. [Afterwards,] He sent Moshe, His servant, [and] Aharon, whom He had chosen."

At first sight, these verses are difficult to understand. The psalm sets forth the kindnesses that Hashem did for Israel since they became a nation. Why, then, should it mention that He changed the hearts of the Egyptians so that they would hate Israel? This was not one of Hashem's favors to us. On the contrary, it would appear that this diminishes the greatness of the redemption from Egypt, since the slavery did not begin through any fault of Israel themselves, but only because the Holy One, Blessed is He, changed the hearts of the Egyptians! What sin had Israel committed to deserve this?

The answer would seem to be as follows. Israel had a known tradition that they would be enslaved in Egypt for four hundred years. After Yosef died, all realized that the days of servitude were soon coming, and this would be the beginning of the exile. They began to fear the future. Who knew how lengthy [the servitude] would be, and what the Egyptians would do to them and their children over such a long stretch of time? They searched for a solution, and decided that the answer was to befriend the Egyptians, and not to seem dissimilar to them. Thus, they would not appear as foreigners and aliens among them. The physical closeness, they thought, would cause emotional closeness and reduce hatred. And certainly, by human logic, this was all correct.

Now, the main difference between Israel and the Egyptians was circumcision, a constant sign in one's very body. . . So they devised a plan that immediately after circumcision, they would pull the foreskin forward. . . Thus it would not be obvious that they were circumcised, and they would satisfy all concerned. They would fulfill the *mitzvah* according to the law of the Torah, yet at the same time their differentness would not be evident. . .

And in fact Israel did not violate any prohibition by doing this. . . Yet in spite of the fact that the act itself did not violate any prohibition, nevertheless it was likely to cause them to mix with the Egyptians over the course of time, and to become sunk in their impurity, since there would be no obvious difference between them. This is actually the complete opposite of the intent of this *mitzvah* [circumcision], which was [given] to distinguish between the Israelites and the Egyptians.

On the verse (*Shir HaShirim* 1:3), "your oils are good for fragrance," *Midrash Rabbah* comments: "Just as oil does not mix with other liquids, so, too, Israel does not mix with the other nations (*Bnei Noach*). And the difference forever remains firmly in place, for the Holy One, Blessed is He, gave the Torah and *mitzvos* to Israel so that they would be distinguished from *Bnei Noach*, as it is said, 'I shall distinguish you from the peoples' (*Vayikra* 20:26)." But if Israel tried to eliminate the difference, then God reinforced the difference by instilling hatred in the hearts of the non-Jews. And all this was a favor to Israel, so that they should not become intermixed with the Egyptians. . .

And this is what we experience today, in this long exile in countries such as Russia. Every day the hatred becomes greater and more intense. By logic and nature, the hatred should constantly decrease, as is the way with everything: At the beginning it is in full force, and afterwards it steadily decreases. . . The real reason for this, however, is as we have explained. The Torah gives Israel distinguishing features through fulfilling Torah and *mitzvos*. The more Israel decreases those distinguishing features, the more the Holy One, Blessed is He, increases hatred in the hearts of the gentiles, to the required degree, so that Israel should remain differentiated.

Assimilation and Rebuke — the Cycle of Exile

IN R' YAAKOV EMDEN'S *siddur*, *Beis Yaakov* (*Dinei Tishah B'Av, Chalon Shevi'i, Chalon Hamitzri*), we also find stinging words against the assimilation that had spread in his day. Writing during the beginning of the *Haskalah,* he declares that "The vast majority of the common people have only one goal: to become like the gentiles and to follow their laws and ways"— to the point, even, of mixed marriages. Of intermarriage, he goes on to write:

This is a go-between to enable people to depart from following Hashem, to abandon His covenant and deny His Torah. This is what darkened the eyes of Israel during the days of the First Temple, and was the source of the overwhelming evils that overtook our fathers during the time of the Second Temple, too. This is what cut off the descendants of Israel from the land of Spain, where they had maintained a lofty position. Hashem is righteous and His judgment is just. The virtuous and learned ones in the generation of the expulsion from Spain justified Hashem's decree upon them, testifying that the children of men who had taken non-Jewish wives had killed their fathers.

He emphasizes that assimilation had brought the downfall of Spanish Jewry. He explains at length how the Jews' preoccupation with Greek philosophy caused them to abandon the Torah, and attributes the catastrophes of 5408 (1648) to the same evil:

Bnei Yisrael were annihilated from the Ukraine, where they had also become great and wealthy. But to the degree that they were elevated — to that same degree was their downfall, for they were uprooted from that whole land. Although some men of great righteousness lived there, it appears to me that this annihilation, too, occurred because of the spreading infection of philosophy in that generation, as implied in the responsum of Marshal to Maharam, in his responsa (sec. 7). The Holy One, Blessed is He, does not pass a verdict without reason.

Thus, according to R' Yaakov Emden, the history of exile is little more than a perpetual cycle of assimilation and rebuke. "With wrath poured out, I shall rule over you" (Yechezkel 20:33) — the central calamities of our exile result primarily from the betrayal of our special role as the chosen people.

A FAMOUS PIECE on this subject is found in Meshech Chochmah, written by R' Meir Simchah of Dvinsk, the author of Or

"Berlin Is Jerusalem"

Sameach. Meshech Chochmah was first published in 5687 (1927), twelve years before the Second World War. As part of his lengthy survey of Jewish history, the author writes:

Soon they will be saying, "Our fathers inherited falsities" (*Yirmeyahu* 16:19). The Israelite will altogether forget his heritage and will be considered a new, inexperienced citizen. He will leave the study of his own Law to study languages that do not belong to him. He will learn from the worthless, rather than from the worthwhile — believing that 'Berlin is Jerusalem'; imitating the worst of [the gentiles]. . .

"Do not rejoice, O Israel, and do not exult like the peoples!" (*Hoshea* 9:1). Then will come a rushing stormwind, uprooting him from his source, carrying him to a distant nation whose language he has not learned. Then he will know that he is a stranger, that his language is our Holy Tongue, and foreign languages are like clothing that one casts off; that his heritage is the root of Israel, and his consolations are those of Hashem's prophets, who prophesied about [David] the son of Yishai at the End of Days (*Meshech Chochmah, Parashas Bechukosai*).

THE *NETZIV* OF VOLOZHIN[1] also writes at length to explain how assimilation arouses hatred against Israel. His essay was written

The Netziv's Analysis about one hundred years ago, during the awakening of European anti-Semitism, a phenomenon which prepared the background for the rise of Nazism. At that time, it had seemed that in the countries of western Europe, where assimilation was more prevalent, anti-Semitism was weaker than in eastern Europe. The *Netziv* writes:

The main cause of this hatred [anti-Semitism] is that Israel does not wish to live apart and to be like strangers. Instead, they compete with one another in their efforts to make themselves as much like the gentiles as is possible. Still, though this is the main reason, there are other [aspects] which are "the hidden things of Hashem" — including the reason why the punishment does not come upon that country where the people are most [assimilated] (p. 63a).

In hindsight, however, we see that the Holocaust — the climax of European anti-Semitism — originated precisely from Germany,

---

1. In *She'ar Yisrael*, an essay published at the end of his commentary on *Shir HaShirim*.

the area of greatest assimilation. The "hidden things of Hashem" have become "the revealed things for us and our children" (*Devarim* 29:28). Although, writes the *Netziv*, anti-Semitism is eternal, nonetheless, this hatred is not always translated into deeds. When it is, it is activated primarily by Israel's desire for assimilation:

> Divine Providence is more strict in its reaction to this than to other sins which are widespread among Israel. And it is logical that this should be so, for Divine Providence is more exacting concerning something which alters the purpose of creation and the existential form of the created being than about that which goes against the will [of Hashem] but does not change this. . .
>
> And so it is with *Am Yisrael*, the Jewish People. With the giving of the Torah they became the people of Hashem, [destined] to guard the keeping of His Torah. Moreover, He gave them the strength and the obligation to rectify and perfect humanity — to help the other nations recognize the unity of Hashem, to teach them proper conduct and eternal rules of behavior. As Yeshayahu (42:6) said: "I formed you and made you a covenant for the peoples, a light to the nations". . . This is the existential form of Israel, that they should be separate and distinct from the nations.
>
> Therefore, when Israel tries to break down the distinction and imitate the actions of the nations — in the end to remove the form of Judaism — how does the Holy One, Blessed is He, react in order to return them to their essential form? He awakens an active hatred on the part of the nations, and they push away the Jewish People — their occupations and their places of residence — until, even against their will, the form of Israel becomes distinct. And the word of our God endures forever.
>
> The nature of this process necessitates yet another result: When Israel destroys their existential form — Judaism — they become contemptible in the eyes of the nations. It is a rule of nature that if something has a high form, when its form is destroyed, it becomes inferior even to those things of lower form. Consider, for example, the mineral, vegetable, animal, and human orders of existence. When something in the

vegetable kingdom loses its power of growth, it wilts into an entity far inferior to a mineral object. Likewise an animal, after it dies and its vitality ceases, rots to a greater extent than a wilted plant. Similarly, a human being who has lost his mind is subordinate to an animal, and a destructive man is more harmful than a wild beast. . .

The same principle applies to Israel. When they lose their Judaism — their essential form — they become inferior to other living persons, becoming like an imitative ape. [It is] then that the other nations look upon the Jew as upon something altogether without human form (Ibid., sec. 4,5).

When we recall the twisted philosophy of the Nazis, the words of the *Netziv* take on a ring of prophecy. In Nazi Germany, the Jews were indeed considered "sub-human," a type of creature that failed to merit the title of "man." Consequently, in the German eye, to destroy the Jew was to do no more than to exterminate an insect. In fact, the killing schemes were carried out in precisely such a fashion. In Nazi documents, terms like "cleaning," "purification," or "hygienic project" were routinely used to refer to murder.

The Ramification

CLEARLY, THEN, THE Torah and the words of the sages contain evidence that assimilation is potentially the central sin of Jewish history. It thus follows that the more serious the sin, the more severe the punishment. If in the last century our people distanced themselves from the Torah and betrayed their unique role, it would not seem unlikely that the Holocaust was in some way a response to this. Indeed, the connection between assimilation and the Holocaust is betrayed by the very way the events unfolded: The punishment fit the crime "measure for measure"—*middah kenegged middah*. "He dug a pit and excavated it, and stumbled into the chasm he created" *(Tehillim* 7:16) — the national downfall of Israel is nothing more than the natural ramification of their assimilation.

The fate of the assimilated Jew in Nazi Germany was grimly ironic. Even those who tried with all their might to blur their Jewish identity were persecuted and murdered simply for being Jews.

The phenomenon seems to be nothing other than the ultimate example of retribution meted out "measure for measure". The frightful correlation between assimilation and persecution was recognized even by non-observant Jews. The following is an excerpt from an article by Robert Welsh, published in the Zionist journal of German Jewry, *Judische Rundschau*, in April, 1933:

> They [the Jews] thought the only important thing was not to be recognized as Jews. Today we are being reproached with having betrayed the German people; the National Socialist Press calls us "the enemies of the nation," and there is nothing we can do about it. It is not true that the Jews have betrayed Germany. If they have betrayed anything, they have betrayed themselves and Judaism.
>
> Because the Jews did not display their Jewishness with pride, because they wanted to shirk the Jewish question, they must share the blame for the degradation of Jewry. . . ("Wear the Yellow Badge Proudly," quoted in *Out of the Whirlwind*, p. 121.)

R' Dr. Aharon Neuvirth writes:

> At the beginning of Hitler's regime, on *Shabbos*, April 1, 1933, Hitler set up guards in front of Jewish shops to prevent people from purchasing from Jews. The shops were forced to close on *Shabbos*. [Thus, in effect] Hitler intentionally ordered that the Jewish shops be closed on *Shabbos*. This event aroused even liberal Jews to self-examination; many of them remembered *Shabbos* and streamed to the synagogues. Is it any more than right to see this event as the finger of God, teaching a lesson which should be learned for all time? (*Yisrael Veshabbato*, p. 155).

Clearly, the Nazi decree affected shops not only on *Shabbos* but during the weekday as well — in the end, the decrees struck not only at the property of the Jews, but at their very bodies and lives. Nevertheless, it is difficult to discount the symbolism in the fact that the persecutions began with the closing of shops on *Shabbos*. The hand of Providence can sometimes be glimpsed behind its veil: "With wrath poured out, I shall rule over you. . ."

The words of the *Maggid* of Kelm, cited in the previous chapter, take on a redoubled significance:

> Because of the sin of the *Shulchan Aruch* of Geiger [founder of the Reform Movement in Germany], a new, German version of the *Shulchan Aruch* is going to arise against the Jewish People, and there — heaven save us — it will be written: "The only thing to do with even the best Jew is — kill him."

So too, we are reminded of R' Yisrael Salanter's warning: on account of Jews permitting mixed marriages with gentiles, the day would come when the gentiles would write a *Shulchan Aruch* of their own, forbidding gentiles to marry Jews.[1]

R' MOSHE AVIGDOR AMIEL, in *LiNevuchei HaTekufah* (Jerusalem, 5703/1943), writes at length to explain how assimila-

The Meaning of "Ivri"

tion helped to generate the Holocaust. He states:

> What did we get from all our equal rights in the Diaspora? From Berlin — cradle of the secular *Haskalah* and assimilation — went forth the evil, an evil the likes of which we have never seen in our entire history, and from there it spread to most of the lands of the Diaspora. The ghettos returned, and the ghettos became slaughterhouses. We were "like sheep led to the slaughter, to be killed, destroyed, wounded, humiliated" (p. 307).
>
> However, if we look deeper we shall see that it is to a certain degree possible to say concerning this too, "The sinfulness of a man makes his path crooked, and his heart becomes angry at Hashem" (*Mishlei* 19:3). The truth is that the devastation did not begin just now, when all has already been destroyed and demolished to the foundation; when our whole settlement in Europe has become a graveyard. Rather, our demise began with the movement for equal rights itself. It is those very equal rights that have wounded us in this awful, horrifying way. . . Our whole existence in exile was possible only as long as we remained

---

1. (The matter is discussed at length by R' Wolbe in *Bein Sheshes Le'Asor*, pp. 75-79.)

"Hebrews (*Ivrim*)" in the sense that *Chazal* explained: "Why was he called a 'Hebrew (*Ivri*)'? — because the whole world was on one 'side (*ever*)', and he was on the other side." As long as we remained "on one side" — the entire world on the side of the material, and we on the side of the spiritual — we existed, even though our existence always involved pain and hardship. But, when we broke across the barriers with all our body and soul to reach the side of the others, we brought upon ourselves this terrible curse (p. 308).

This is what happened when we began to dream about equal *national* rights. We had never previously dreamt of this, for we would not have been content with it, knowing that "Hashem your God chose you to be a treasured people to Him" (*Devarim* 7:6). We had never asked ourselves whether or not the nations acknowledged us as a people, for we did not depend on their recognition for our life. But when we began to dream about national equality, we became confused concerning this. Then began the pursuit of approval. From one end of the world to the other, we sounded trumpets, [desperately seeking] some chieftain to nod his head to us and say that we, too, were a people like other peoples. And if, God forbid, one of the gentiles denied this and asserted the opposite, we felt inconsolable sorrow.

Hitler, may his name be blotted out, destroyed a large part of the Jewish People, but his era really began ten years earlier with the Nuremberg laws. We still remember the cry of distress that rose throughout the camps of Israel the world over, at the news of *those* decrees. But in fact, what was truly new about the Nuremberg laws? Nothing. They only confirmed the decrees that we ourselves should have passed. These are the Eighteen Decrees which both Beis Shammai and Beis Hillel agreed on: "They decreed [that it was forbidden to eat] their bread and oil because [they did not want people to drink] their wine. And they decreed against their wine because [they did not want them to intermarry]. . ." It was not only sworn assimilationists who wept over these decrees, but extreme nationalists as well. God-fearing people, careful of all the *mitzvos*, also wept over the great insult. The insult was that Hitler had annulled the approval that others had given us — [the recognition] that we, too, were human beings like all others, a people like all the peoples.

We cannot help but be reminded of *Chazal's* words: "You wept over nothing, so I shall establish for you a weeping for generations" (p. 310).

A Causative Relationship THE GENTILE DECLARATION forbidding intermarriage with Jews was a "measure for measure" reaction to the Jewish desire for assimilation and subordination within gentile ranks. It can also be shown that assimilation was itself the logical and natural catalyst to increased hatred of the Jews. We quote from Eliezer Livneh, a leader of the Zionist movement in *Eretz Yisrael*, who drew closer to traditional Judaism at the end of his life.

> Emancipation, the intermixing within gentile society, immeasurably increased the strength and extent of the Holocaust. Wherever Jews receive equal rights, they rise all the more quickly in economic and social ranks. . . A regime based upon the absence of racial, religious, and ethnic discrimination pushes the Jews rapidly upwards. . . This phenomenon appears to confirm the high intellectual, emotional, and ethical qualities which are fostered by the Jewish way of life, and which persist for a certain amount of time even after that way of life is abandoned. However, the success of the Jews cannot but sharpen anti-Jewish tension. . . The social rise of the Jews and their high visibility in leadership roles serves simultaneously to stimulate and to rationalize anti-Jewish anger. The connection between Emancipation and anti-Semitism is substantial and causative, and this includes all aspects of anti-Semitism.
>
> The Jews did not realize what was happening around them and did not sense the seriousness of the reactions they aroused. The Orthodox were enclosed within their own circle, lacking a great deal of social contact with the outside world. As for those who were more involved, including the

assimilated, their supposed close contact with society proved imaginary. . . Even in this liberal society, an invisible barrier stood between Jews and non-Jews. During World War I, the renowned Russian historian, Mikhail Rostovtzov, told a Jewish friend: "I'm surprised at the Jews. They are a wise and understanding people, yet they have no idea how we speak about them amongst ourselves. They don't know at all what feelings other peoples have towards them. . ."

Apparently, the suddenness of the hostile outbursts against the Jews is illusory. It would be more correct to speak of the revelation of a basic, widespread feeling, always ready to surface at the opportune moment. . .

Still, one must ask: Why did this happen precisely among the German people. . . It is difficult to explain this solely on the basis of the characteristics of the German people. . . True, this nation willingly subordinated itself to any authority, seeing the execution of orders as duty. For this reason, no matter what orders [the Nazi regime] gave, the resistance to it was weak. Nevertheless, this does not explain why Nazi sovereignty arose [specifically] amidst the German people, and with its consent. . .

All the same, it is impossible not to see the special Jewish-German symbiosis of the nineteenth and early twentieth centuries as a cause of the Nazi rise to power. The social emancipation of German Jewry — that is, their assimilation into German culture and involvement in German society — was far advanced long before their political emancipation was achieved. . . The assimilating Jews of Germany began to penetrate the areas of literature and criticism, music and entertainment, commentary and social guidance — all the fields which were later included in the title, "communication"— very early on. . . Many of these Jews were engaged in bitingly satirical criticism of the German present and past, and offered far-reaching proposals for the future. They were unaware of their own foreignness to the inner life of the German nation, and to its subterranean roots. . . Is it any wonder that they aroused unfathomed inner antagonism among the Germans? (*Israel Umashber Hatzivilizatziah Hamaaravit*, pp. 56-59).

There is yet another indication that assimilation was one of the harbingers of the Holocaust. The masses of emancipated Jewish Europe had believed in illusory ideals — idols of sorts — which encouraged them to assimilate. Ultimately, it was the Holocaust which shattered these idols. A further chapter is devoted to a discussion of this subject at length, but for the present, it shall suffice to point out that the highly cultured German nation exhibited abysmal moral degeneration. In retrospect, one can raise serious doubts about the overall quality and worth of that culture as a whole. All the humanitarian values of western civilization collapse when we contemplate the Holocaust. As we shall see later, not only did these values fail to prevent the Holocaust, they actually seem to have facilitated its onslaught.

D.

Zionism and the Holocaust

HE DESTRUCTION OF European Jewry and the establishment of the State of Israel were twin historical phenomena — separated chronologically by only a few years. Whether any more substantive link existed between Zionism and the Holocaust has been a subject of dispute among

The Admor of Satmar's Approach Torah leaders. The *Admor* of Satmar, in *Vayo'el Moshe*, writes that Zionism stands in essential contradiction to the Torah. He argues further that the existence of the Zionist Movement was a primary cause of the Holocaust. His principal basis is a statement of *Chazal* in *Kesubos* 101a:

> R' Yosi the son of R' Channina said: "What are these three oaths? One is that Israel should not storm the wall. One is that the Holy One, Blessed is He, made Israel take an oath not to rebel against the nations of the world. And one is that the Holy One, Blessed is He, made the nations of the world take an oath not to excessively oppress Israel."

Rashi defines "storming the wall" as meaning that the Jewish People should not return to *Eretz Yisrael* "together, by force." The Zionist Movement had as its goal the establishment of a Jewish state by force or otherwise; thus, in the Admor's opinion, it constituted a violation of the oath — for it was nothing other than a rebellion against the nations of the world who opposed Jewish control of *Eretz Yisrael*. The *Gemara*, which the Admor quotes, goes on to cite the verse from *Shir HaShirim* (2:7): " 'I administer an oath to you, O daughters of Jerusalem, by the deer or by the gazelles of the field, that you may not awaken or arouse the love until it wishes.' The Holy One, Blessed is He, said to Israel: 'If you fulfill the oath, all is well; but if not, I shall permit your flesh [as prey] like the deer or the gazelles of the field.' Since this ominous warning was carried out fully during the Holocaust, the *Admor* infers that it was indeed the violation of the above-mentioned oaths which caused European Jewry's destruction.

The *Admor* of Satmar further points to certain actions of Jewish leaders, which, he writes, constituted "rebellion" against the nations of the world, and served to increase the wrath of the Nazis. Citing facts which became known through the Kastner[1] trial, he also accuses certain Zionist leaders of cooperating with the Nazis.

Advocates of the Satmar view further claim that it was the aspirations of the Zionist Movement which caused the British to close the gates of *Eretz Yisrael* to Holocaust refugees. The British governors and the Arab occupants of *Eretz Yisrael*, they argue, would have had little reason to prevent the entrance of Jews with no nationalistic ambitions. Furthermore, even as Zionist leaders encouraged emigration, some among them helped ensure that the gates of refuge in other countries remained closed to Holocaust refugees, for fear of diminished immigration to *Eretz Yisrael*.

Along these lines, some also make the claim that Arab anti-Semitism is primarily a result of the advent of Zionism. They point to the role of the Mufti of Jerusalem in the Holocaust. According to statements made by Adolph Eichmann, the Mufti encouraged Hitler to annihilate the Jews of Europe, "so that they would not be able to come to Palestine." R' Weissmandl quotes similar statements to this effect made by the Nazi criminal Dietr Wisleceny.

THE APPARENT ANTITHESIS of the Satmar perspective on Zionism and the Holocaust is adopted by the *gaon* R' Yissachar

Em Habanim S'meichah Shlomo Teichtal, in his book *Em Habanim S'meichah*. R' Teichtal, author of the responsa *Mishneh Sachir*, was one of the important rabbinical figures of pre-war Hungary. Before the war years, he stood as a staunch opponent of Zionism. The events of

---

1. Rudolf Kastner, a Hungarian Zionist leader during the war, had been accused of collaboration with the Nazis. He sued his accuser for libel, but the trial became a lengthy and well-publicized exposé of his misdeeds and those of his colleagues.

the Holocaust, however, caused him to reverse his opinion, and in 5704 (1944), at the height of the European devastation, he published *Em Habanim S'meichah* in Budapest.

In this work, he argues that it was the Jewish desire to settle permanently in the Diaspora — precisely their non-participation in the Zionist buildup of *Eretz Yisrael* — which was the sin that perpetuated the Holocaust. Although, he writes, one must reject the secular ideology of Zionism, one must nevertheless cooperate with the movement in settling the Land, for settling *Eretz Yisrael* is one of the most important *mitzvos* in the Torah. Writing in forceful language, R' Teichtal rejects the claims advanced in Hungary in his day, that the Holocaust was a punishment for Zionism, and that Hungarian Jewry had only been saved from destruction (as everyone thought at the time) in the merit of their non-participation in the Zionist Movement:

> Woe to the ears that hear such a claim, and woe to the generation which succumbs to such foolishness; that is raised and educated so falsely, bringing such a perverted accusation against thousands and tens of thousands of Israel who were killed in sanctification of Hashem. Moreover, this [claim] belittles the value of the *mitzvah* of settling *Eretz Yisrael*, which *Chazal* placed on a very high level, equating it to the entire Torah. To such claims one can only say, as King Shlomo, the wisest of all men, advised, "Do not argue with the fool on the level of his foolishness" (*Mishlei* 26:4). May Hashem forgive them (*Em Habanim S'meichah*, p. 229).

R' Teichtal further quotes the words of R' Yaakov Emden:

> Every Jew must make a fixed and unshakeable resolution in his heart to go and live in *Eretz Yisrael*. . . They should not consider settling permanently in other lands, where they would, God forbid, witness the fulfillment of the verse, "The land of your enemies shall consume you" (*Vayikra* 26:38). This was the sin of our early forefathers, who caused a "weeping for generations" because of their rejection of the desirable Land. This is what has accompanied us through our bitter exile: Not just one has risen against us, but in every generation we have had no peace or rest. We have

completely forgotten about living in *Eretz Yisrael,* and thus we have been persecuted mercilessly and without pause, and have been like one long ago considered dead and forgotten. Not even one in a thousand considers acquiring a holding there, to settle and live there. Only once in a generation an individual in a lone country or two remembers and acts. No one gives heed to seek the love of the Land, to care about its welfare; no one expects ever to see it.

As we sit contentedly in other countries, we imagine that we have already found another *Eretz Yisrael* and another Jerusalem just like the original. This is why all the evils came upon us. . . [The people of] Israel were in Spain and other countries, where they had dwelled contentedly and with great honor for a long time, since the destruction of the *Beis Hamikdash* nearly two thousand years ago. But then they were expelled, until no remnant of Israel remained in [these] lands. Hashem is just, for [the Jews] had completely forgotten that they were in exile; [they] had mixed with the gentiles, imitated their deeds, and done reprehensible things. The holy [nation] had mixed with the peoples of the lands (*Siddur*, Introduction).

Elsewhere, R' Yaakov Emden writes even more emphatically:

If there was no other sin in our hands but this, that we do not mourn as we should for Jerusalem, this would be enough to prolong our exile. In my eyes, this is the most obvious and strong reason for all the fearsome and unthinkable annihilations that have overtaken us in all the dispersed places of our exile (Ibid., *Shaar Hadelek, Chalon Shishi*).

R' Teichtal also establishes the seriousness of regarding exile as permanent, by citing from *Seder Hadoros* (part 1, year 5380/ 1620). When Ezra the Scribe built the Second Temple, he sent letters to the communities of the Diaspora instructing them to return to *Eretz Yisrael*. *Seder Hadoros* quotes the *Sema* (*Sefer Me'iras Einayim*), who records that the Jews of Worms replied: "You settle in the Great Jerusalem, and we will settle here in Little Jerusalem." *Sema* concludes that on this account evil decrees befell this community more than others.

R' Teichtal maintains that the dimensions of the Holocaust were increased by European Jewry's reluctance to participate in the settlement of the Land, since many Jews would have been saved had they moved to *Eretz Yisrael*. The Holocaust, in his view, thus constituted a Divine call to leave the exile and to seek the refuge of our Holy Land. He continues:

> Through the sanctification of the Name (martyrdom) by thousands and tens of thousands of Israel at their death, the barriers (*klipos*) against holiness have been weakened, and the gate has been opened to enter our Holy Land (p. 209).

The ashes of our calamity, in R' Teichtal's opinion, are the spiritual keys to *Eretz Yisrael*. The Holocaust, then, is not simply punishment for a localized sin, but is *chevlei Mashiach* par excellence — the beginning of the conclusion of our exile. R' Teichtal goes on to connect the explanation for *chevlei Mashiach* with his overall theme:

> If the Redemption were to occur in good, peaceful times, when quiet prevailed among peoples, many of our brothers, *Bnei Yisrael*, would not want to leave the exile, for what would they be lacking there? (p. 67).

Thus, in contrast to the view set forth by the *Admor* of Satmar, R' Teichtal connects the Holocaust with what he sees as European Jewry's failure to fulfill the imperative to settle *Eretz Yisrael*.

This is not the place, nor does the present author consider himself qualified, to take sides in this fundamental debate. The response of the sages of the previous generation was divided: Most did not adopt the viewpoint of the *Admor* of Satmar; nevertheless, most also refrained from involving themselves in the Zionist Movement, primarily because they did not wish to lend their support to those who had rejected the yoke of Torah and *mitzvos*.

BOTH OF THE ABOVE positions have been questioned. The Satmar approach seems difficult, for the Zionist Movement

Is There a Medium? claimed only a small minority of European Jewry as its members before the Holocaust. It became a central force among the Jewish

People only after the disaster. Also, one cannot deny that the great majority of Jews killed in the Holocaust were not Zionists. It is likewise difficult to see non-participation in the settlement of the Land as a fault of the general community as R' Teichtal does. Whether because of difficult economic conditions, British limitations on immigration or the hostility of the Arab occupants, most European Jews had little true option to emigrate to *Eretz Yisrael*. We tend to forget the Arab riots of 5696-9 (1936-9), when Polish Jewry prayed as one for the safety of their brethren in *Eretz Yisrael*. Was so severe a punishment as the Holocaust really brought about by those who took caution from these disturbances and postponed their move to *Eretz Yisrael*?

The very fact that Torah leaders have found it possible to interpret the significance of these events in opposite ways points to the inherent complexity of the issues at stake. Nonetheless, "both these and those are the words of the living God"— it is worth seeking the elements of truth contained in each of the conflicting views. Clearly, part of the Jewish People refrained from participating in building up the Land. Likewise, another element was swept along with all aspects of the Zionist Movement. Both facts are connected with the Holocaust, and this involves no contradiction.

It is true that many Jews were — and still are — indifferent to the settlement of *Eretz Yisrael*. In many cases, a prime cause of this indifference is pursuit of the relatively luxurious standard of living which the Diaspora offers, as well as the subtle alienation from spiritual values which often accompanies it. Love of *Eretz Yisrael* is enhanced by an appreciation of holiness, and both of these sensitivities are aspects of love of Hashem. One who loves Hashem and desires to cleave to Him can do so to the fullest extent only in the portion of Hashem, the Holy Land. One who truly yearns for the spiritual rectification of the world, yearns also for "the air of Your Land, which gives life to the soul." But one who does not aspire to self-perfection and attachment to his Creator flees the difficulties, the *yisurim*, which are the necessary prerequisites for the acquisition of *Eretz Yisrael*. The lack of even a hope to settle in *Eretz Yisrael* is significant to the extent that it is an expression of alienation from spirituality as a whole. It could be said that, in a sense, the sin is an aspect of assimilation with the gentile nations of the world; for to reject the importance of settling *Eretz Yisrael,* to an extent, is indicative of a certain passive repudiation of the unique role of the Jewish People.

R' Shlomo Wolbe, *shlita*, writes:

> No one has the right to discuss what brought us to the Holocaust. Only someone who has personally suffered all those torments — only he is permitted to conduct the self-examination of the generation of the Holocaust. R' Avraham Grodzinski, a *gaon* and *mussar* authority, lived in the Slobodka ghetto, and experienced the tormented existence of all the inhabitants of the ghetto. [During the Holocaust] he searched through the sources in *Chazal* and found causes that led to the Holocaust. He presented these to his students, former students of the glorious Slobodka Yeshivah, who had since become slave laborers. He found twelve reasons, and exhorted his students that in order to merit salvation from the [enemy], they must remedy shortcomings in these areas . . . The following are the sins:
>
> 1) Lack of faith
>
> 2) Failure to keep the *Shabbos*
>
> 3) Failure to maintain family purity
>
> 4) Carelessness regarding forbidden foods
>
> 5) Usury (*ribis*)
>
> 6) Neglect of Torah education
>
> 7) Neglect of Torah study (*bitul Torah*)
>
> 8) Failure to love one's fellow Jew and the Jewish People
>
> 9) Insufficient Kindness (*chessed*)
>
> 10) Unwillingness to make do with little (*histapkus*)
>
> 11) Lack of trust in Hashem (*bitachon*)
>
> 12) *Eretz Yisrael*
>
> (based on *Toras Avraham*,
> Jerusalem, 5723/1963, p. 17)

> R' Avraham explained the whole matter in the light of sources in *Chazal*. Had we been worthy, we would have been able to study the matter more deeply and see for ourselves

how *Chazal* indicated the Holocaust that threatened to result from the neglect of these areas. However, these writings, hidden away before the destruction of the ghetto, were stolen immediately after that destruction, and the world did not merit their light (*Bein Sheshes Le'asor*, pp. 77-8).

R' Avraham points principally at general weakness in all foundations of the Torah: faith, trust in Hashem, *Shabbos*, *kashrus*, family purity, Torah study, and the *mitzvos* that govern conduct between man and man. *Eretz Yisrael* is only one of the many important *mitzvos* he listed, and only from the overall perspective of Torah and *mitzvos* can one discuss the neglect of this *mitzvah* specifically. It is clear, however, that according to R' Avraham, the Holocaust is, among other things, a grim reminder that *Klal Yisrael* must improve with respect to the love of *Eretz Yisrael* as well.

HOWEVER, EVEN THE desire to settle *Eretz Yisrael* can be marred by the context within which it appears. Precisely because

The Earth Bereft of Heavens

of the importance of building the land, one can view secular Zionism as a neglect of this *mitzvah* as well. Indeed, the *Eretz Yisrael* inscribed on the banner of the secular Zionist Movement was no more than a small stretch of land on the Mediterranean coast, devoid of all religious or truly Jewish significance. The Israel of Herzl's dream was an anonymous land of refuge; a kind of homeland which was only incidentally our nation's birthplace. As is known, the Zionist leader at first wished to establish the country of the Jews "in Argentina or in Palestine," and later favored accepting the British proposal to set up the state in Uganda. In the end the substitutes were rejected, but the decision amounted only to a geographical switch, not an essential change. In principle, the Zionist aspiration remained to establish a kind of Jewish Uganda in the Land of Israel; a homeland built upon the *earth* of Israel, bereft of its heavens or essential spirit. The fact that the basic thrust of popular Zionism was secular, is indicative of a certain failure on the part of the Jewish People — a weakness in recognition of the true worth of *Eretz Yisrael* and the value of self-sacrifice on her behalf.

Just as indifference to settling *Eretz Yisrael* stems from the subtle penetration of gentile values, a de facto consequence of exile, so too does the counterfeit love of a so-called "*Eretz Yisrael*" stem from these same faults. Indeed, classic secular Zionist ideology, if taken to its logical conclusion, maintains that one must produce in *Eretz Yisrael* not only a new state, but a new people and a new society as well. The new people would not be the natural culmination of the Jewish People, but a kind of one-dimensional national entity; a people that would trade the vibrant "meta-history" of Torah for a vague kind of "historical heritage." In a certain sense, assimilation of this sort is more insidious than the personal assimilation of Jews in the Diaspora, for here we have not the private acts of individuals, but a perversion of the essence of our very nationhood.

IT SEEMS CLEAR, then, that the indifference towards settling *Eretz Yisrael* expressed by one segment of the people, and the

Two Faces of Assimilation

love of the land expressed by others in alienation from Torah and *mitzvos*, were two sides of the same coin. Each of these phenomena developed from a blurring of the unique task of the Jewish People. The issue of Jewry's relationship to *Eretz Yisrael*, then, should not be seen as a separate and distinct issue, but rather as an integral outgrowth of the sins of assimilation and abandonment of Torah discussed earlier in this chapter.

The *gaon* R' Elchanan Wasserman, too, identifies secular nationalism with other secular movements of his day. In his work, *Ikvasa DeMeshicha* we find:

> In our days the Jews have chosen two idols to which they offer their sacrifices: Socialism and Nationalism. The philosophy of Nationalism can be summed up very briefly: "Let us be like all the nations." Nothing is demanded of the Jew except a feeling of patriotism. If one gives his donation and sings *Hatikvah*, he is exempt from all the *mitzvos* of the Torah. Clearly, this approach is considered idolatry in

the opinion of the Torah.

These two idols have poisoned the minds and hearts of Jewish youth. Each idol has a general faculty of false prophets, writers and speakers, who faithfully perform their duties. Now, a miraculous thing has happened. Heaven has combined these two idols into one, and it is called National-Socialism [Nazism]. From this has been produced a horrible staff of anger, which wounds Jews in every corner of the earth. The impurities to which they have bowed down are the ones that are wounding us, as it is written (*Yirmeyahu* 2:19): "Your evil will torment you" (*Ikvasa DeMeshicha* p. 27).

The essential defect of blind nationalism, then, is its separation of the holy ideal of Jewish nationalism from its life-source. Similarly, the flaw of the socialist movement was not that it struggled for equal rights and social justice, but that it severed these great ideals from the Torah of Israel.

IN CONCLUDING OUR discussion of Zionism and the Holocaust, let us respond to a standard accusation sometimes leveled against

The Heart of the King. . .

the observant public: "Your Torah leaders — the heads of yeshivos and the rabbis — are to be blamed for the deaths of tens of thousands of Jews, for they discouraged emigration to *Eretz Yisrael* before the Holocaust."

The genuinely believing person understands that the events of the Holocaust was not a natural historical process, and thus its prevention was impossible by ordinary, natural means. Even had the Torah leaders (or others who opposed *aliyah*) taken a different stand, the Holocaust would not have been prevented. "The heart of the king is in the hand of Hashem" (*Mishlei* 21:1).

Just before the destruction of Jerusalem, Rabban Yochanan ben Zakkai was given the opportunity to ask anything he wanted from Vespasian. He requested only: "Give me Yavneh and its Sages." In retrospect, *Chazal* said of his request that it fulfilled the verse (*Yeshayahu* 44:25), "He turns the wise backwards, making their minds foolish"— for Rabban Yochanan ben Zakkai should have asked that Jerusalem itself be spared (*Gittin* 56b). Clearly, though, *Chazal* did not hold Rabban Yochanan responsible for the destruction of the *Beis Hamikdash*. Rather, it is the Holy One, Blessed is He, Who "turns the wise backwards." He gives the sages wisdom in accordance with the plan of Divine Providence.

There is no guarantee of infallibility given to even the saintliest of men. This, however, does not detract from the legitimacy of leadership by the Torah sages, for they are nonetheless fit to stand at the head of the people on account of their Torah knowledge and righteousness. Whatever the ultimate result, our duty is to act according to the imperatives of the Torah. If it is the will of Hashem that harsh decrees should come upon us precisely through the leadership of Torah sages, then so be it; we must lovingly accept His will.

IT WOULD SEEM, however, that in our case there is no need to apply the verse, "He turns the wise backwards." First of all, the

A Clarification

allegations themselves are incorrect. Who exactly are these heads of yeshivos and rabbis who supposedly ruled against emigrating to *Eretz Yisrael*? Agudas Yisrael was the generally recognized organization representing the anti-Zionist segment of the Orthodox public prior to the Holocaust. But all the recognized leaders of Agudas Yisrael — the *Admor* of Gur, the Chafetz Chaim, R' Elchanan Wasserman — were themselves preparing before the war to emigrate to *Eretz Yisrael*. The *Chazon Ish*, perhaps the most vehemently anti-Zionist of them all, moved to *Eretz Yisrael* in 5693 (1933). The fact that the other Torah leaders just mentioned did not succeed in reaching *Eretz Yisrael* only underscores the almost insurmountable obstacles that stood in the way of *aliyah* — the same obstacles which prevented a great number of Zionists from realizing their aspirations as well.

It is true that the Torah leaders mentioned above dissociated themselves from the Zionist Movement, primarily in response to its markedly secular orientation. However, they did not oppose *aliyah* to *Eretz Yisrael*. Indeed, just the opposite is the case. The *Chazon Ish* ruled that it was obligatory to move to the Land, and this was the opinion held by most other Torah sages as well. Zionism, no; *Eretz Yisrael*, certainly. There can be no doubt that the Torah leadership of pre-war Europe separated these two concepts.

The most adamant opponent of Zionism in *Eretz Yisrael* was R' Yosef Chaim Sonnenfeld, chief rabbi of the *Eidah Hachareidis* of Jerusalem. Nevertheless, he too at every opportunity called for *aliyah* to the Holy Land, as is described at length in his biography, *Ha'Ish al Hachomah* (vol. 2, pp. 144-156). Let us quote the summary of a secular historian's discussion of Polish Jewry before the Holocaust:

> The Agudas Yisrael also did not brush aside the rebuilding of Palestine. The Agudists were, of course, dissatisfied with the religious, or irreligious, attitude of official Zionism, but *Yishuv Eretz Yisrael* ("Resettlement of Palestine") stood forth as a Biblical command and found the warmest support among leading Agudist rabbis (Prof. Ismar Elbogen, *A Century of Jewish Life*, p. 539).

It is correct that the Torah-observant public played a relatively small role in the new settlement of *Eretz Yisrael*. But this was not due to any opposition in principle to building up the Land. Rather, its primary cause was the organizational weakness of the religious sector. Orthodox European Jewry did not have, and did not create for themselves, the organizational tools and institutions necessary to enable large-scale *aliyah*.

Speaking personally, this author does not understand the basis upon which the Torah leadership is accused of opposing *aliyah*. I have personally heard stories from Holocaust survivors relating how a particular rav or *rosh yeshivah* in Hungary told his students not to emigrate to *Eretz Yisrael*, but it would seem that these incidents were the exception to the general rule. A decisive majority of Torah sages did not take such a stand. The widespread misconception to the contrary is most likely due to popular confusion between the battle against Zionism with an imagined battle against emigration to Israel. The position of a minority of sages (such as the *Admor* of Satmar and his followers) is mistaken as the position taken by all opponents of secular Zionism.

Forty years after the fact, confusion still prevails concerning these concepts; this author has devoted a chapter of an earlier work, *Tzion Beis Chayeinu*, to elucidating the topic in greater detail.

Another point should be dealt with here. World War Two was not a confirmation of that basic tenet of secular Zionism, that the Jewish People are safe from anti-Semitism only in their own land and state. True, *Eretz Yisrael* escaped the day of wrath, but the escape was only through a miracle in the Battle of El Alamein. Had events unfolded as the calculations of relative troop strength would have dictated, Rommel's troops would have easily conquered *Eretz Yisrael*. If the Nazis, God forbid, had conquered the Land, the fate of the Jews living there would have matched the fate of their brethren in other countries that suffered Nazi conquest. The advent of the Holocaust is less a validation of the political positions of secular Zionism than it is cogent evidence that Hashem guards his Holy Land.

In fact, however, it was not only the religious public which delayed emigration to *Eretz Yisrael*. The greater part of non-Orthodox European Jewry also remained in the Old Country, as did most of the Zionists themselves. No one foresaw the dimensions of the approaching catastrophe, and by the time disaster became apparent, escape from the horror was no longer possible. Any serious historical investigation of the Holocaust must thus conclude that there is little room for the claim that the Torah leadership recklessly misadvised European Jewry, or that they neglected to act through appropriate channels to prevent the disaster. For in hindsight, the sequence of events surrounding the Holocaust — the extent of the impending catastrophe as well as the relative safety of *Eretz Yisrael* — was not only unpredictable, it defied the very pattern of normal historical process.

We quote R' Moshe Blau, a leader of Agudas Yisrael during the Holocaust:

> In recent days our brothers, the Zionists, have begun to take advantage of the destruction of the Diaspora for political purposes — they wish to use it to show that their approach to the issue of *Eretz Yisrael* is correct. They even go so far as to

take advantage of spilled Jewish blood to attack the Orthodox for what they consider their apathy towards *Eretz Yisrael*. More than once we have read newspaper pieces claiming that the Orthodox rabbis and the *admorim*, who did not preach Zionism, are responsible for the blood of ten thousands of Israel who remained in Europe because their religious leaders did not espouse Zionism.

I don't know if [the Zionists] intend by this to say that they foresaw the tragedy of the Diaspora — that the spirit of prophecy, *ruach hakodesh*, appeared in their *"beis midrash"* and revealed that Hitler would decree annihilation upon the Jews. According to [the view of] true faith, this terrible decree came precisely because whole sections of the nation, under the influence of the Zionists, systematically and brazenly raised the banner of rebellion against the God of Israel and His Torah. The fact is that even the Jews who lived in Germany itself did not see what was developing. Not only did they not suspect a decree of annihilation, but even when Hitler boasted about such a prescription, they did not believe him, [for they] continued living in Germany — and in this matter there was no difference between the Orthodox and the non-religious (*Kisvei R' Moshe Blau, "Matzpunah shel HaYahadus Hachareidis Naki!"* pp. 250-251).[1]

---

1. For more on the issue of faith in Torah sages (*emunas chachamim*), see *Michtav Me'Eliyahu*, Part 1, p. 75.

E.

In Conclusion

I N CONCLUDING THIS chapter, it is appropriate to re-emphasize several points which may be lost in the scope of the more detailed discussions. First, all that is quoted in the name of Torah leaders is meant only so that practical lessons may be drawn from the disaster. The Torah leadership, for

Prophets and Mortals

all their saintliness and scholarship, dealt with the questions not as prophets, but as mortals: They attached no claims of certainty to their analyses. Their statements were not made to uncover the definitive rationale of Divine justice. Rather, they were intended only to bring the ways of Hashem closer to our comprehension — to enable us to see Divine Providence in the midst of the terrible *hester panim* — and to impress faith upon our hearts by highlighting the hand of Providence in history.

MORTAL MAN IS NOT capable of knowing if in fact the Holocaust constitutes *chevlei Mashiach*. Neither can we hope to understand

A Crucial Era

the true significance of *chevlei Mashiach*. Nevertheless, it is proper to wonder whether we do not stand at a crucial era in our history, and to evaluate if our conduct is worthy of the role Providence has dealt us. No man can assert with confidence that the awesome punishment of the Holocaust — the utter obliteration of European Jewry, observant and assimilated alike — resulted from the *Haskalah* or from assimilation. The mortal mind is helpless even to comprehend the enormity of the verdict; it is all the more inadequate to definitively explicate the sins which were its cause. Nonetheless it is proper not to ignore at least the visible connections between assimilation and the Holocaust, and to wonder whether indeed the two may be substantively correlated. Likewise, we cannot point to the other sins mentioned in this chapter, and claim with certainty that they were causes of the Holocaust. Just the same, we cannot shirk the obligation to search our deeds, and — as our fathers did throughout the generations — to recite the *vidui*, and seek to correct our shortcomings.

IT WOULD SEEM accurate to summarize that according to all opinions, a message of the Holocaust for the generation after is

Strengthening Awareness that we must strengthen our awareness of our role as Jews. We must strengthen observance of all aspects of Torah: the duties of the heart and the obligations of the body; the *mitzvos* that apply between man and God and those that govern conduct between man and man; the *mitzvos* that pertain to *Eretz Yisrael* and those that apply outside of the Land. Only in this way shall we bring ourselves ever closer to complete Redemption.

ALL STAND SPEECHLESS and terror stricken before the profundity of Divine justice revealed in our most recent calamity.

Sculpting History Likewise, all believe that it is impossible to let such an enormous historical event pass in silence or apathy. Hidden in the depths of the awesome *hester panim* of the Holocaust lies the longing Divine call: "Return to Me and I shall return to you" (*Zechariah* 1:3). The potential is here, but the future lies only with us. If we only heed the call wholeheartedly, we can be sure that the events of our century will have been those of *chevlei Mashiach*, the birth pangs of mankind's universal return to its Creator.

The extraordinary responsibility which befalls our generation emerges as the unifying theme of all the statements we have thus far seen. R' Dessler writes powerfully on this theme:

> In my humble opinion, at a time like this, anyone with a heart must disengage himself from all self-centered activity and thought concerning his material future, and give himself up completely to disseminating Torah among the Jewish People. Due to our many sins, so much has been destroyed, and it is

therefore clear that our obligation is to build. We have lost not only the physical selves of our Jewish brothers, but also their holy souls have departed from us, and many centers of Torah have been uprooted and destroyed. If we do not strengthen ourselves, to build with all possible energy — and beyond — our sin will certainly find us. Great portions of the World to Come lie about as jewels in the street, and no one has the understanding to pick them up. Each person turns to his own private gain, and even after the terrible destruction we have witnessed, everyone [still] only considers his future income.

How is it among all the nations? In a time of danger to his people, is the individual — for the sake of his own life — permitted to shirk acting to save the people? Why should we, the Jewish People, do any less? Why should we not do as well as the best among the nations? So much has been destroyed in front of our eyes, and we remain silent. How can an individual dare to think about his private concerns? Only a rebel does that, and earns the name of a contemptible traitor. Living Torah scrolls are burned in front of our eyes, and we — our hearts think about a loaf of bread? Alas for that shame! Do we not understand that to behave like this, is to [behave] like beasts?

The Torah screams and cries out to her children: "Save me!" Let us rise up, please, a little bit. Let us make ourselves activists for the sake of heaven, for we are then assured of certain success. Let our words go forth from the depths of our heart, and then, clearly, they will enter the hearts of others. The people do not listen unless they see great deeds, done with self-sacrifice (*Michtav Me'Eliyahu*, letter written in 5704/1944, part 3, p. 345).

Although these words were written in the midst of the Holocaust, they are still relevant today, nearly half a century later. By the kindness of Hashem, new Torah centers have been built in *Eretz Yisrael* and in America. But it is precisely at this juncture that we can see even more clearly the difference between our generation and the one lost in the Holocaust. Statistics indicate that the number of those studying in yeshivos today exceeds the amount of Jews studying on the eve of the Holocaust. Nevertheless, in quality, content, and sheer self-sacrifice, the yeshivah world of today still lags behind its counterpart of fifty years ago. When we evaluate the present state of the Jewish People as a whole, we are confronted with intermarriage which claims a near-majority of our people as victims. Among the rest of our nation, assimilation continues at an alarming rate.

All Israel are held accountable for one another — when those of ability, those capable of carrying others upon their shoulders are reduced in number, the extra burden falls equally upon those who remain. We know from tradition that the Holy One, Blessed is He, does not send a man trials beyond his capability to endure. Clearly, then, the contemporary observant community has the ability to bear the extra burden of its nation. If one acts truly, selflessly, and with faith in his Creator, Hashem will grant success to his undertakings. How great is the responsibility, how monumental the obligation. May it be His will that we fulfill our charge.

5

The Human Response

A.

Nazi Germany – Exception or Rule

THE HOLOCAUST CLEARLY represents the greatest outbreak of unrestrained evil that this century, perhaps even this millennium, has witnessed. The central question it raises, however, is not "Where was God?" but "Where was man?" Prof. Lucy Dawidowicz writes:

Where Was Man? The annihilation of six million Jews, carried out by the German state under Adolf Hitler during World War II, has resisted understanding. The question persists: How could it have happened? That question embraces several questions, each charged with passion and moral judgment. They are:

1. How was it possible for a modern state to carry out the systematic murder of a whole people for no reason other than that they were Jews?
2. How was it possible for a whole people to allow itself to be destroyed?

3. How was it possible for the world to stand by without halting this destruction?

(The War Against the Jews 1933-1945, p. x)

These are indeed the essential questions at stake in the query: "Where was man?" It is to the first of these issues that we shall devote the present chapter.

HOW COULD A highly cultured people, such as the Germans, fall so quickly and easily to the depths of moral depravity? Was a

A Unique Failing? failing of this magnitude unique to the German people — could it perhaps have stemmed from the basic education of this nation, or from its

particular structure of authority? Or are similar phenomena also possible among other peoples? How can one reconcile the idea of genocide with the great scientific advances and philosophical genius produced by German culture?

This author is not expert enough in German history and literature to decipher whether a poisonous tendency toward murder existed in this culture from earlier times, or whether the outer and inner struggles of German history are essentially similar to those of other peoples. Many historians attempt to find in German legends and history a tendency towards violence and an admiration of brute force. One cannot know, however, whether this is merely the wisdom of hindsight and whether the evidence adduced is taken out of context. The fact is that Germany did not project a genocidal image before the Holocaust, and no one then foresaw the depths to which this nation would eventually fall. One who searches hard enough will find similar legends and ideas among other peoples, and indeed a great distance lies between folk legend and actual participation in murder.

OTHER HISTORIANS ARGUE that the flaw is to be found within the basic education of the German people. They see in German

A Second Theory history an essential alienation from Western democratic tradition, and a tendency instead toward blind obedience. Only in Germany, they

maintain, did the people accept upon themselves, almost eagerly, such absolute dictatorship — a dictatorship which eventually led to the murder of the Jews.

It would seem, however, that this theory is superficial. Germany's effort to murder the Jews was not confined to a narrow segment of its population. Many people engaged in the killing, not through blind obedience, but with dedication and even zeal. It was not the dictatorship or its control of the military that made possible the murder of the Jews, for even a dictator is not free to carry out whatever he wishes. The fact is that when Hitler attempted to murder the mentally ill in Germany, such a great popular protest ensued that he was forced to abandon the plan.

Likewise, democracy is not the only guardian of moral rectitude: During World War II, the Spanish dictator, Franco, saved more Jews than most democratic states. In the final analysis, the theory that Germany committed the Holocaust because of alienation from Western values smacks of self-righteousness: "The Holocaust won't — or couldn't — happen here, because atrocities are not possible in a democracy." This, however, is unfortunately not true.

THE QUESTION INTENSIFIES when we contemplate the great accomplishments achieved by German culture in all fields of

The Nation of Kant
human endeavor. For a substantial time, Germany was considered the foremost representative of enlightenment and progress. From her midst went forth the greatest minds of Europe — scientists, poets, writers, and philosophers. Among them was Immanuel Kant, who wrote at length to establish the binding force of the moral imperative. A high percentage of Nobel Prize winners were German. Indeed, it was only Germany's advanced level of technological development which allowed it to wage war for long years against half the world. How is it possible, then, that this people engaged in murder on a scale unmatched in the history of mankind?

With hindsight, of course, it is possible to find traces of Nazi ideology among the very German philosophers and scientists which her culture had claimed as prize jewels. William Shirer, in

The Rise and Fall of the Third Reich, writes:

> There had been among the Germans, to be sure, some of the
> most elevated minds and spirits of the Western world —
> Leibnitz, Kant, Herder, Humboldt, Lessing, Goethe, Schiller,
> Bach and Beethoven — and they had made unique contribu-
> tions to the civilization of the West. But the German culture
> which became dominant in the nineteenth century and which
> coincided with the rise of Prussian Germany, continuing from
> Bismarck through Hitler, rests primarily on Fichte and Hegel,
> to begin with, and then on Treitschke, Nietzsche, Richard
> Wagner, and a host of lesser lights not the least of whom,
> strangely enough, were a bizarre Frenchman and an eccen-
> tric Englishman. They succeeded in establishing a spiritual
> break with the West; the breach has not been healed to this
> day (p. 97).

This argument, though, appears weak. First of all, the assertion
that it was precisely "Fichte and Hegel" and their followers who
"held sway" is based only on the hindsight which the Holocaust
provides. Second, even those philosophers would not in their
worst nightmares have suggested that the purpose of the German
state is to become a slaughterhouse for millions of human beings.
All the subsequent passages cited by Shirer are open to various
interpretations, and must certainly be weighed in the overall
context of those writers' philosophical systems.

Third, and most importantly: The assumption that the roots
of Nazism existed in German culture a century before the
Holocaust does not reduce the question — it only magnifies it.
How is it possible that one and the same people could produce on
the one hand truly worthwhile schools of thought, and on the
other hand philosophers who preached murder and pillage?
Neither group stood on the margins of society — instead, each
squarely occupied the foremost ranks of the nation's leaders. The
mass murderers came from among the admirers of Beethoven no
less than from among the followers of the anti-Semitic Wagner;
some of the most sadistic killers were members of societies for
prevention of cruelty to animals. In the eyes of many Germans,
there was no contradiction between admiring the great German

philosophers and believing in the ideology of violence. We must ask ourselves if indeed the contradiction is all that real.

IN ANALYZING THE theories which deal with the subject, we find that most of them attempt to locate a defect unique to the German

Enlightenment's Frontier

people. It would appear, though, that the validity of this assumption is questionable; in truth we have little guarantee that other peoples could not degenerate similarly.

The fact is that tens of thousands of people of other nationalities took part in the murder of the Jews: Poles, Ukrainians, Lithuanians, Latvians, Rumanians, Russians, Hungarians, Dutchmen, Frenchmen, and others. Even in our day, Nazi parties exist in Britain and the United States. True, Germany was the prime source of the evil, but this does not mean that Germany was an aberrant exception among the community of nations. On the contrary, it is possible that the German nation was simply the avant-garde, the concrete expression of feelings and views which had not yet reached actualization in other nations. Could it be that precisely because Germany was a highly cultured nation, standing on the frontier of enlightenment, that she also stood on the frontier of all trends to which nations are susceptible — including sadism? Could it be that the moral degeneracy of Germany stands not in contradiction to its culture, but on the contrary, is the very product of that culture? If so, the Holocaust constitutes an unshakeable indictment of all the values of German culture — values held dear by other nations as well. Few wish to draw the logical conclusions of such criticism, and perhaps it is for this reason that so few schools of thought have taken this approach. However, as we shall endeavor to show, the evidence which supports it cannot be ignored.

B.

Nazism and the Abandonment of Religion

Avraham said: "For I thought, 'It is only that there
is no fear of God in this place, and they will kill me
because of the matter of my wife.' "
(*Bereishis* 20:11)

He gave him an irrefutable answer. . . "It is true
that there is correct conduct (*derech eretz*) here,
but this stems, not from fear of God,
but from human intelligence. . .
for if a person does not have fear of God,
he cannot overcome his urges and govern his human will.
Therefore I feared that they would kill me."
(*Ha'amek Davar, ad loc.* And see *Malbim, ad loc.*)

F WE SEEK THE root of the moral degeneracy which caused the Holocaust, we must first investigate the foundations of moral consciousness in general.

It would seem that in the final analysis, there are only two possibilities. Morality may be based either on absolute Divine com-

A Fundamental Principle mand, or upon the human vantage point. The imperative to avoid murder, for example, can gain validity either because "Thou shalt not kill" is one of the Ten Commandments uttered by the Master of the universe, or because there is some independent logical reason which asserts why it is not proper to murder. The difference between the two is this: The obligation to obey Divine commands does not rest on the foundations of deductive reasoning. It is a fundamental principle which stands on its own accord; thus, by definition, it cannot be proved, nor does it require proof. Such basic principles, precisely because they are so fundamental, cannot be substantiated by reference to a more basic premise. If the Creator Himself, Who breathes life into His creatures at every moment, makes a demand upon His creations, it is simply self-evident that they are obligated to obey. One can no more easily deny this basic truth than he can deny any other self-evident assumption, such as the reality of his own existence. The question 'why' is simply meaningless.

THE LOGICAL BASIS of man-made morality, on the other hand, cannot be called a fundamental principle. It is true that every **A Frail** nation and people has a prohibition against murder, **Sense** but it is also true that since the beginning of time, humanity has been continually preoccupied with incessant warfare. A number of primitive tribes still permit murder for the sake of eating human flesh, and in modern states it is acceptable to destroy a fetus in its mother's womb. "Mercy killing" is another example of modern man's curious ability to rationalize murder. But there can be no stronger illustration of the frailty of man's moral sense than the Holocaust itself. Apparently, even the prohibition against taking human life is not a self-evident principle.

THE *ADMOR* OF PIASTCHENE writes the following concerning the verses (*Tehillim* 147:19-20), "He tells His words to Yaakov, **Direct** His statutes (*chukim* beyond reason) **Comprehension** and judgments to Israel. He did not do this to all the nations, and did not let them know His judgments."

> We need to understand why it says only, "He did not let them know His judgments," rather than, "He did not let them know His statutes and judgments."
> The answer is that people imagine they understand logical matters purely according to their reason. But the truth is that every person is bound to his own essence, and everyone understands in accordance with his essence. This applies even to theft and murder, which have always been consid-

ered logical prohibitions, or what the verse calls "judgments." But today we see that there are nations which invent arguments to prove that one must murder and steal.

Chazal tell us: "Do not say, 'I don't want pork,' but say, 'I want pork, but what can I do? The Almighty prohibited it.'" *Rambam* in *Shemoneh Perakim* explains why *Chazal* chose for their example this type of *mitzvah*, the type which is beyond reason (which our verse calls "statutes") rather than, "I want to steal or to murder, but what can I do? The Almighty prohibited it." *Rambam* says that anyone who would say he wants to do such things is an "inferior soul." In other words, an "inferior soul" does wish even to steal and to murder, although these are logical prohibitions. But a man's ways always seem just in his own eyes. Only someone with a "good soul" understands that it is forbidden to steal and murder.

Therefore, when the Jew brings himself closer to the Holy One, Blessed is He, and to Torah, he understands that even the *mitzvos* which are "statutes" must be the way they are. This understanding is not [arrived at] by means of his human intelligence, according to this or that reason; one needs reasoned explanations only for things which are foreign to him. But things which belong to one's essence, he comprehends directly and simply, just as he comprehends his own existence. This is why [the Torah] says, "He tells. . . His statutes and judgments to Israel." It means that even His "statutes" are like reasonable "judgments" to the Jewish People, since the Jews in their essence are close to the Torah. "He did not do this to all the nations, and did not let them know His judgments." That is, this special ability of knowing even the "statutes" as if they were "judgments"— this He did not grant to all the nations, but only to Israel (*Esh Kodesh*, p. 33).

Can Reason Be a Guide?

CLEARLY, PEOPLE POSSESS an intuitive moral sense which opposes murder and other immoral acts. Some refer to this sense as "conscience"; in Torah literature it is known as *yetzer tov* — the good inclination — or *neshamah elokis* — the Divine soul. Yet in opposition to this, man also possesses a baser nature. He has an evil inclination (*yetzer hara*) as well, an appetite for power and dominion which knows no limits if left unbridled. The question becomes: What is to tip the balance between these two urges; what ultimately determines how a man shall act? Can human understanding be a guide to man, the creature who is pulled simultaneously towards good and evil? Can reason ever establish clear boundaries between the two?

To this day morality remains one of the most elusive areas of the philosophical spectrum. There is little agreement on standards of good and evil — indeed, philosophers do not even agree on the essential nature of morality. Some maintain that one cannot give an absolute definition to good and evil, for the moral good is only a reflection of the conventions of each society. Others identify "good" with pleasure or benefit to the individual or society. Still others argue that morality cannot be defined rationally at all, for perception of good and evil is intuitive, not intellectual. One wonders, if the unclarity is so great among scholars, how is the ordinary person to avoid wrongdoing? If great and learned men have reached the conclusion that good is "that which causes me pleasure," why shouldn't one indeed give higher priority to his personal happiness than to a vague imperative which obligates him not to harm others?

THE BUILDING BLOCKS of morality have eluded the otherwise penetrating eye of human intellect. Historically speaking, the **A Divine Framework** foundations of morality were given to mankind by religion, not by the achievements of reason. While Greek thinkers debated definitions of good and evil, no one ever raised the question within the framework of Judaism. Even medieval Jewish philosophers who dealt extensively with problems raised by Greek philosophy did not debate the foundation of morality. Indeed, within a Divine system, the question does not begin. Jewish philosophy has always known that there is no truly founded morality outside of Divine morality; that only within its framework can man find the unshakeable standards with which to evaluate his deeds.

IF MAN-MADE MORALITY rests on shaky philosophical foundations, its power of enforcement is even weaker. The practice of

Conscience Can Be Quieted such an ethical system is ultimately voluntary, and it has little to rely on other than a dubious faith in man's enduring good will. One who acts contrary to man-made morality has nothing to fear but his conscience, and conscience, as we know, can be quieted. Fear of God, by contrast, provides a firm practical basis for ethics. Although one who accepts Divine morality seeks to be motivated by love of his Creator and awe of His grandeur, he cannot help but fear the consequences of his actions as well. Fear of God — and the intent here is to its most simple and widespread form, i.e., fear of punishment — is an incomparably strong psychological force. Throughout history, it has guarded millions from moral degeneration.

IF MAN ULTIMATELY determines good and evil, then he stands, as it were, above ethics — beyond the concepts of good and evil

Eternal Validity which he himself created. If morality is defined by humans, it can also be put aside for various human needs. Man is at liberty to tinker with his inventions. Divine morality, however, stands eternally. Ordained by Him Who created both man and the world, this morality transcends the vicissitudes of mortal whims. It is forever valid, and man accepts it upon himself in reverence and awe.

IT WOULD SEEM, then, that a prominent reason for the moral degeneration of Europe during the Holocaust stands quite clearly

A Shift of Focus before us. In the modern era, European society underwent a fundamental spiritual revolution. It severed itself from the religious faith which dominated all aspects of life during the Middle Ages. Millions, of course, remained faithful to religious ceremony and principles, but at the core, the status of religion was fundamentally altered. Religious faith, once the center of European life, was replaced by the striving for personal happiness, and religion became only one of the ways to achieve this happiness. The inherent stability of Divine morality, with its boundaries protected by fear of God, was replaced by the infirmity of man-made morality. Eternal reward or punishment was no longer a matter of great consequence, as suddenly the very foundations of morality became open to attack. Is it any wonder that the abandonment of Divine morality should inevitably bring moral anarchy in its wake?

Undoubtedly, atrocities and criminal acts of unfathomed magnitude also occurred during the predominantly religious Middle Ages. No people knows this better than the Jews — suffice it to mention merely the Crusades, the Spanish Expulsion, and the "holy" Inquisition with its forced conversions. Yet true Divine morality did not hold sway even during this period. Christianity, though it rests on *Tanach* and the Divine revelation of Judaism, nevertheless introduced additions and changes to the Jewish faith. These deviations were all man-made, alterations of the Divine Torah. Christianity thus does not represent pure Divine morality, but a mixture of truth and falsehood; Divine morality and man-made morality — a world in which night and day prevail at once.

STILL, CHRISTIANITY REMAINED somewhat of a deterrent. All the atrocities of the Middle Ages pale in comparison to the infamy

Religion as a Deterrent
committed by "progressive", modern man. All those killed during the entire span of the Crusades make up only a small percentage of those murdered in a single German concentration camp. Not one of Israel's enemies during the Middle Ages attempted to annihilate her as the Nazis plotted. The goal of medieval persecutions was not murder for its own sake, but forced conversion. Even the religious persecutions of the Middle Ages were generally not conducted by the Christian or Moslem religious authorities themselves. The official religious line opposed the murder of Jews. It was by and large the masses that took false advantage of religion to give vent to their lust for murder. Indeed, anyone familiar with the history of the period knows that Jews sometimes took refuge from the crusaders in the castle of the local priest, who tried to defend them. Likewise, within the country of the Pope the situation of the Jews was usually better than elsewhere. The

man-made morality of our day, by contrast, did not prevent a cultured nation from murdering assimilated or even converted Jews. Genocide — a concept unthinkable to even the most fanatical Christian monarch of the "dark" Middle Ages — became something perfectly permissible, even a high duty, during our more "enlightened" era.

ONLY THROUGH THE desertion of religion and the separation of religion and philosophy was it possible for the Nazis to produce a

Nietzsche "philosophical system" advocating violence and murder; a system which based itself, accurately or inaccurately, on citations from the writings of great philosophers. Most notorious are the references in Nazi ideology to the writings of the German philosopher, Nietzsche. In carrying Enlightenment philosophy to its logical extreme, Nietzsche wrote vehemently against the "Judeo-Christian slave-morality," and argued in favor of the concept of "superior man" — man who would be "beyond good and evil," as the concepts are defined by conventional morality.

It makes little difference whether Nietzsche and others actually intended what the Nazis found in their words. The "superman" ideal, the concept of life "beyond good and evil" — all this could only have become reality in a world in which religion was no longer a central force.

THE PRACTICAL CONNECTION between atheism and violence seems incontrovertible. The Nazis themselves made no attempt to

Atheism and Violence hide that they opposed not only Judaism, but also popularly accepted forms of Christianity. Let us not forget that the closest modern equivalent to the Holocaust was the purges of Stalin in the Soviet Union. There too, Communist doctrine opposed all religion, and it seems hardly a coincidence that in the Soviet Union literally millions of innocent people, including many Jews, were also murdered. Quite a number of Nazi practices, including concentration camps, were simply imitations of methods used in Russia — except that the Nazis outdid their teachers.

Similarly, while Communist ideology — Dialectical Materialism — is distinguished by its thoroughly materialistic approach to human events, the Nazis spoke of "returning to nature" and of obeying man's animal urges — the "laws of the blood." Nazism denies the existence of man's soul and, consequently, his spiritual superiority over beasts. Thus, German racist theory saw man as just another species of animal, to which the laws of "natural selection" apply in full. The moral degeneracy of Nazism and Communism thus flows naturally from their rejection of religious thought.

The *gaon* R' Elchanan Wasserman writes:

> The Chafetz Chaim used to say: "If Torah ceases, faith must also cease; and without faith in Hashem, the world cannot exist." This idea is found explicitly in the Torah: "It is only that there is no fear of God in this place, and they will kill me because of the matter of my wife" (*Bereishis* 20:11). The expression "it is only" indicates that nothing in the world has the power to hold back the animal within man, except fear of Hashem. In the modern era, when non-belief has spread throughout the world, human beings have become serpents who bite each other, and the most healthy among the nations of the world are those that believe in the holy Scriptures (*Kovetz Maamarim*, p. 70).

It is not by chance that of the few gentiles who saved Jewish lives, a high percentage were people of deep religious faith. By and large, the isolated individuals who had the courage to protest Nazi policy were religious persons.

All this, of course, does not explain why Germany degenerated more rapidly than other nations which had also abandoned Christian faith. Our point is simply that the casting off of religion prepared the background for the heinous crimes of the Hitler regime. It may be that those who actually believed Nazi ideology were a small extremist group. But the madness of the fringe is the expression of urges and phenomena which exist in society as a whole. Only the departure from religion can explain the apathy of the collective German society towards the wholesale murder of the Jews, or the population's passive — and sometimes active — participation in that murder.

The Value of Life ONLY ONE WHO recognizes that life itself is given to man as a trust — as only a means to a Divine end — understands that he has no right to destroy any human life, his own or another's. How instructive is it that in Jewish law, the prohibition against suicide is only a subcategory of the general restriction against murder (*Rambam, Hilchos Rotze'ach* 2:2). *Halachah* similarly rules that one cannot be executed on the strength of his own confession alone, for "a man's life is not his own property, but the property of the Holy One, Blessed is He — as it is written, (*Yechezkel* 18:4), 'All the souls are Mine'" (*Radbaz* on *Rambam, Hilchos Sanhedrin* 18:6).

Our century has been the witness that once man rejected the Divine origin of life, the practical prohibition against murder fell away as well. When man usurped the place of God in creation, he also seized the authority to take or give life. It is only because of their historical roots in religion that other societies which have abandoned fear of God have thus far refrained from giving tacit sanction to murder as well.

We have come to see, then, that from both the side of the murderer as well as the side of the victim, one of the central causes of the Holocaust was the rejection of religious faith. As we have shown in earlier chapters, the assimilation of European Jewry and the growing abandonment of Torah seem to have been precursors of the impending disaster. Likewise, it appears that more than any other force, it was the denial of God which removed the moral restraints which stood between the Nazi party and genocide.[1]

---

1. (See also *Binesivos Hazman Vehanetzach* ch. 2 by Yehudah Leib Girsht, for extensive treatment of this issue.)

C.

The Christian Role

ALTHOUGH THE MORE direct causes of the Holocaust center around the abandonment of religion in general, it is nonetheless true that without Christianity, the success of Nazism would not have been possible. As we have indicated earlier, although Christianity is based on the Divine Law, the distortions and changes it introduced into that Law led to moral failings of the first order. As we shall see, the Holocaust was apparently nurtured by one of these failings.

IT IS A FACT that Hitler and his cohorts abandoned Christianity. Their persecution of the Jews was carried out for racist, not

Religious Hatred — a Historical Legacy

religious, reasons. Nevertheless, the role Christianity played in the historical roots of the Holocaust is not to be overlooked. Were it not for the fact that dozens of generations in Europe had been imbued with religious hatred, the growth of racist hatred towards Jewry in modern times could not have taken place.[1]

Furthermore, throughout the Holocaust, the Vatican refrained from protesting the murder, and by and large, stood aside, rescuing only a tiny few. To this day, the Vatican refuses scholars full access to documents of the period. It has been established, however, that the Vatican was among the first in the world to know about the genocide, and it did nothing to publicize the information (see Walter Laquer, *The Terrible Secret*).

---

1. This subject is dealt with at length by Jules Isaac in his book, *The Christian Roots of the Holocaust*.

INDEED ROLFE HOCHHUTH'S play *The Deputy*, which sharply illuminated the Vatican's response to the Holocaust, aroused in its

The Apathy of Silence day a worldwide public storm. Some critics defended the Vatican, but it is difficult to avoid the conclusion that the Pope's inaction indicated tacit approval. One is reminded of *Chazal*'s words regarding Pharaoh's plan (*Shemos* 1:10), "Come, let us deal wisely with them." Our sages write that Bil'am (Balaam), Iyov (Job), and Yisro (Jethro) were consulted by the Egyptian ruler. "Bil'am, who offered advice, was [eventually] killed. Iyov, who remained silent, was condemned to suffer" (*Sotah* 11). The apathy of silence carries with it the harsh responsibilities of approval.

R' WEISSMANDL, WRITING in *Min Hameitzar* (pp. 18 ff.), relates that the Jews of Slovakia, a state under the rule of a Catholic

R' Weissmandl's Account priest, tried to stop the shipments to the death camps by appealing to the Vatican:

> Immediately, a letter of reply arrived from Rome to their faithful servant, the priest Tiso, head of the government of this Catholic state. In smooth language, they put forth two basic principles. One was: Do not ship out the Jews and do not cause them suffering *through the breaking up of families*. The second principle was: Do not under any circumstances ship out *the Jews who had converted to Christianity*.
>
> Tiso called a special assembly of the government to make known the Pope's reply: the message that was implied in the first principle, and the explicit instruction contained in the second principle. By this means, he calmed the small doubt that had existed concerning the expulsion law [which enabled shipping the Jews to the camps]. Those who had opposed it, either because of their conscience or due to the influence of the Jews, were quieted. Tiso extracted the "*halachah*" from this letter with true scholarly acumen. He fathomed the profound wickedness contained therein, realizing that the second principle, which forbade the shipping out of Jews who had converted to Catholicism, implied something about the first principle: namely, that it was a *mitzvah* to ship out the

other Jews, and the only prohibition was, not against shipping them out, but against breaking up families — i.e., leaving a single soul behind. Therefore this wicked one said: "Come, let us give satisfaction to our father, the Pope, in two ways. We will not break up families, but will ship them all together to Lublin. And those who have converted to Christianity, we shall completely exempt from the decree" (pp. 20-21).

Another incident concerning an appeal to Catholic authorities is related in R' Weissmandl's work. When a group of Jews asked a certain archbishop to prevent an expulsion order, they still believed that their fate was only expulsion. R' Weissmandl records:

> That wicked archbishop answered our teacher, may his merit defend us, and told him: "This is not just expulsion! There you will not die of hunger and epidemic! There they will slaughter all of you together, from the old men to the babies, children and women, in one day, and this is the punishment you deserve for the death of our Redeemer. You have only one course: Convert to our religion, and then I will act to have the decree canceled" (Ibid., p. 24).

On another occasion, R' Weissmandl appealed to the nuncio, the Pope's emissary in Slovakia, and received this reply:

> This wicked man, the emissary of the Pope, his face full of hatred, eyes flashing vengeance, answered: "There is no such thing as the blood of innocent Jewish children! All Jewish blood is guilty, and they must all die. This is the punishment that awaits them for that sin" (Ibid., p. 25).

Even when the Church engaged in isolated rescue activities, the motive seems to have been to bring the rescued Jews into the bosom of Christianity. Thousands of Jewish children were taken into monasteries, and after the war, many were not returned to their people and faith even after relatives pleaded for their release.

With unparalleled cynicism, many Christians still see the Holocaust as a heavenly punishment for the Jews' failure to accept Christianity. Some still claim that the killing is a testament to the righteousness of the murderer and the sin of the victim. Mindless hatred of this sort needs no refutation; however, the hypocrisy which it betrays is truly shocking. In a certain sense, it is perhaps more contemptible than the murder itself.

HOW DID CHRISTIANITY, which professes unbounded love and unflinching moral conduct, deteriorate so profoundly? The issue is

Ethical Standards complex, but we have touched upon one of the main reasons earlier: this religion grafted man-made principles onto the Divine Law. Let us explain:[1]

It is known that Christianity prided itself, and still prides itself, on its supposed moral superiority to Judaism. Throughout history, the charges have been numerous: The Jewish faith teaches that one must "love one's fellow-man as oneself," Christianity calls for unlimited love of one's fellow-man. Where Judaism praises one who "is insulted but does not insult, hears himself belittled and does not reply," Christianity demands that one who is slapped turn his other cheek to his attacker. While Judaism emphasizes concrete *mitzvos* — among them "statutes" (*chukim*) whose reasons man cannot never fully fathom, Christianity annuls these concrete obligations and emphasizes the faith of the heart. Judaism distinguishes between Jew and non-Jew, while Christianity places all humanity on an equal plane. The list can continue.

In truth, however, Christianity's moral standards are the roots of their own demise. The fundamental error is the extreme character of the ethical demands which this religion makes upon its followers — standards which can never be met by the masses of humanity. The Jewish Torah, by contrast, is given by man's Creator, Who understands the fundamental nature of human character. Thus, while the Torah calls on man to reach spiritual heights, it remains keenly aware of the baser drives he must struggle with. Included within *Halachah* is the law of the *Eishes Y'fas Toar*, the "beautiful captive woman" (*Devarim* 21:10-14). *Chazal* tell us that this law

---

1. This is not the place to discuss at length the fundamental errors of Christianity — the corporeality of the Divine, its division into a trinity, and the belief in a false messiah. We limit our present discussion to the ethical aspects of Christianity alone.

was given only "to assuage the evil inclination," which, in this particular situation, the average man is deemed incapable of resisting. From this case the classical commentators deduce that everywhere else in the Torah — where no such permission is granted — man is indeed capable of resisting his lower impulses. The Torah's ethical standards remain thoroughly practical, and hence, are eminently relevant.

The same, however, cannot be said of Christianity. Being a religion constructed by man himself, it cannot lay claim to a truly profound knowledge of the human soul. Hence it demands of man to turn the other cheek, to love one's fellow man more than oneself, and to put another's life before one's own. The priests of Christianity are forbidden to marry, and its monks, living lives of self-affliction, isolate themselves from human society. The religion is not one which can easily be put into practice by individuals, much less so by society at large. The notion that it can be, leads to incomparable hypocrisy.

Society must exist, and in order to do so it must routinely commit various acts defined by Christianity as sinful. The result is that faith becomes only lip service. A people cannot exist without waging war in self-defense; it simply cannot make due with turning the other cheek. When a soldier goes to battle, and afterwards attends the Sunday prayer-service to hear Christianity's opposition to war, the value of this prayer-service progressively diminishes in his eyes. In this way, ethical standards quickly lose their relevance.

PROF. YITZCHAK JULIUS GUTMAN writes:

Beyond the Love Ethic

The theology of the Christian Church attempts to explain the difference between the place of law in Jewish life and in Christian life, between legal commandments and non-legal commandments. However, the truth is that in the end Christianity also has laws, but with one difference: The laws do not have a definitive quality; they lack the seriousness found in Judaism.

And more: The pure ethic of love [in Christianity] is limited to the personal and internal relationships between one individual and another. In its view, the only important relationship is that between one soul and another. Moreover, it is impossible to govern the life of society and the state with the morality of love. The indifference towards society and state that one finds in evangelism remained the heritage of Christianity, though of course it has to give these matters some place in its world. And when Christianity became the ruling religion, it could not be content with just accepting and tolerating the existence of society and state. It was compelled to construct an ethic for these aspects of life too. Outside of the absolute morality of love, they gave recognition to a law of relative morality, which applied in everyday life, and especially in the life of the state.

This separation entailed great danger. True, they saw the Ten Commandments as the basis of this morality, but what they built upon it was in many cases a jurisprudence of mercy, in which human feelings held no sway. Thus we find in the Middle Ages an extremely exalted religious ethic, side by side with a system of criminal law which is among the cruelest ever known. . . This double approach to morality could even go so far as to abandon, with regard to political life, not only the ideal of love, but even that of justice, leaving the conduct of the state in the hands of completely secular institutions, for whom the supreme value was the advantage of the state. . .

It is true that Judaism, too, distinguishes between various levels of morality — but it does not *separate* them. The morality of love and that of justice exist in mutual interaction. Together they make up one moral world, just as the God of justice is also the God of kindness and mercy *(Dat Umada,* pp. 279-80).

IN ADDITION TO these problems, Christianity's declaration of the annulment of the Torah opened the door to the undermining of

Discarding Obligation religious authority. If it was possible for the early Christians — who were born and raised as Jews — to simply discard the *mitzvos* of circumcision and *Shabbos*, it is also possible to eventually annul the binding force of "Thou shalt not kill." Historically speaking, Christianity gave rise to a surprising number of major reform movements.

Each of these successfully eliminated more and more of its commandments. Even the Jewish Reform Movement — itself an aberration of Judaism, not an organic product of it — is modeled after Christian counterparts.

Furthermore, the Christian attempt to base religious actions on feeling alone led to a myriad of deviations from the accepted faith. Over the years, Christianity gave rise to a number of mystic cults, some of which distinguished themselves by their affinity for the lowest forms of moral abomination. The Christian process of repentance also led to the commission of grave crimes. When automatic atonement is offered to those who confess before a priest, the temptation to sin is greatly increased. How characteristic it is that in the Divine system of Judaism, man confesses to God, while in man-made religion, the sinner confesses before a human being!

A Mystic Salvation

PRACTICALLY SPEAKING, THE difference between Jewish and Christian ethical systems was evident wherever Jews and Christians lived side by side. While murder, robbery, and rape were all but unheard of within medieval Jewish communities, these acts were commonplace within devoutly Christian medieval Europe. The spiritual salvation promised by Christianity found no concrete expression. This was pointed out by *Ramban* in his debate with a Jewish convert to Christianity, in front of the king of Spain:

> The prophet says that in the time of the Messiah. . . "they shall beat their swords into plowshares . . .and nation shall not raise sword against nation, and they shall no longer study war" (*Yeshayahu* 2:4). But from the days of Yeshu until now, the entire world is full of oppression and violence, and the Christians spill more blood than the other nations, and also indulge in illicit relations. And just think how difficult it would be for you, my lord the king, and for these knights of yours, if they could no longer study war (*Sefer Havikuach*, in *Kisvei HaRamban,* ed. Chavel, part 1, p. 311).

The conclusion is all but self-evident — Christian morality has failed decisively in its attempt to educate mankind.

D.

Enlightenment Idols

HE EUROPEAN DEPARTURE from religion discussed above was connected with the Enlightenment, a major cultural movement which effectively transformed all of Europe. In Judaism, this movement took the form of the *Haskalah*. Despite its distinctive Hebrew name, the *Haskalah* was

Enlightenment only one aspect of the phenomenon which encompassed whole schools of thought in Western nations. The essence of the movement was the belief that human intelligence is ultimately all powerful; thus, all values are to be based upon the dictates of human understanding. The Enlightenment is the force which gave birth to Liberalism and Humanism, while accelerating the abandonment of religion. It also spurred the development of technology, a process which continues to progress rapidly today.

PROPONENTS OF THE Enlightenment saw themselves as "citizens of the world." They were in their own eyes part of a collective

Citizens of the World world movement which would in the end bring permanent peace to humanity. Indeed, the Enlightenment spirit continues to leave its mark on modern society. Many still believe that the spirit of pure science will eventually bring about mutual understanding among previously hostile nations. A widespread faith continues that bloodshed is a relic of man's primitive past; that as mankind progresses ever further in science and technology, war will fade away of its own accord.

THIS FAITH IN THE unbounded power of the human mind is connected with a parallel belief in the progress and development

Darwinism — a Social Theory of the human species. Advocates of the Enlightenment view of man maintain that our forefathers were relatively primitive and intellectually weak. Modern man, by contrast, moves with giant strides towards the bright future of a wiser, more advanced humanity. The development of technology, in this view, means improvement in the basic character of humanity.

It is Darwin's Theory of Evolution which became the foremost symbol of this faith in the constant progress of the world. In the beginning, Darwin claims, the world contained only reptiles. From these species evolved birds and mammals, and from them came nothing less than man himself. Imaginative Enlightenment thinkers went on to speculate that perhaps even wiser, more refined creatures are one day destined to replace the human species of our day.

The Theory of Evolution did not limit itself to consideration of biology and zoology alone. Darwinism slowly became the symbol of "science" in all areas of its endeavor. Evolutionary theorists turned their gaze to the social sciences, and postulated "Social Darwinism." This theory proclaims that societies evolved from primitive forms, where might makes right, into cultured ones in which law reigns supreme. Ultimately, the study of religion itself became permeated by Darwin's influence. Earlier forms of worship, it was claimed, were products of primitive man's fear of nature; only as time progressed did these forms slowly evolve into more complex and abstract religions.

EVOLUTION STILL REMAINS the model for most secular approaches to these "sciences" today. There can be no stronger

Evolution and the Holocaust

refutation of its truth, however, than the Holocaust itself.

To the eyes of Enlightenment Europe, Germany represented the very embodiment of high culture; the pinnacle of human progress. In science, culture, and technology, it stood at the fore of the European community. Yet Germany's awesome moral failure stands without a parallel in history. When "cultural progress" locks arms with genocide, one must look again at its real value.

In the case of the Nazis, not only did scientific and technological advances fail to prevent the terrible murder, they actually provided the means to carry it out. Only in such an advanced state as

Germany was it possible to kill so many people so quickly, with such limited manpower. It was only Germany's technology which allowed it to mass produce Zyklon-B for the gas chambers. Only in cultured and organized Europe was it possible to identify the Jews to be murdered so rapidly, and with such ease. Likewise, it was only the railroad, the invention that brought the Industrial Revolution to Europe, that made possible the transport of the Jews to the death camps.

But more: Enlightenment science not only made mass murder technically possible. Its pervasive influence upon society was actually one of the direct causes of the crime. Prof. Yaakov Talmon writes:

> Darwinism brought down one of the strongest barriers protecting "thou shalt not kill." For this reason alone, its great diffusion and enormous influence make it a turning point in the history of mankind. Darwinism deprived man of his uniqueness in the order of creation. Man was no longer created by God; he did not emerge from the womb of nature *ex nihilo*, a final and completed product with a soul that elevates him above other creatures, all creation his footstool. Man no longer enjoyed a direct and special relation with his all-merciful heavenly Father, Who spreads the canopy of His peace over man and accompanies him in all his ways, provides him with sustenance, sees into his heart, rewards him for keeping His Commandments, punishes the sinners or visits the iniquities of the fathers upon the children.
>
> Not any longer. Nature, it turns out, is not benevolent, it does not take care of everyone, and most important, it does not take care of the crown of creation, man himself. There is no Providence to look after man; nor can one speak of Nature as having been planned by a Creator or by some cosmic intelligence. The universe was not wrought by God, nor is it the handiwork of abstract reason. There is no order in the universe, no plan, no harmony, that could prove the concern of a Creator. Rather, it is characterized by confusion and contradiction, by waste and antagonism and by the struggle of all against all.
>
> Such ordered harmony as does strike the eye and provoke

wonder and gratitude — because it seems to indicate the possibility of progress and harmony — is in fact only the product of a struggle for existence, paid for in blood, pain, and suffering. There is no end to this desperate struggle in which the strong, the fit and the talented rule the roost, while the weak, the botched, the unfit and the inefficient bow themselves out or else become the tools of those with greater vitality, and the instruments of their will. The notion of the sanctity of life therefore has no meaning. The whole earth, man's battleground, is strewn with the corpses of creatures that have been obliterated because they could not adapt to or resist their betters.

Now if mankind is not distinctive, it becomes difficult to speak of the unity of mankind. If there is no soul, then there is no reason either, for reason is the only quality that distinguishes man from the rest of the animal kingdom. Reason is but the one of the tools evolved in the course of the struggle for existence, a particular expression of animal vitality.

It also becomes impossible to acknowledge objective morality, for the only purpose of morality is to safeguard existence by cementing the unity of the race in its struggle against rivals and enemies. In a Nature "red in tooth and claw," the sanctity of life is a contradiction in terms. Not only are the weak doomed to die, but the progress of the universe virtually demands their extinction or extermination, so that the fittest shall survive to employ the power that Nature has given them for the conquest of Nature, its resources and its potentialities and possibilities, turning individuals inferior to themselves to use.

. . .Although one cannot equate Darwinism with racist theory, it would be impossible to imagine racism without Darwin. And I am speaking here not of an indirect affinity but of a direct connection.

In the "Descent of Man," Darwin writes:

"With savages, the weak in body or mind are soon eliminated; and those that survive commonly exhibit a vigorous state of health. We civilized men, on the other hand, do our utmost to check the process of elimination; we build asylums for the imbecile, the maimed, and the sick; we institute poor-laws; and our medical men exert their utmost skill to save the life of everyone to the last moment. There is reason to believe that vaccination has preserved thousands who from a weak constitution would formerly have succumbed to smallpox. Thus the weak members of civilized societies propagate their kind.

"No one who has attended to the breeding of animals will doubt that this must be highly injurious to the race of man. . . Care, or care wrongly directed, leads to the degeneration of a domestic race; but excepting in the case of man himself, hardly anyone is so ignorant as to allow his worst animals to breed."

Darwin states this more explicitly in a letter of July 3, 1881, where he writes: "Looking at the world at no very distant date, what an endless number of the lower races will have been eliminated by the higher civilized races throughout the world" (lecture by Prof. Talmon, printed in the pamphlet, *European History as the Seedbed of the Holocaust*).

"MY STRENGTH AND THE might of my arm produced all this wealth for me" (*Devarim* 8:17). Exaggerated faith in the power of

The Primal Dream

human reason leads to moral downfall: "lest. . . your heart become haughty, and you forget Hashem your God" (ibid. v. 12,14). As in his early sin of eating from the Tree of Knowledge, Enlightenment man once again dreamt the primal dream: ". . .and you will be like gods" (*Bereishis* 3:5). And if in fact man is to be a god, then life and death also do not evade his grasp. Ultimately, "Thou shalt not kill" falls to the axe as well.

Just as eating from the Tree of Knowledge brought death to the world, so too has technological progress without moral restraint brought mankind to the brink of self-destruction through nuclear weaponry. It does not seem coincidental that nuclear development was connected with the Second World War, and that it was pursued firstly by the nation that perpetrated the very tenuous connection between nuclear and Holocaust. The outlook which brought humanity to genocide is also capable of bringing it to complete self-destruction.

The chief rabbi of Antwerp, R' Moshe Yonah Zweig, wrote:

Ideals bearing the seal of sanctity from time immemorial were desecrated by depraved men [during the Holocaust] and disappeared as if they had never existed. Basic assumptions which had served as the building blocks of human philosophy, solid molds which had forged the laws and judgments regulating interpersonal and international relations were broken and ground to dust like discarded vessels. And yet, at the very same time, mortal man began to imagine that he had succeeded in penetrating the heavens, that all the secrets of the universe were being revealed to him, and that he had entered the holiest sanctuary of Creation. Because of his tremendous achievements in every branch of science, he pictured himself as having risen above the sky, as having found a vantage point beyond his own world. He thought that he could embrace the extremities of the universe in human arms, and with his mighty strength, wrench the globe from its axis, changing its orbit as he wished.

Like one violating a covenant, he did not hear the words of Hashem, carved out of flame, "From the Tree of Knowledge of Good and Evil you shall not eat, for on the day you eat from it you shall surely die." Today, all of us have been shown that technology and science, despite their great development, have not brought the hoped-for happiness. They do not at all bestow absolute good upon man who produced them. On the contrary, it seems they were made for his harm, for good and evil are indiscriminately mixed together in them.

From the day when man ate the fruits of these sciences, he has been hounded by the shadow of death wherever he goes. Atrocious fantasies and insecurity have nested in his heart, robbing him of peace, stealing the blessing of Hashem from him, so that he is a wanderer on the face of the earth. The Holy One, Blessed is He, put before him two paths, one of life and one of death, and he chose the path of death. Man could have stretched forth his hand and taken from the Tree of Life, eating its fruit and being satisfied by its goodness. He could have chosen pure faith in the One Who gives vitality to all the worlds — Who does good and grants life to all, Who contains the world and is not contained by it, for no place is devoid of Him. He bestows intelligence on man, showing the way of happiness and contentment among the bewildering paths of the world. He tells man, "Choose life." But man listened to the voice of the tempter and ate — *and goes on eating* — from the Tree of Knowledge of Good and Evil. It arouses vain fantasies and appetites within him, misleading him from the path of perfection to that which leads him and everyone with him into a bottomless pit. Then his handsome ornament — i.e., the image of God with which he was created — was removed from him, and he became a destructive creature, his sword unsheathed in hand to annihilate all (Introduction to responsa *Ohel Moshe*, part 2).

Technology Is Blind

THE FOLLY OF Enlightenment philosophy is its insistence that science in and of itself holds the keys to human happiness; that the pursuit of technology itself will somehow bring man to the path of truth. In fact, however, science is only the lifeless tool of its creator. Technology itself is blind. Whether these forces are indeed productive or destructive depends only upon how they are used. Nuclear fission can warm homes, or destroy civilizations. When fixed ethical standards guide its use, technology can be man's greatest blessing. When left unbridled, however, there is virtually no limit to the evil which it can unleash.

R' Dessler writes:

> In their pride, people believe that the more they develop the world — the more the sciences produce inventions to improve the world and help people enjoy it — the more they will perfect it. But this is a great error — all their "progress" is only regression. All of this civilization simply adds more destruction the more it develops.
>
> People don't wish to understand that it is man's evil traits which harm everything. . . They grab, quarrel, make war — and of course use all the latest inventions for destruction and ruin. For example, the reduction of distances through the invention of traveling and flying machines — it is obvious how much damage this has caused; warfare was formerly limited to one locality, but now the destruction is worldwide. . . Every invention or development has a potential for good —

but only if righteous people use it. This is people's error. They think that the improvement of character will follow automatically. This is nonsense, a mistake which even the most foolish of men should not make. . .

That outlook on worldly wisdom is dealt with explicitly in the Torah (*Bereishis* 4:22): "Tuval Cain, who honed brass and iron." What would we have said about an invention like this in ancient times? Tuval Cain succeeded in inventing the use of metals, instead of the sticks and stones that had been used for plowing the ground. How this eased their labor to sustain themselves! But *Chazal* tell us that the Torah saw this as a destructive development — one that increased ruin in the world, as *Rashi* records: "[He was called] Tuval Cain because he was perfecting (*tibbel* תִּבֵּל) the profession of Cain. The word *tibbel* is a form of the word *tavlin*, "spice." He "spiced" and perfected the profession of Cain, producing weaponry for murderers" (*Michtav Me'Eliyahu*, part 1, p. 270; and see ibid., p. 66).

IN HIS *BINESIVOS HAZMAN VEHANETZACH*, R' Yehudah Leib Girsht writes:

The Ambivalence of Scientific Achievement

Certainly the material advantages of most scientific achievements are clear and obvious. Scientific research in itself, inasmuch as it seeks to aid men, improve their situation and fill their needs, is certainly desirable and valid. This applies, however, only when these advantages are utilized by good people for righteous purposes. But it must not be forgotten that scientific inventions also serve wicked people for evil purposes. The invention of gunpowder, for example, is used not only for good, but also for evil. The novelist Tolstoy, as is known, dealt at length with the extent of the damage which technological achievements are causing and can cause. . .

Among the great scientific discoveries of all time, certainly an important place is held by the [discovery of the] release of atomic energy. Without a doubt we have here the possibility of great blessing in the supply of man's economic needs. Yet how many possibilities for disaster to all mankind, disaster of almost unimaginable scope, are embodied in this power? During the Second World War, German scientists worked day and night to produce an atomic bomb, and they came close to achieving their goal. A miracle happened, and the American scientists preceded them. But just imagine what would have happened if the outcome had been reversed, and German science had been the first to reach its goal! It would have meant [God forbid] the destruction of humanity and the complete annihilation of the nation of Israel. (pp. 25-26)

Technological Man

SINCE THE INDUSTRIAL REVOLUTION, science, the rightful servant of mankind, has slowly become the master. The advance of technology has led to a new type of man, a "technological man," more occupied with specific details than with their larger purposes. In primitive civilizations, the artisan produced a complete implement; but the twentieth-century worker stands at an assembly line, mindlessly inserting identical pieces into a mold. Man's labor, once an expression of his creativity, became an anonymous statistic of national productivity. In industrial society, the laborer became little more than a tool of his tools, hardly more significant than the machine he creates.

Technological man loses himself in detail, creating bureaucracies which swallow his uniqueness in a shuffle of paperwork. Franz Kafka's *The Trial*, an epic of modern society, describes a man who is brought to trial without any possibility of finding out the charges or the identity of the prosecuting authorities. In futility, he runs from office to office, but in the end, he is helplessly condemned to death. The artistic portrayal is of course an exaggeration, but more than a grain of truth is contained therein.

The Banality of Evil

THE BANAL, MECHANICAL aspects of "technological man" showed themselves in full force during the Holocaust. Many Germans who murdered Jews were only technical functionaries, men with no interest in murder itself. Those who remember the trial of Eichmann, may his name be blotted out, will affirm that the most shocking aspect of the entire ordeal was the persona of the accused. The man on trial seemed anything but the sadistic murderer of millions; he was an aging clerk, bespectacled and intelligent, with no outstanding features. Had he been put in charge of German agriculture problems, he undoubtedly would have performed this bureaucratic function successfully as well. A common element among Nazi officers was a twisted ability to concentrate on performing functions with simply no concern for their moral significance. It is apathy, more than hate, which characterizes the twentieth-century murderer.

Technique or Purpose?

ONE CANNOT UNDERESTIMATE the value of contemplating the profound wisdom contained in nature. Let us not be misunderstood — none of the above points are meant to detract from the importance of scientific study and accomplishment. When technology is guided by a firm ethical system, when science allows man to stand in awe at the grandeur of God's creation, it is one of man's greatest assets. The error of Enlightenment philosophy is its confusion of means and end, technique for purpose, and ultimately, material for spiritual. In the absence of religion, Enlightenment man was forced to find a new faith; thus, he worships at the altar of technology.

More than any analytical argument, the events of the Holocaust themselves refute the Enlightenment's view of science and its place in society. The Holocaust clearly demonstrated that in itself, the study of science has no positive influence upon scientists themselves: There is no connection between scientific accomplishment and moral decency.

Science and Ethical Refinement

IN HIS BOOK, *Hitler's Professors*, Dr. Max Weinreich establishes that the German scientific community, with few exceptions, cooperated with those who murdered the Jewish people. Among them were many Nobel prize winners. This fact comes as no great surprise to the believing Jew. He understands that it is only study for the sake of heaven that refines one's character. Scientific study, on its own, holds no sway over man's personality and soul. In modern society, however, the scientist is still commonly envisaged as a morally superior personality. In every matter of public concern, his opinion is given prominent attention, as if the very fact of his knowledge would yield him wisdom as well.

THE TREACHERY OF Nazi medical doctors is most shocking of all. By their profession and by the Hippocratic Oath they had

The Medical Technician

sworn, they were obligated to save human lives. Yet, they actively participated in the murder and torture of millions. Unflinchingly, many of these doctors used living people and the bodies of the murdered for scientific experimentation. As is typical of the Enlightenment, the doctor transformed himself from savior of human life into mere medical technologist — one who sees the particular organ or disease he wishes to cure, but misses the larger picture entirely.[1]

The technique of the gas chamber was developed by Nazi physicians in charge of exterminating the crippled and mentally ill. Anyone familiar with the medical profession knows that in our day, too, the temptation to take human life frequently arises. Many modern doctors become involved in murder by participating in abortion. Even though they are unaware of the severity of their acts, one wrongdoing leads to another: The insensitivity to the sanctity of human life becomes compounded.

Here, too, we see the danger inherent in transforming the physician into a "technologist of medicine", and the patient into a mere medical "case." The Nazi's satanic idea of using human

---

1. Again and again we witness instances of insensitivity in the modern medical community. Research concentrates on the physical aspects of sickness, on its biochemical and physiological causes, while the patient's emotional state is sometimes all but ignored. The fact that "a man's spirit enables him to bear his illness" (*Mishlei* 18:14) is forgotten. The advance in medicine in our age has meant that more and more ethical questions, actual life-and-death issues, are placed before doctors for verdicts. The doctor of a terminal patient is sometimes required to make a decision about his continued treatment which will determine whether he will live or die. The "medical technician" is hardly equipped to make such a choice.

beings as laboratory rats had its roots in the dehumanization of medicine, in the treatment of the disease rather than the person. One recalls the grim joke: "The operation was successful, but the patient died." Here too, as in all the decadence of Nazism, the underlying basis of the abomination is a materialistic ideology — an outlook which sees man as only a more developed species of animal. If in the end, man is no more than an intelligent monkey, what indeed is to keep medical experimentation from using men as monkeys?

No one can deny the blessing that modern medicine has brought, and still brings, to the world. Many of the great sages of the Jewish People were doctors, and there is no need to spell out the great *mitzvah* inherent in the proper practice of medicine. However, cutting off medical wisdom from faith, treating it as just another natural science, brings death rather than life.

IN THE END, goodness and blessing draws only from the Divine source. There is no wisdom, no understanding, no knowledge of

The Shell of Science

ethical conduct, except from Hashem. "Let not the wise pride himself on his wisdom but only on being enlightened about and knowing Me" (*Yirmeyahu* 9:22-23). Life and healing can only come from Him Who heals all flesh, Who is the source of life itself. Likewise, knowledge comes only from Him Who is both the Knower and the known, Who is one with His Knowledge. In the wake of the Enlightenment, scientific pursuit ceased to draw its nourishment from the source of true life. Hence, we have been left with only the shell of science, not its heart. Its wisdom has become merely external, and it has been used as a tool of destruction. Our world will find remedy only when all forms of knowledge are once again united with their Divine source.

E.

Confronting the Moral Dilemma

W E HAVE DISCUSSED the moral failures of man-made ethical systems with reference to the pursuer, Nazi Germany. But one also sees the limitations of these systems from the agonizing situations which the pursued were forced to confront.

"Do not judge your fellow-man until you reach his situation" (*Avos* 2:5). One who did not experience the sufferings of Nazi oppression has no right to judge the actions of those who did. This feeling is shared to a great extent by the public at large; after the war, almost none of the Jewish "kapos" who cooperated with the Nazis were brought to trial. In conditions of imminent threat to life, under incessant terror, and in an atmosphere of mutual suspicion deliberately fostered by the Nazis, there were many who broke under the strain. We cannot condemn them.

Nevertheless, even in these hellish conditions, some seemed to have been better equipped than others to stand the test. Israel Efroikin, a Jewish author who as a result of the Holocaust became observant in his later years, writes:

> Those thousands of Jews who served the Germans as policemen and assistants in the ghettos and the camps — where did they come from? From which circles was this army of criminals recruited? From the Jewish underworld, and from the ranks of the *Maskilim* . . . Those same *Maskilim* had always despised their fellow-Jews for their traditional clothing. Didn't they feel towards these Jews the same feelings of contempt, and perhaps even hatred, that their lords and officers, the Nazis, felt? Ask the Jews of the ghetto and the camps, and they will confirm that the blows they received at the hands of these "golden Jewish youths" contained a great deal of contempt. The victims sensed that the Germans' orders were not just being carried out through obedience, but

the cruel blows were invested with a bit of additional devotion and independent energy. . .

What we don't understand is that for a Jew to throw off his Jewishness is also to throw off his humanness. Removing the image of the Jew from his face also involves removing the image of man and the value of man. And here it is proper to note a fact confirmed by all those who witnessed and recorded the events, from Communists and Bundists at one extreme, to Zionists at the other: that Jews who remained faithful to Torah, Jews dressed in long-coated rabbinic garb were not found among the Jewish policemen; they formed no part of the kapos and the special brigades. Even those gentiles who look favorably upon us, when they want to describe shining characters and sublime acts among the Jews of the camps, are forced to look for these among Torah-observant Jews. [These were the Jews] who did not give beatings, who went hungry rather than contaminate themselves with non-kosher foods, who shared their last piece of bread with the sick and the weak. . . (*Kedushah Ugevurah Etzel HaYehudim*, as cited in *Serufei Hakivshanim Ma'ashimim*, p. 4).

A SIMILAR ACCOUNT is given by Dr. Hillel Seidman in his *Yoman Ghetto Varsha*:

The Sense of Self It is important to note a widely accepted point: The Orthodox Jews stood up better than others under certain kinds of tests. This does not mean that they are holy or that they have extraordinary spiritual strength. They fight for their lives and want to save themselves. But they are outstanding in two ways: First, they hold on to their sense of self. They became "shoemakers" and pulled nails out of German boots, but they put on *tallis* and *tefillin* every day, prayed, studied, kept *Shabbos*, and for all this, risked their lives, under tremendous danger. . .

Secondly, Orthodox Jews wanted to save their own lives just like everyone else, but not completely in the same way — they never did so at the expense of others. They consistently remembered the principle: "What do you see [which makes you think] your blood is redder [more valuable] than his?" (*Sanhedrin* 74a). Among the Orthodox Jews there were no kidnapers, taskmasters, Gestapo agents. Not even one.

This is a fact admitted even by opponents of the Orthodox. In the camps, too — in Auschwitz, in Buchenwald, in Bergen-Belsen — the position of the Orthodox Jews was honorable. Often they risked their lives to save others. Especially praised are the good deeds done by the teachers and students of the Agudas Yisrael [girl's] school, Beis Yaakov.

The horrible destruction, the mass murder, did not dull their feelings of mercy. While others paid exaggerated attention to the principle "Your life comes first" (*Bava Metzia* 62a), the Orthodox Jews did not forget the verse, "Your brother shall live along with you" (*Vayikra* 25:36).

Hillel Leivik, a member of the Bund, visited survivors immediately after the Holocaust. He provides a third testimony:

> Comrade Kaplan informed me that in the area of mutual aid under conditions of forced labor in the concentration camps — with regard to taking pity on the aged and the sick, and defending them — the behavior of the religious youth was better and more humane than that of the non-religious. The enlightened outlook of members of non-religious parties, and their party affiliation, had no influence whatsoever upon their personal behavior in the camps, upon their relations with their fellow Jews. This does not mean — Kaplan indicated — that the enlightened individuals in general acted badly. It simply indicates that the religious acted better.
>
> In forced labor, under lashes of the whips, it frequently happened that an aged Jew fell behind in his work and could not keep up with the labor's murderous pace. This meant danger to the whole group. Because of the slowness of the elderly, all would have to work more. In this situation, non-religious youth usually lost their temper and become angry at the elderly. By contrast, the religious youth were accustomed to go up to the older person and say: "Reb Yid, pretend that you are working. Don't squeeze the last drop of strength out of yourself. I will make up for your quota."

I conclude from Kaplan's words (and I heard this from many) that almost none of the kapos came from among the religious Jews, something which unfortunately cannot be said for the various non-religious parties (*Mit Der She'eris Hapleitah*, pp. 199-200, quoted by Yehoshua Eibeschitz, *Bikedushah Uvigevurah — Bein Adam Lechaveiro*, pp. 3-4).

In the free world, too, it was observant Jews who were at the forefront of rescue efforts. Their representation in these campaigns far exceeded the numerical and organizational strength of religious Jewry.

A Basic Moral Strength

THE SWEEPING TESTIMONIALS of these writers are not, perhaps, to be accepted unquestioningly. It would seem unlikely that no religious Jews at all were to be found among the kapos. Similarly, it is clear that not all the kapos and Jewish policemen acted reprehensibly. However, it is probable that the impression conveyed by these eyewitnesses is based on reality. Apparently, a vast number of religious Jews did withstand the awesome ethical trials of the Holocaust. No observant Jew holds a guarantee that he will not stumble in his relationships with other men or with God. However, in contrast to secular humanist education, the basic moral strength of Torah education appears evident. The religious Jew is imbued with faith in His Creator, Who alone is the source of true morality and justice.

Who Shall Live?

ANOTHER POINT IN the history of the Holocaust stands out strikingly. The ghastly reality of mass murder forced Jews to decide excruciating moral dilemmas. The harrowing issues they were made to confront were all but impossible to solve using human "conscience" alone. To this very day, there is unresolved public debate concerning the propriety of the actions of the *Judenrats*, or Jewish councils, which governed Jewish communities under Nazi rule. Even their most extreme critics, however, admit that many *Judenrat* leaders were of high moral and intellectual standing. The agonizing life-and-death choices which confronted these men were simply impossible to resolve through conventional logic.

The same applies to other situations which often arose during the Holocaust. Men were forced to choose between their own lives and those of others. A sadistic German officer forced a Jewish mother to choose which of her children would be allowed to survive. Who among us could honorably pass such a trial? How would we have reacted had we been hidden in that famous bunker where the occupants could remain alive only by smothering a crying infant to death? Is it possible at all to reach logical decisions on moral questions of this nature?

One whose moral foundations are in any case vague stands absolutely helpless when confronted with ethical decisions such as these. The Divine morality of Torah, however, provides fundamental and clear-cut criteria with which even the most difficult of questions can be approached. The Talmud is not silent on life and death issues: "What makes you think your blood is redder [more valuable] than his? Perhaps his blood is redder?" (*Sanhedrin* 74a). And: "All must die rather than turn over a single Jew [to the enemy]" (*Rambam, Hilchos Yesodei Hatorah* 5:5). The applications of these and other principles are both numerous and complex. As with all *halachos* of this type, when it is possible, a qualified authority must be consulted for practical rulings; nevertheless, these questions come firmly within the realm of halachic decision. Judaism does not abandon the subtleties of life-and-death issues to the whims of individual moral uncertainty.

WE DO NOT CLAIM that an obvious halachic ruling exists in each of the cases outlined above. Halachic disagreement exists in all

Words of the Living God

areas of Jewish law, no less so in issues of life and death. Certainly, the questions are difficult, and differing rulings could be rendered. But each ruling has a firm basis in the Divinely-given Torah. Torah, and Torah alone, serves as the foundation for ethical decision-making. If differing rulings are given, then to the extent that each is truly based upon the Torah, each possesses validity: "Both these and those are the words of the living God". The doubt which is the product of such halachic disagreement differs fundamentally from the contradictory notions of ethical responsibility fostered by man-made ethical systems.

IN TRUTH, *HALACHAH* offers guidelines for action even in cases when there is no clear-cut ruling. One who follows halachic

Uncertainty and Halachah

principles is thus assured of acting properly. R' Tzvi Hirsch Meisels relates the following incident in his Introduction to Responsa *Mekadshei Hashem*.

> On the eve of Rosh Hashanah (5705/1945), they rounded up and took . . . fourteen hundred boys to an isolated, closed block (at Auschwitz). The next day, the first day of Rosh Hashanah, the rumor spread through the whole camp that in the evening the youths would be taken to the furnace. Many people in the camp had an only son among these youths, the only child left to them . . . and all that day they ran in confusion around the closed block, in the hope that perhaps they could catch some glimmer of light to save their precious son from there. . .
>
> A simple Jew came and said to me: "Rabbi! My only son is in there among the boys condemned to the furnace, and it is within my power to purchase his release. Since it is known to us, without any doubt, that they will take someone else in his place, I present before you a halachic question. Tell me what the law is according to the Torah. Am I allowed to redeem him? I shall act according to your decision."
>
> When I heard this question, the thought of rendering a decision on a matter of life and death caused me to tremble. I replied: "My dear friend, how can I give a clear-cut ruling on a question like this? When the Temple was standing, a question like this would have been brought before the Sanhedrin. And I am here in Auschwitz, without a single book of *halachah*, without other *rabbanim*, and without a calm and settled mind, due to the many disasters and troubles. If it were the practice of these wicked ones to first release the

redeemed one, and afterwards to take another in his place, there would be some room to lean toward a permissive [ruling]. . ."

But the man wept greatly, and begged me very much. He said to me: "Rabbi, you must tell me the *halachah* now." I in turn pleaded with him: "Release me from this question, for I cannot tell you anything at all." But he continued to beg me, saying: "Rabbi, does that mean that you do not permit me to redeem my only son? If so — I accept the ruling with love."

I pleaded with him and objected to his inference, but he went on begging me and trying to make me give him a clear answer. When he saw that I stood my ground and did not want to give a halachic ruling, he answered me with emotion and with tremendous inspiration:

"Rabbi, I have done my duty as the Torah requires me to do. I brought my question before the *Rav*. There is no other *Rav* here. If His Honor, the *Rav*, cannot answer that it is permitted for me to redeem my child, that is a sign that he is not completely sure that the *halachah* permits [it]. If it were permissible without any doubts, certainly you would tell me so. To me this means that according to the *Halachah* it is forbidden to me. I accept this with love and joy, and I shall not do anything to redeem him, because that is what the Torah commanded. . ."

All my pleadings to him not to put the responsibility on me were to no avail. He only repeated what he had said, with heartrending weeping. He fulfilled his words, and did not redeem his son. That whole day, Rosh Hashanah, he walked and spoke to himself joyfully, saying that he merited to sacrifice his only son to Hashem, since even though it was in his power to redeem him, he would not, seeing that the Torah did not permit him to do such a thing. This would be considered by the Holy One, Blessed is He, like the Binding (*Akeidah*) of our Father Yitzchak, which also had taken place on Rosh Hashanah. (Cited in *Ani Ma'amin*, pp. 63-64. Another eye-witness account of this incident is recorded in *Zichron Kedoshim*, p. 380.)

As exemplified by this father's conduct, in awesome questions of life or death, the existence of doubt is sufficient to tip the halachic scales. Is it conceivable that man-made rules of morality could be so definite? Is there any man-made system of morality capable of bringing a man to sacrifice his son *with joy*, "that he merited to sacrifice his only son to Hashem?"

LITTLE IS KNOWN to us about halachic responsa of this type during the Holocaust. Those who asked the questions were

Responsa of the Holocaust

murdered and burned along with those who answered. Of the written responsa, their letters flew heavenward as the sheets that contained them turned to ashes. Only a few remnants survive the flames, mainly collected in R' Efrayim Oshry's *She'elos Uteshuvos Mimaamakim*. The volume contains a number of responsa given by R' Oshry himself, who served as a member of the rabbinate in Kovna, Lithuania, during the Holocaust.

In one of these responsa, the author relates that the Nazis commanded the *Judenrat* of Kovna to publish notices calling upon the Jews to assemble in Democracy Square. The Jews would then be transported to the death camps. The *Judenrat's* refusal would endanger the lives of all the occupants of the ghetto. The heads of the *Judenrat* turned to R' Avraham Dov Kahana-Shapiro (author of *Dvar Avraham*) for a halachic ruling. When the aged *Rav* first heard the question, he fainted. Then, after prolonged deliberation, he permitted the *Judenrat* to obey, so as to prevent the murder of all the Jews of the ghetto.[1]

In his book entitled "Judenrat", the historian of the Jewish councils in the ghettos, Dr. Isaiah Trunk, records several accounts of similar halachic questions put before *rabbanim*. According to one, a group of four *rabbanim* were sent to the chairman of the Vilna *Judenrat*, Yaakov Gans, to protest against the *Judenrat's* participation in one of the German "operations." The *rabbanim* argued that it was halachically forbidden to turn a Jew over to the Germans, even if refusal endangered the entire ghetto.[2]

---

1. A similar account is given by a head of the Kovna *Judenrat*, Leib Garfunkel, who wrote *Kovna HaYehudis Bechurbanah*.

2. Other correlating accounts are contained in the same book.

At first glance, it would seem that disagreement on this issue existed among various *rabbanim*. In fact, however, it is difficult to know the exact details of the various incidents, and this author does not consider himself qualified to make a definitive judgment on the issue. However, it would appear that there is a difference between the Vilna Jewish policemen's actual physical assistance in turning people over to the Germans, and the *Judenrat's* relatively passive action of publishing notices to assemble. Furthermore, the publishing of notices did not constitute actual aid in sending people to the camps, since everyone knew that the *Judenrat* was a Nazi instrument and its notices were not to be believed. Also, one must consider: Was it clearly known then, as it is now, that these people were being sent to certain death, or did an element of doubt exist? Different communities became aware of these realities gradually, and at different times.

IN ANY CASE, as shown earlier, even if halachic disagreement existed, such doubt differs fundamentally from the contradictory

The Framework of Halachic Disagreement

notions of right or wrong which cloud the questionable moral judgments of individuals. The disagreement here concerns the correct interpretation of sources given at Sinai. Regarding such disputes the Talmud states: "Both these and those are the words of the living God". Even in cases of sharply differing views, all sides are based on the same Torah, the same basic principles of Divine morality. All aspire to the same goal: to do the will of the Creator, Who gives life and rules everything. In the final analysis, there is no comparison between one who acts a certain way because he believes it is halachically correct, and one who chooses the very same action in desperation after man-made morality has left him at a moral impasse.

❧ ❧ ❧

We have explored how an advanced, cultured nation sank to the lowest levels of moral decadence. Historically, the process of its downfall was connected with an outlook which enthroned human reason in God's stead. Man, on whom all faith was now placed, turned into a creature deprived of the image of God. As if to fulfill Darwin's prophecy, he became a kind of highly developed ape; a creature living in a world without reward and punishment, devoid of good and evil.

Technical progress occurred with no parallel spiritual development. With little psychological or moral preparation, man was given awesome tools of destruction — tools which require of their holders an intense sense of responsibility. Like a malicious child, mankind suddenly discovered cannons and artillery, his new playthings. Concentration on technology transformed men into technicians, men who did not interest themselves in "Why?" or "To what end?" but only in "How?" Man's preoccupation with exploring the physical nature of the world caused him to forget its spiritual aspect. The devastating result was not long in coming.

Man's pride became the source of his downfall. He was led to enthrone himself in place of God, and to take into his hands decisions which belong to his Creator alone. Believing that he had the right and duty to "improve" the human race, man engaged in mass murder. Concurrently, pride deluded him into thinking that morality comes from within him; that objective, Divine ethical standards do not exist.

"Where was man during the Holocaust?" He was tasting the fruit of the Tree of Knowledge, attempting to create and destroy worlds. Man fell once again, reaching futilely for the dream that lies so emphatically beyond his grasp: "And you shall be like gods". . . (Bereishis 3:5)

Only when man returns to his God, when he once more enthrones the Creator as King over himself and the world, will he again become the creature formed in the image of God. Only when man comes to grips with his insignificance before his Creator's presence shall he become truly great; a creator of worlds rather than their destroyer.

Those who publicly sanctified the name of Hashem; those who were killed, but accepted the Divine decree with love; those who preserved the image of God with which man was imbued, showed us the heights man can reach through his faith. Their murderers demonstrated the depths to which he may fall:

> After all, man is that being who has invented the gas chambers of Auschwitz; however, he is also that being who has entered those gas chambers upright, with. . . the "*Shema Israel*" on his lips (Viktor Frankl, *Man's Search for Meaning*, pp. 213-214).

6

"Like Sheep
to the Slaughter"
or "Kiddush Hashem?"

N THIS CHAPTER we shall discuss the second question raised by Prof. Dawidowicz, quoted at the beginning of the previous chapter. "How could an entire people allow itself to be exterminated?" We shall, however, somewhat change the wording of the question. The Jewish People did not "allow itself" to lose one-third of its members. It must be remembered that those who died were civilian victims, not military men. There was no war between balanced forces — defenseless men, women and children were massacred by policemen and armed soldiers. The behavior of the victims could not in any way have prevented the killing.

The question we shall discuss is: In what manner did the Jewish People behave during the fearsome extermination, and what can we learn from their behavior? Did our sanctified ones go to their death "like sheep to the slaughter?" Was their death in itself an act of *Kiddush Hashem*, a sanctification of the Name? And beyond this: Did the generation of the Holocaust behave as their ancestors did in earlier times of religious persecution such as the Crusades? Is the Holocaust to be seen as another link in the chain of evil decrees and persecutions, or is it a new phenomenon, a new type of decree and a new type of Jewish reaction? In this chapter, we shall focus upon these and other issues connected with the question: "Where was man — Jewish man — during the Holocaust?"

A.

"Like Sheep to the Slaughter. . ."

WHY DIDN'T THE JEWS put up any opposition?

Undoubtedly, this is one of the most popular questions raised about the Holocaust. The question was brought up by the prosecutor in the Eichmann trial, who asked witnesses time and again, "Why didn't you resist?" It is to this day

Question or Accusation? raised in almost every discussion of the Holocaust among our youth. Sometimes it is not simply a question, but an accusation. The implication includes a charge of cowardliness, faintheartedness; even foolishness.

The beginnings of the accusation can be found as early as the Holocaust itself. Zionist leader Yitzchak Gruenbaum said that the Jews died "like rags," not men. The charge was continued by others, including important historians like Raul Hilberg in his book, *The Destruction of European Jews*. These historians claimed that the lack of resistance to the Nazis and the cooperation of the *Judenrats* with the German authorities stemmed from a traditional Jewish policy of non-resistance to oppressors. In Zionist phraseology, this was called "exile mentality," an ingrained spirit of submission to gentile mastery. The final outcome of these accusations is a tendency among Jewish youth to shy away from memory of the Holocaust because of the supposed "shame" of our "exile behavior." This humiliating behavior is even said to have been a cause of the destruction itself.

THIS TENDENCY OF our youth to reject the memory of the Holocaust has caused consternation among Jewish leaders. It is

Juxtaposing Holocaust and Heroism the main reason why many Jewish historians have put great emphasis on the phenomenon of armed Jewish resistance against the Nazis. Yad Vashem is the Israeli

government agency for perpetuating the memory of "the Holocaust and heroism (hasho'ah vehagevurah)". The twenty-seventh
of Nissan has likewise been established as "the memorial day of
the Holocaust and heroism." The juxtaposition seems to imply
that we are dealing with an equivalent pair; the Holocaust (of
"exile Jews") and the heroism (of other Jews). It is not by chance
that this exact date, the twenty-seventh of Nissan, was chosen for
the day of memorial. The date alludes to the Warsaw Ghetto
uprising, the symbol of heroism and bravery. Seemingly, the
Holocaust of our people is only worth commemorating because of
its ties with heroism and bravery.

In recent years, Holocaust research has reached a turning point.
Studies now deal increasingly with "the Holocaust" and less with
"the heroism". Gradually, historians are coming to realize that the
concept of heroism is not limited to the idea of armed resistance; it
can include various aspects of spiritual courage as well. It is
difficult, however, to know whether the educational and historical
damage already done can be repaired.

IT IS INTERESTING TO NOTE that the issue of "sheep to the
slaughter" has not been raised with the same intensity among the

The Profundity of Divine Judgment

Torah-observant public. Many have
wondered, of course, how only a few
S.S. personnel were able to guard
thousands of Jews on their final journey. However, the feeling
expressed is more one of astonishment at the magnitude of the
catastrophe and the profundity of the heavenly judgment. "How
could one pursue a thousand, and two make ten thousand flee,
were it not that their Creator sold them, and Hashem handed
them over?"(Devarim 32:30). No accusation against the Jews
who perished is implied.

In the Passages of Rebuke (Tochachos) it is written (Vayikra
26:36): "I shall put faintness into their heart in the lands of their
enemies, and the sound of a rustling leaf will pursue them." Even
if the Jews of the Holocaust did show faintheartedness or
helplessness — and we shall presently discuss whether they did or

did not — perhaps such failings were themselves an integral part of the terrible Divine decree.

Ibn Ezra, in his commentary on *Shemos* 14:13 (also see his comments on *Shemos* 2:3), speaks about *Bnei Yisrael's* fear of the Egyptians after the Exodus from Egypt:

> It is surprising: How could a large camp of six hundred thousand men be afraid of those pursuing them? Why didn't they fight for their and their children's lives? The answer is that the Egyptians were the masters of the Israelites. This was the generation that went out of Egypt, and they had learned from childhood to bear the yoke of Egypt. Their soul was lowly. How could they now fight against their masters? And Israel was weak, and not trained in war. One can see, after all, that Amalek attacked them with a small force, and were it not for the prayer of Moshe, they would have defeated Israel. Hashem alone, Who does great things, and for Whom all events are directed, brought it about that all the males who went out of Egypt would die, for they did not have strength to wage war against the Canaanites; until a new generation arose, the generation of the wilderness, who had not seen exile and who had exalted soul[s].

IBN EZRA'S UNDERSTANDING thus differs sharply from the secularist viewpoint. In denigrating the "exile mentality" of

A Sharp Difference

European Jewry, the secularist places a superficial faith in "my strength and the might of my arm." He believes such strength to be capable of unlimited accomplishment. The secularist motto in time of crisis is, "Let us take our fate into our hands," for he believes only in the undaunted power of man. The "exile mentality" put forth by Ibn Ezra, however, derives from a different context entirely. He teaches that part of the decree of exile was that the nation would feel subservient to its Egyptian masters. This was not an outgrowth of exile, but *part* of it; and *Ibn Ezra* adds that they took this vestige of exile with them when they left Egypt. "Hashem alone, Who does great things, and for Whom all events are directed" also determines whether the community at large shall be fainthearted or courageous. If the victims of the Holocaust did not fight back, this too may have been part of the Heavenly decree. As the Talmud writes, "All is in the hands of heaven except fear of heaven."

IT WOULD SEEM, HOWEVER, that the accusation of "sheep to the slaughter" is more fundamentally flawed. The entire charge of

Timidity is Not a Failing

"faintheartedness" and the corresponding adulation of "heroism" is rooted in cultural values alien to Judaism. Timidity is not a moral failing; it is a character trait like any other. The Torah recognizes it as a legitimate reason for exemption from battle (*Devarim* 20:8). It is simply a fact of human nature: some people are naturally fainthearted, and they are not to be blamed for it.

Contempt of "cowards" has its roots in a culture which idealizes physical or psychological strength, a culture in which "strong" somehow equals "good". Let us not forget that it was the Nazis themselves who deified sheer physical strength; it was from them that we heard the epithets "rag dolls," "gutless" and the like. How terrible is it to discuss the Holocaust using the moral standards of a culture which gave birth to Nazism itself!

WHO THEN IS STRONG in a Jewish context? One who acts with restraint and patience; one who, in the words of *Pirkei Avos* (4:1),

Who is Strong?

"controls his desires." His is not external might, but exalted internal strength. He does not require the endorsements of war or concrete struggle. When necessary, he makes use of force, but if he does so, might never becomes an ideal in itself. Where force is not required, he sees acts of physical prowess as a descent to the level of the enemy. He does not wish to fight terror with terror, murder with murder, for fear that he himself will lose his sensitivity to human life. Sometimes he has no choice but to follow the dictum of the Talmud, "If someone comes to kill you, kill him first." But when he does, he knows this is not heroism.

The desperate rallying call to "die honorably" is very far indeed from the Torah lexicon. Concealed within this appeal is the premise that there is little hope in life; that since death must inevitably come, "let me take some of them with me." Judaism does not share this pessimism. The Jews have always known that, "even if a sharpened sword is poised over your neck, do not despair of justice." In the darkest moments in the death camps, Jews with true spiritual strength repeated to themselves and others that "the salvation of Hashem comes as the blink of an eye." In the merit of this enduring hopefulness and patience, many were indeed saved from a death which only moments earlier had seemed so certain.

HOWEVER, IT IS NOT ONLY from a Torah perspective that the question of "like sheep to the slaughter" is refuted at its source.

Historical Refutation Secular thinkers have disputed the charge on historical grounds. One of the more convincing arguments is presented by K. Shabtai (Shabtai Keshev-Klugman) in his book, *Katzon Latevach*. A summary of his points follows:

K. Shabtai initially combats the charge that the Holocaust showed "the cowardliness of the exile Jew," by pointing out that it was not only Jews whom the Nazis murdered — many gentiles were killed in like fashion. Included among these were three million Russian and one million Polish prisoners of war — trained soldiers who can hardly be accused of faintheartedness. None of these men rose up in rebellion.

From another angle, scores of Jews joined partisan forces against the Germans and distinguished themselves for their bravery in armed struggle. In the Red Army, Jews received more medals for valor than any other national group. By the same token, numerous Holocaust survivors later emigrated to *Eretz Yisrael*, where they fought in the War of Independence. In combat, their bravery and prowess was indistinguishable from their Israeli-born brethren.

ALL THE SAME, one is tempted to ask: The Jews numbered millions; their assailants, only tens of thousands. Why didn't the

Millions vs. Thousands

Jews revolt?

There is no question. The killers were a highly organized army of young, healthy males. They were equipped with advanced weaponry, and possessed virtually unlimited mobility. The millions who perished at their hands were civilians. They were either geographically dispersed, or were imprisoned in ghettos and concentration camps. These millions included old people, women and children, and constituted the most undernourished population in Europe. It has been calculated that even if the Nazis had not directly annihilated the Jews of Europe, the ghetto populations would have perished shortly from sheer starvation.

Above all: The murderers included not only those who participated directly in the crime, but the entire German people, as well as other anti-Semitic national groups. Even among the partisan militias who fought the Germans, there was rabid anti-Semitism. It happened very often that a Jew fled from the Germans into the forests, only to be murdered there by the partisans.

FURTHERMORE, THE ANNIHILATION was carried out using sophisticated psychological trickery. Elaborate systems of decep-

Elaborate Deception

tion were meticulously planned and executed. Such an organized, systematic destruction of an entire nation had never before been attempted in human history. It is no surprise that no one believed that it could happen.

The plans for mass murder, were, until the end, shrouded in secrecy by the Nazis. The Germans took advantage of people's natural, inherent hopefulness by indicating that not everyone would be sent to the camps; that not all Jews were considered "superfluous." The "selections" were carried out with suddenness, allowing no time for planned reaction. In general, the Nazis used advanced techniques of terrorization, paralyzing the Jews' will, even before the actual murder.

ABOUT A MILLION and a half Jews — some estimates put the figure as high as two million — were killed during mass-murder

No Warning operations in territories conquered from the Soviet Union. Since the Soviet Union had formerly been an ally of Germany, the Russians had avoided publicizing information about German persecution of the Jews. As a result, Russian Jews knew little of the Germans' intentions.

The mass murders were generally carried out without warning. One morning, a delegation of troops would call on the Jews of a city to assemble in a synagogue or town square. Nearly all the Jews innocently obeyed the order. From there they were taken in trucks to a site outside the city, where they were shot before an open mass grave. Resistance was simply not an option.

THE NAZIS ALSO EMPLOYED systems of collective punishment. A town that rebelled was burned to the ground and its inhabitants

Collective Punishment executed. When a German was killed by the underground resistance, a hundred hostages would be collected and summarily executed unless the underground fighter responsible for the killing was turned over. In the ghettos, the practice was to murder the family of any person who escaped to join the partisans. It is understandable that many avoided taking any such step.

ONE CAUGHT ENGAGING IN resistance activities was subjected to agonizing torture by the Nazis. Survivors tell of the ghastly

R' Aharonson's Testimony deaths invented by the German imagination. Even those sure of their imminent demise would avoid bringing upon themselves such fearsome agony. R' Yehoshua Moshe Aharonson, a concentration camp inmate, writes in his diary:

> I see fit to first answer the question of historians who ask, after the fact, why we did not defend our lives, avenging ourselves on the angels of death who came to take us into the valley of the shadow of death. The answer is as follows:
>
> (1) At first, many did not believe that they were being taken to their death. They believed what they were told, that they

were going to perform light work, or that they were to be hospitalized. (2) Even the minority, who understood what was happening, did not wish to take responsibility for the entire community. [By encouraging them to rebel, they would be putting their lives in danger.]

In the end (except in Warsaw): After being under their control for four years, and in forced labor for sixteen to twenty-five months, our spirits and bodies were weakened to the point that we had no initiative for anything. We lacked the strength and might, the daring and strong spirit. The precautions taken to guard us were very strict, and everything was done suddenly, in the blink of an eye. Also, many had already become weary of living a life of such slavery. They preferred death to life, looking forward to the end; they waited for the angels of death, as if seeing them as angels of redemption from their dreadful suffering — the sufferings of Job in the full sense of the term (*Ani Ma'amin*, pp. 81-82).

DR. HILLEL SEIDMAN, a Holocaust survivor, writes in his *Yoman Ghetto Varsha* (pp. 264-268):

Disbelief How could such a thing happen? Why did we let them take us like sheep to the slaughter? Couldn't we defend ourselves?. . .

First of all, it has not at all been proven that the Nazis planned from the beginning to annihilate us, that this was their intention when they established the ghetto. I personally witnessed the tragedy. I carefully watched their schemes throughout all those years. I cannot say that this was their premeditated intent. At least, not all of them; for there were various lines of thought about the Jewish question. . .

It is probable that when Hitler and his cohorts spoke of the annihilation of European Jewry, they meant it literally. But the Jews couldn't believe it — actually to kill and destroy. They thought annihilation meant the kind of thing that went on every day: to make them go hungry, to cause them suffering, to persecute them, harass them, rob them, conduct periodic pogroms — but not total annihilation. . .

And when it reached the stage of deportations, and all during the time of the deportations, they still calmed themselves. Nearly everyone thought that it wouldn't affect him personally. In their deportation order of July 22, the Germans listed so many different kinds of exemptions that everyone thought he fit into one of the categories. Either he was an official of the community (there were ten thousand of these lucky ones), or an official of the ghetto (another ten thousand), or he was employed in a workshop either inside or outside the ghetto. In theory, the deportation order affected only a small part of the Jewish population. They thought their identity cards, work cards, or passports would save them. They thought that the annihilation would not strike everyone; for, after all, what was the purpose of all the selections and the workshops? They believed that at least a small number would be saved, and each one believed that he would be included in those few. They believed, hoped, dreamed. Did they have any alternative?

And there was something else they believed in; the world, the conscience of the world. If what was happening here could only be verified in the free world — and despite the tight blackout, some knowledge did penetrate to other countries — then the world would be shocked. When the terrible cruelty became known, could any conscientious person in the world be at rest? Wouldn't they tear down walls, shake the world, in order to save the remnants?

How would they save them? That no one asked himself. They were sure that the strong, mighty world, with its tremendous spiritual and material powers, would find a way to stop the slaughter. Sanctions against the Germans, legal means of defense, defense through the agency of neutral states, through the International Red Cross, through the intervention of the Pope. . . They would recognize the Jews as international citizens, would give them passports. And in any case can we, here, chained in prison, give the world advice how to save us? Is there any lack of Jewish organizations, influential men, statesmen (such as Morgenthau, Baruch, Rosenman, Hore-Belisha, and others for whom the Nazis consider us responsible) — judicial figures, diplomats? They will find ways to save us.

If so, what is the point of immediately endangering the lives of relatives — children, parents, brothers and sisters — and entering into a struggle against hopeless odds, a struggle against a major power which dominates most of Europe and which to this day has never been defeated by any army?

And why should just we be the ones to fight? We, the starved, the tormented, the untrained, with our wives, our children, our sick, and our aged? After all, there were also death camps for Russian military prisoners. Did one of those camps ever break out in rebellion or uprising?

It is possible to cite ever more details, but here is not the place to elaborate. No one who studies the historical record can seriously pose the question of why the Jews did not rebel.

THE REAL QUESTION which arises is: What is the source of the charge "like sheep to the slaughter?" Why is it repeatedly raised

The Accusation's Roots

with such intensity, when it in fact has no historical foundation? This curiosity is addressed by Prof. Yehudah Bauer:

All this leads to the great question, the one which arises in every discussion-group with soldiers, schoolchildren, and even college students. The question generally centers around the phrase, "like sheep to the slaughter."

This phrase is very interesting, in that it is used only by Jews. One must ask: Did anyone ever raise this question regarding the two-and-a-half million Soviet captives who were murdered by the Nazis, without, of course, rebelling? Did anyone ever raise it regarding three million Poles who were murdered, or regarding many thousands of people of other nationalities who opposed the Nazi regime? We have never encountered any historical book, speech, or other document of any kind in which a non-Jew asks, "Why did they go like sheep to the slaughter?" concerning the tens of millions of people who were killed during the Second World War. The question is purely and exclusively a Jewish one. Apparently it expresses self-hatred, a demand made upon ourselves to be super-human; heroes, as it were, altogether above nature.

The fact that this question is asked with such intensity, and sometimes with such venom, requires some sort of explanation. The explanation is to be found, it would seem, in a unique Jewish tendency to probe and criticize ourselves in particular, while at the same time forgiving others (*Teguvot B'eit Hasho'ah*, pp. 164-5).

Prof. Bauer's question is a valid one. His answer, however — that there exists "a unique Jewish tendency to probe and criticize ourselves" — is neither sufficient nor correct. If there were legitimate grounds for accusation in the first place, it is possible that the Jewish People would distinguish themselves for their self-criticism. But when such libel is groundless from the outset, its source requires further investigation.

THE TRUE ROOTS of the "sheep to the slaughter" argument seem to derive from a tacit acceptance of a foreign concept of heroism.

A Foreign Concept As noted earlier, Jews throughout the ages have recognized that the true hero is the master of internal fortitude, not the wielder of physical brawn. We have, however, come to live in a world which glorifies the external trappings of power. Money, technological prowess, and brute physical force have replaced inner fortitude and perseverance as the foremost symbols of strength. In denying heroism to the Jews of the Holocaust, we succumb to the vacant contentions of Western doctrine.

The above is not intended to detract from appreciation of the valor and self-sacrifice shown by those few who managed, here and there, to strike at the Nazis. Their honor remains unquestioned. However, there is little justification to belittle the behavior of the vast majority of the victims, who could not physically wage war against the enemy.

THE DISTORTED SENSE of perspective involved in emphasizing only the "heroism" of the Holocaust has its roots in a mythic, and

A Mythic Ideology ultimately false, nationalist ideology. Unfortunately, to this day, this ideology stands as the basis of secular Zionist education. If we do not correct the injustice it has brought to the memory of our martyrs during the Holocaust, we will have let pass an extremely serious historical error. The error is a national, no less than a religious one. We will have broken the chain of generations by denying the memory of our fathers. After all, we are only their heirs.

IN CONCLUSION, I wish to state that this author has not found an unequivocal consensus among this generation's Torah leaders

Armed Resistance and Halachah

regarding the question of resistance during the Holocaust. Apparently, the halachic validity of such actions depends on particular circumstances, and on the question: Would resistance lead to saving, or destroying, Jewish lives? Certainly, however, the issue is not one of "honor." Within *Chazal* we find various approaches to similar issues of resistance, and the approaches are even more varied among the sages of later generations. As for the period of the Holocaust, there seem to be precedents for differing approaches. The halachic validity of armed resistance, for example, seems to be supported by the following incident, told by Dr. Hillel Seidman about the *gaon* R' Menachem Ziemba:

> Then R' Menachem Ziemba said in a serious tone: "There are various ways of doing *Kiddush Hashem*. If today they were forcing the Jews to convert, and it were possible to save one's life by converting, as in Spain or during the persecutions of 4856 (1096), our death in itself would be *Kiddush Hashem*. *Rambam* even writes that if a Jew is killed because he is a Jew, that is *Kiddush Hashem* — and the *halachah* is in accordance with his words. But today, the only way to do *Kiddush Hashem* is through active armed resistance" (*Yoman Ghetto Varsha*, p. 221).[1]

On the other hand, the leader of Agudas Yisrael in Warsaw, R' Zisha Friedman, author of *Maayanah shel Torah*, firmly opposed the Warsaw Ghetto uprising. He saw it as an act of despair,

---

1. R' Simchah Elberg, in his article, "*Merred Hagettaot Lefi Hahalachah*," in the newspaper *Hamodia*, Friday, 15 Sivan, 5744, denies the claim that R' Menachem Ziemba supported the Warsaw Ghetto uprising. He bases this assertion on his personal acquaintance with the *gaon* R' Ziemba, and on the fact that in the memoirs of R' Avraham Ziemba from that period there is no hint that R' Menachem Ziemba supported the resistance.

arguing that to the Jew who believes that "the salvation of Hashem is like the blink of an eye," resistance of this sort is indicative only of lack of faith.[1]

R' Moshe Blau was the leader of Agudas Yisrael in *Eretz Yisrael*. During the Warsaw Ghetto uprising, he wrote the following:

> Only people weary of living could undertake an uprising under these circumstances, where there is no chance of victory. Of course it cannot be denied that the situation in Poland is sufficient to cause a person to become weary of living; it could drive young people out of their senses, making them do things which bring closer the day of death. But it is clear that this is suicide, and such a conclusion could be reached only by those groups that are capable of deciding in favor of suicide. To die a hero's death simply for the sake of dying a hero's death — this has no basis in Jewish faith, even if doing so does not put others in danger. All the more so, when it threatens to endanger the lives of others, for whom each extra minute of life has great value. [Even in] the most desperate situation, [these others] do not despair of Hashem's salvation, knowing that its ways are hidden, and it can come like the blink of an eye.
>
> Believing Jews do not try to make their death come earlier than it has to, and all the more so, they do not try to hasten the death of others simply because of their difficult situation. This kind of act *is* performed, however, by people who have lost their faith, and who judge the situation according to the laws of nature. People such as these are capable of all kinds of suicide, even this kind; and people like these are not deterred by the threat that their own suicide might hurt the lives of others (*Kisvei Rabbi Moshe Blau*, p. 241).

Similarly, it is known that great sages of the Jewish People have, throughout the ages, generally taken a similar position regarding rebellion against the gentiles. Still, one cannot know whether in such extreme circumstances they would have preferred submission to rebellion. The matter is not a simple one, and its full resolution cannot truly be attempted in a work of this nature.

---

1. He is quoted in *The War against the Jews*, p. 302.

B.

Racial Persecution and Kiddush Hashem

E HAVE SEEN THAT THE "heroism" which is some times associated with Jewish Holocaust resistance is not always, or necessarily, a *Kiddush Hashem*, sanctification of the Name. We must now ask whether within a general framework, the death of Jews during the Holocaust can be considered a *Kiddush Hashem*.

OF THE MANY persecutions which have previously befallen the Jewish People during their exile, most were set against a religious

Past Persecution background. Thus, *Kiddush Hashem* was always a central motif. As R' Yehudah HaLevi writes in *Kuzari*, it was very easy for a Jew to say a single word and accept Christianity or Islam; in doing so, he would rid himself of all troubles. Such was indeed the goal of the gentiles in decreeing their persecutions. Although many Jews did not stand the test, the vast majority of our people clung firmly to their faith despite the most difficult of trials.

> All this has come upon us, and we have not forgotten You. We have not denied Your covenant. Our heart has not retreated, nor have we swerved from Your path. When You put us down in a place of serpents, and covered us with the shadow of death, we did not forget the Name of our God, nor spread out our palms to a foreign deity. Behold, God can probe this, for He knows the hidden things of the heart. We have been killed for You every day. We have been considered like sheep for the slaughter (*Tehillim* 44:18-23).

IN THIS RESPECT, the Holocaust stands as singular in Jewish history. It was not a religious persecution. With the same sadistic

Racial Anti-Semitism bent, the Nazis murdered all Jews: children of mixed marriages, assimilated Jews — even those who had converted to

Christianity. For the first time, the determining factor was not religion, but race. Thus, the question haunts us: Where is the *Kiddush Hashem*? A significant number of those killed did not even believe in Judaism, much less desire to give their lives up for its sake. Racial anti-Semitism appears to be a new phenomenon in Jewish history. In what sense can its victims be said to have perished in *Kiddush Hashem*?

A preliminary approach to this question is often taken by citing the words of *Rambam* — a Jew, who is killed simply because he is Jewish, sanctifies the Name by his death itself. (See the quote from R' Menachem Ziemba, in the previous section.) This author has not found this statement in *Rambam*'s works, but a similar idea is expressed in *Sanhedrin* 47, where *Tehillim* ch. 79 is cited: "O God, nations have intruded into Your inheritance, defiling Your holy Temple. . . They have left the corpses of Your servants as food for the birds of the skies, the flesh of Your pious ones to the wild animals of the land." The *Gemara* comments that the term "Your servants" refers to Jews who were wicked during their lifetime. Because they were killed by gentiles, however, their sins were atoned for, and they are deemed worthy of the name "servants" of Hashem. Although one normally does not observe mourning for a *mumar* (one who has rejected the Torah), this *Gemara* serves as the source for the *halachah* that a *mumar* who perished at the hands of gentile authorities, is indeed mourned for (*Rama, Yoreh De'ah* 340:5).[1]

FROM *SANHEDRIN* 47, it appears that victims of persecution achieve not only atonement, but are classified even as "servants

The Akeidah of Hashem." The *Admor* of Piastchene explains:

> The Binding (*Akeidah*) of Yitzchak was not just a test for him; it was the beginning of the work of self-sacrifice for Hashem and Israel. This trial of Avraham and Yitzchak involved thought and will which were not totally completed in action; for the angel told him, "Do not put forth your hand to the youth

---

1. The *halachah* is mentioned only to illustrate the point presently under discussion. Practical applications must be decided only in consultation with a halachic authority.

and do not do anything to him" (*Bereishis* 22:12). Therefore, every [subsequent] incident in which Jews are killed by gentiles in the opposite situation — i.e., the act without the will and thought — constitutes a completion of the Binding of Yitzchak. That was the beginning, the thought and the will; and here is the conclusion and the act. Thus, the *Akeidah* and all subsequently killed Jews all constitute one act (*Esh Kodesh*, p. 72).

According to the *Admor*, the Holocaust is not to be seen as an isolated historical event. It is rather to be perceived against the background of all Jewish history, as a direct sequel to the *Akeidah* of Yitzchak and the many *akeidos* of all the generations.

THE *KIDDUSH HASHEM* of those who perished in the Holocaust can be substantiated on other levels as well. As explained at length

Chosenness — Two Aspects in this author's previous work, *Am Segulah* (ch. 2), it would appear that there are two aspects to the uniqueness and chosenness of the Jewish People. One is a revealed sanctity, acquired through the active acceptance of Torah and *mitzvos*. The other is an additional, more hidden element of sanctity which is implanted in the Jewish People from their very inception. This second aspect of sanctity is one which comes not from action, but from being: it is not contingent upon any subsequent choice or deed.

"I MADE THIS people for Me; they shall tell My praise" (*Yeshayahu* 43:21). If the purpose of Israel's chosenness is to

A Latent Sanctity sanctify the Name of Heaven in the world, then it is also clear that *Kiddush Hashem* also has two aspects, one revealed and one hidden. A Jew can sanctify the Name of Heaven through open sacrifice for the fulfillment of Torah and *mitzvos*. But there is also *Kiddush Hashem* latent in the very uniqueness of the Jew. The existence of the Jewish People itself creates potential for the Divine Presence (*Shechinah*) to dwell in the world. When a Jew is killed or suffers simply because he is Jewish, the uniqueness of the Jewish People is thus underscored, and Hashem's Name is sanctified.

Thus, we are also led to understand why even a wicked Jew

who is killed by gentiles is classified as "Your servant." A servant of Hashem is one whose life serves only to fulfill the will of his Master; one who acts as an extension of his Master. If one is killed for being Jewish — even if he did not do the will of his Master during his lifetime — his entire life is sanctified. The very fact of his death is a tragic but exalted link in the process of sanctifying Hashem's Name within our world.

IT IS NOT ONLY the *Kiddush Hashem* of the Holocaust which points to this essential aspect of sanctity within the Jew. The very

Racial Anti-Semitism — Attacking the Essence

nature of the anti-Semitism displayed in the Holocaust highlights it as well. No longer are we witness to persecution based upon behavior — the Jew's religion, commercial activities, or social standing. Instead, we are confronted with racial hatred. For perhaps the first time in our history, persecution was connected not with deeds of the Jew, but with his very nature and unique essence.

With a kind of satanic sixth sense, the Nazi movement realized that within every Jew, righteous or the opposite, nationalist or assimilationist, is hidden a spiritual kernel of Divine good. It was this essential element of holiness which made the very existence of the Jew antithetical to that movement. Hatred was no longer directed against the deeds of the Jewish people, but against their essential being. It follows that the struggle of the Jewish People during the Holocaust constituted *Kiddush Hashem* in itself, independent of the particular deeds of individuals.

THE VIEW THAT all those murdered in the Holocaust are to be seen as holy has been adopted by many Torah leaders of the

"Who Commanded Us to Sanctify His Name"

present generation. Many of their writings are dedicated to the memory of community members or family who perished — all of whom they refer to as "holy." The same position can be inferred from the words of R' Elchanan Wasserman, who, when taken to be killed, said that he was about to "fulfill the greatest of all the *mitzvos*" (Introduction to *Kovetz Shiurim*). It is related of R' Elchanan that he instructed the people who were to be killed with him to recite the blessing: ". . .Who commanded us to sanctify His Name in public," using the full Name of Hashem (*shem u'malchus*). Many followed his ruling (See *She'elos Uteshuvos Mimaamakim*, part 2, sec. 2).

A Hidden Sacrifice

WHY WAS IT decreed upon our most recent generation in particular to sanctify Hashem's Name in this way? If they were to perish for *Kiddush Hashem*, why was their sacrifice hidden, while earlier generations sanctified Hashem's Name by dying openly for the sake of Torah and *mitzvos*? It is difficult, perhaps impossible, to know. It may be that the final outburst of evil in our world, before the coming of *Mashiach*, must be directed precisely towards the most essential aspect of Jewish chosenness. On the other hand, perhaps their identity was all that a spiritually impoverished generation had left to sacrifice:

> Tell me, my fellow Jews, what would have happened if Hitler had given the Jews the option offered by oppressors throughout all the periods and eras — to convert or be destroyed? Would the Jews of our generation, the deniers, the non-believers, have stood the test, as did previous generations? Only isolated individuals would have preferred death to conversion, sanctifying the Name of Hashem publicly. This time, the issue was not religion, but "blood," "race." Here there was no room for evasion. Believer, denier, assimilationist, convert down to the third generation, Jews who had forgotten their origin, non-Jews who did not even know they had Jewish ancestry — all paid in blood. All suffered the same verdict.
>
> "The Jewish People are held accountable for each other." Can it be that the doctrine of racism reveals the finger of God? Is it mere coincidence? (*Ani Ma'amin*, pp. 252-3, citing an article by Moshe Kahanovitch).

IN EVERY LOCALITY, the Nazis first and foremost attacked the *rabbanim* and *admorim*, the Torah scholars who seemed to represent Judaism in its pure form. With fury, they devoted special effort to desecrate Torah scrolls and other sacred books. Innumerable synagogues were burned at their hands. The innermost essence of the war against *Klal Yisrael* was hatred of the Divine; all the rest was merely accessory. By its very nature, the struggle was one of *Kiddush Hashem*. The *Admor* of Piastchene writes:

The War Against God

> How can we know whether the troubles are purely due to our sins, or whether they are for the purpose of sanctifying His Name, Blessed is He; whether the enemy simply tortures us, or whether the essence of his hatred is towards the Torah, and because of this he also tortures us?
>
> Regarding the decree of Haman, the *Gemara* asks (*Megillah* 12): "On what grounds did 'the enemies of Israel' [a euphemism for the Jewish People] of that generation deserve to be annihilated?" But regarding the decree of the Greeks [in Hasmonean times], the *Gemara* does not ask this question — even though [the Greeks] killed several thousands of Jews, conquered nearly all of *Eretz Yisrael*, and entered the *Beis Hamikdash*.
>
> Haman aimed his decree only at the Jewish People; hence it surely must have been due to sin, and the *Gemara* [thus] asks which sin was its cause. Of the Greeks, on the other hand, it is said: "In the days of Mattisyahu, when the wicked kingdom of Greece rose up. . . to make them forget Your Torah and violate the statutes of Your will. . ." Hence there is no need to ask which sin was the cause; the suffering was for *Kiddush Hashem*, even though it also brought atonement for their sins (*Esh Kodesh*, p. 191).

During the Holocaust, the Nazis plotted not only against the Torah-observant public, but against their fulfillment of *mitzvos* as well. In the ghettos the law forbade growing a beard or *pe'os* (sidelocks). The *mikvaos* were closed. Even to pray with a *minyan* was to risk one's life. People were forced to desecrate *Shabbos*. A special calendar of the Jewish festivals was distributed to the S.S.

so that they could plan their "actions" precisely for those days. In short, the holier the person or thing, the more energy the enemy devoted to destroying it.

BY NATURE, EVEN the most sadistic murderers are somewhat compassionate towards the helpless young; but in the terrible

Targeting the Youth
reality of the Holocaust, the Nazis directed their most vicious actions precisely against children. The *Admor* of Piastchene sees significance in this, too:

> The eternal existence of Israel in this world, too, is only [attained] by means of the children. Therefore Pharaoh, the first anti-Semite, attacked the Jewish children: "Every boy who is born, cast into the river" (*Shemos* 1:22). In the same way, the enemies of Israel always focus their greatest cruelty on the Jewish children, either to kill them, God forbid, or to force them to deny the Torah, as is known from the persecutions of earlier centuries, may the Merciful One save us. And to our sorrow we see the same today. Of all the horrible cruelty and killing which is poured upon us, the House of Israel, the most terrible [is that directed] against the little children. Alas, what has happened to us! (*Esh Kodesh*, pp. 185-6).

Elsewhere, he writes:

> We are persecuted, not because we have stolen, nor because we have done evil to any man, but simply because we are Israelites, attached to our God and to His Torah, Blessed is He. And our enemies are not satisfied just to extinguish the spark of godliness that is in us; they want to destroy both together, the body and the soul of the Jewish person. (ibid., p. 141).

From all angles — the nature of the racial anti-Semitism, to the particulars of its awful realization — the Holocaust challenged the essential nature of the Jew. Thus, the very flames which engulfed the victims endowed their lives with eternal sanctity.

IT WAS NOT ONLY in death that the Jews of the Holocaust sanctified the Name of their Creator. The goal of the Nazis was to

The Struggle for Life physically annihilate the Jews, and it thus follows that the struggle for life itself also constituted *Kiddush Hashem*. Among the sanctified ones we must include not only the murdered, but also the survivors.

As a rule, most persons will pay any price to stay alive. But the destitution in the ghettos and concentration camps was incomparable, and many simply lost the will to live. There were others however, even more numerous, who persevered. With their last remaining strength, they clung to life, if only to oppose the utter annihilation plotted by the enemy. Not all of them succeeded. Many who tried so desperately to live, eventually fell. But their very love of life, their struggle for the continued existence of the Jewish People must certainly be deemed a *Kiddush Hashem* as well.

In the diary he kept while imprisoned in a German work camp, R' Yehoshua Moshe Aharonson writes:

> Many had already become weary of living a life of such slavery. They preferred death to life, looking forward to the end and waiting for the angel of death, seeing it as the angel of redemption from their terrible suffering — sufferings of Job in the full sense of the word. The only question was: "What is the point of living, when we have lost our families, and we know what awaits us? Why aren't there sensible people among us who commit suicide? Why do we just keep on serving our oppressors with our last shred of strength, doing all their backbreaking work in the house and in the field?"
>
> In my opinion, the answer is: Because of that awesome feeling hidden deep within us from earliest youth, and implanted in our heart, to be repulsed by suicide. And because in our exile we have become accustomed to live in hope of a better tomorrow. And also — for some — a desire for revenge, even though the moment of vengeance may be very far away. And because we are controlled by a feeling of cowardliness to take the action, even in the way King Shaul took his life (*Ani Ma'amin*, pp. 81-2).

DR. HILLEL SEIDMAN also addresses the issue:

The Will to Live

In the Warsaw Ghetto, one of the factors that increases the desire for life — exerting such strong influence that even those condemned to death cling to life with superhuman powers — is a fierce faith in the ultimate victory of justice. They believe and know that the wicked regime will be defeated, and they want to merit to see it happen. They declare: "May it come, and may I see it."

This explains the amazing fact that despite the dire suffering, there were almost no suicides in the Ghetto. . . Rooted within us is the knowledge that suicide is defeatism and despair, a kind of desertion. No one despaired and no one wanted to desert — so strong was faith, so strong the desire for life.

The director of the bureau of statistics told me, in amazement, that the number of suicides among the Jews in the years 1940-42 decreased by 65% in comparison with the year 1939 (*Yoman Ghetto Varsha*, pp. 134-5).

Other sources provide further evidence:

The will to live of Jews in the ghettos contrasted dramatically with the passivity and total resignation that characterized the Russian prisoners of war. Even ghetto Jews who encountered them at forced labor and who often risked their lives to give them bread were appalled at the transformation of human beings into wraiths of wretchedness (*The War against the Jews 1933-1945*, p. 347).

DR. MEIR DWORZECKI writes:

"Uberleben"

During the days of the ghettos and the camps, a new concept came into being: "the sanctification of life." The community and the individual, each and every one, did everything in their power to nullify the Nazi plot to annihilate the Jewish community and the Jewish individual. R' Nissenbaum said: "The enemy demands the Jew's body, and the Jew has an obligation to defend it — to protect his life." The Jews spoke of "fulfilling the *mitzvah* of life," of "living to spite the enemy." It was a kind of game, to deliberately infuriate the enemy by violating their command of death. In earlier generations, when the enemy wanted to negate our souls, we would sacrifice our bodies. Now, when the enemy wants to take away our bodies, we shall guard our lives at all cost.

From this stemmed the aspiration: *"Uberleben!"* ("Outlive them!"). "Moshe, halt sich!" ("Moshe, hold on!"). Calls like these, designed to encourage people to bear their suffering and hold out until the moment of redemption, found expression in most of the songs of the ghetto (Dr. Meir Dworzecki, *Sho'at Yehudei Eiropa*, p. 281).

The descriptions give the clear impression that a difference existed in this area between East European Jewry, who were much closer to their roots, and West European Jewry, who were more distant. Among the Jews of Western Europe there were apparently many more who despaired of their fate and lost the will to persevere. One can only speculate that perhaps the will to live becomes strengthened as the individual perceives that his life carries meaning. The Torah Jew who remains cognizant of his true worth, of his cosmic purpose, thus clings to life with undaunted tenacity.

C.

In Death's Shadow

S WE HAVE SAID, each and every victim of the Holocaust, regardless of his personal level of observance or righteousness, was beloved, heroic, and sanctified. However, there is no doubt that *Kiddush Hashem* in the usual sense of the word — giving up one's life for the sake of Torah and *mitzvos* — is the Jew's most sublime sacrifice. Through such sacrifice, thousands of European Jews etched their names into the fabric of eternity. It is our duty to attempt to absorb within us at least a fraction of their legacy's precious light.

PROF. DAWIDOWICZ WRITES:

The Refinements of Cruelty

The refinements of cruelty were reserved for pious Jews and rabbis, whose traditional Jewish garb — hat and long coat — and whose beard and sidelocks identified them as quintessentially Jewish. . . the Germans deliberately chose observant Jews to force them to desecrate and destroy the sacred articles of Judaism, even to set fire to synagogues. In some places the Germans piled the Torah scrolls in the marketplace, compelling the Jews to set fire to the pile, and dance around it, singing, "We rejoice that. . . is burning." Another German pleasure was "feeding" pork to pious Jews, usually in the presence of an invited audience. The most popular German game, played in countless variations, was "beards." In its simplest versions Germans seized bearded Jews and beat them. A more sophisticated entertainment involved plucking beards, hair by hair or in clumps. Sometimes Germans herded bearded Jews into barber shops, ordering them to be shaved and making them pay for the service. Sometimes the Germans themselves hacked off Jewish beards with bayonets, often along with parts of cheeks, chins, faces. In some places, Jews were assembled in the town square and shorn in a ceremony of mass mockery; else-where, beards were set afire (*The War Against the Jews 1933-1945*, pp. 201-202).

The Germans, denying that Jews were a religious group, had rendered the entire public existence of the observant community illegal. Not only were observant Jews singled out for German sport and persecution, not only were most synagogues destroyed or desecrated, but all functions pertaining to the observance of Judaism were outlawed: public and/or private worship, religious study and religious teaching, *shechitah* [kosher slaughtering].

Like *kashrus,* the Sabbath was nearly impossible to observe. In Lodz, Warsaw, Vilna, and Kovno, the Sabbath was a permitted day of rest for brief periods or in certain communal institutions, but for the most part the Germans, with deliberate sadism, forced the Jews to work on Saturdays and the High Holy Days. . . the Germans had forbidden ritual baths [*mikvaot*] (Ibid., pp. 248, 250,251).

HOW DID THE great majority of the Jewish public react to these decrees? Clearly, they were obligated by *halachah* to desecrate

Secret Minyanim   *Shabbos*, or eat non-kosher food, if there was any threat to life. But beyond what people were required to do to preserve their lives, there were incidents of unparalleled *mesirus nefesh*, self-sacrifice.

All through Poland, Jews prayed in secret. On August 12, 1940, on the eve of Tisha B'Av, the fast-day commemorating the destruction of the Temple, Chaim Kaplan noted: "Public prayer in these dangerous times is a forbidden act. Anyone caught in this crime is doomed to severe punishment. If you will, it is even sabotage and anyone engaging in sabotage is subject to execution." But Jews prayed in thousands of secret *minyanim*, some six hundred in Warsaw alone. They prayed in cellars, attics, back rooms, behind drawn blinds, with men on guard. . .

Prayer took on new solemnity and urgency, with the special petitionary prayers augmenting the regular service. In the Kovno ghetto it became customary after the morning and afternoon prayers to recite Psalms 130. . . and 142. . . Also the petitionary and penitential prayers of the *Tachanun*, reserved normally for Mondays, Thursdays, and fast-days, used to be recited daily. Composed for the most part during the Crusades, these prayers now expressed a tragic immediacy. They were uttered to the accompaniment of weeping and lamentation, especially at the *"Shomer Yisrael"*: "O Guardian of Israel, guard the remnant of Israel, and suffer not Israel to perish." Everywhere the rabbis called to penitence and prayer, since Jewish tradition regards these as indispensable for the redemption of all Israel. . .

Hundreds of secret yeshivot and houses of study came into being in the Generalgouvernement and the occupied eastern territories. . . In the Warsaw ghetto, some two hundred yeshiva students "learned" in at least eleven yeshivot. Most yeshiva students had no legal existence in the ghettos, since they were not registered with the Judenrat, and so were relieved of the onus of forced labor. But that meant that they had no ration cards. Some well-to-do families supplied them with food in quantity, as did some welfare agencies. Students took turns begging on the streets or soliciting food and money among people of means. . . (Ibid., pp. 248,249,251).

A Further Motive

WITH DELIBERATE INTENT, the enemy aimed to sow discord among ghetto residents. Using the strategy of "divide and conquer," the Germans attempted to ensure that Jews would direct their little remaining strength against one another. Even in the death camps themselves, the Germans consistently created situations in which one man's life would depend on another's death. With unsurpassed sadism, they forced Jewish mothers to decide which of their children would be left alive. There is no doubt that beyond the Germans' basic intent to destroy, there lay another motive. Systematically, the Nazis sought to destroy the essence of the Jew's Divine image, turning him into a creature whose only interest is self-preservation.

One stands amazed at the spiritual fortitude revealed by the Jewish public as a whole. Certainly there were those who failed, and it is not for us to judge them. But if one weighs the actions of the public as a whole, we will find a monumental revelation of *mesirus nefesh*, self-sacrifice. There is no doubt that herein lies a genuine *Kiddush Hashem*. The *Admor* of Piastchene writes:

> One who sacrifices his life for the Jewish People is greater than one who does so for Hashem alone. This is like one who sacrifices his life for the king's son. From this, people see that his love of the king is so great that he not only sacrifices his life for the king himself, but even for his son (*Esh Kodesh*, p. 23, in the name of the author's father).

Even Jews whose "love of the King" was not outwardly visible gave up their lives for "the King's son." But this, too, reveals the *kedushah*, sanctity, of the Jewish soul.

EVEN BEFORE THE Jews were sent to death camps, they were imprisoned in ghettos, where they faced virtual starvation. The

Black Bread and Sand daily food ration allotted by the Germans consisted mainly of black bread, frequently mixed with sawdust, and potatoes. Even this portion was distributed irregularly. Under these conditions, it was impossible to stay alive without smuggling food, an activity which itself involved imminent risk of life. There was an appalling lack of space. In the ghetto's crowded, deprived conditions, epidemics of typhus and dysentery spread with lightning speed. Mutual aid organizations in the ghettos cared for orphans and the sick under unimaginably difficult circumstances.

One source states:

> Never has there been the possibility of examining so many acts of selflessness and sacrifice as during this time. Innumerable Jews hurry to answer every appeal from the Jewish community or from the Jewish Self-Help Organization [*Haezrah Ha'atzmit HaYehudit*].
>
> Under the auspices of the Jewish Self-Help Organization, a special division of social aid has been organized, comprising the following departments: money; collection of clothing; urgent help; sanitation and housing for the homeless. . . (*Hashoah Beti'ud*, p. 165, citing a newspaper which appeared in the Warsaw Ghetto, the largest of the ghettos).

In many places, the young and healthy had the option of escaping the ghetto and joining the partisans in the forests. Only a few, however, chose to do so.[1]

Most Jews chose to remain within the Nazi snare, for they knew that their flight would endanger the remaining Jewish public. As noted earlier, the Germans imposed collective punishments for the rebellion of individuals. In certain areas, the practice was to murder the family or neighbors of those who joined the partisans. But even where there was no such danger, many young people stayed so as not to leave the old and sick behind; to help their family and community bear the burdens of existence. We speak here not of exceptional individuals, but of the great majority of Jewish youth.

IN THE INTRODUCTION to *Dvar Avraham*, it is recounted that R' Avraham Dov-Ber Kahana-Shapira found himself in Switzerland

The Dvar Avraham

for medical reasons on the eve of World War II. His son, a United States citizen, appealed by telegram to his father to come to America until the danger passed.

The son writes:

> My great father, as was afterwards told to me, showed the telegram to a few of his friends who were with him at the time. Even though they begged him to agree to my request, he refused them, saying: "The ship's captain is the last to abandon the burning ship, not the first. In this time of danger, this time of trouble for Israel, my place is with my community. I'm going to Kovno." And, like a shepherd devoted to his flock, he returned to Kovno and cast himself into the jowls of the furnace, as the conflagration of war spread throughout Eastern Europe (*Dvar Avraham*, Introduction to Part 3, New York, 5706/1946).

---

1. According to Dr. Meir Dworzecki about a hundred thousand Jews tried to join the partisans, but most were murdered by local populaces or anti-Semitic partisan factions. Of the one hundred thousand, only about ten thousand survived. (See *Iyunim Bitekufat Hashoah*, p. 25.)

BY THE END OF winter, 5703 (1943), only three *rabbanim* remained in the Warsaw Ghetto: the *gaon* R' Menachem Ziemba,

Three Rabbanim R' Shimshon Stockhammer, and R' David Shapira. Through international Jewish efforts, the Catholic Church agreed to rescue them and hide them in a safe place until the danger passed. It is related that all three *rabbanim* refused to leave the community. R' David Shapira said at the time: "It is perfectly clear to all that we have no power to help these people in any way. But the very fact that we are here with them, that we have not abandoned them, gives them encouragement — their only encouragement." (See *Ani Ma'amin*, p. 22.)

Similar accounts are given of many other Jewish leaders. They shunned the beckoning opportunity to leave their communities, even in situations in which *halachah* did not firmly obligate them to remain. (See *Sefer Hazikaron* for the *Chasam Sofer*, Jerusalem, 5717, pp. 36 ff.)

ACTS OF *MESIRUS NEFESH* were also performed by Jewish public leaders. Many men who bore responsibility for contacts with

Between Hammer and Anvil the Nazi authorities tried with all their might to save as many lives as possible. The words "*Judenrat*" and "kapo" are generally associated with negative images; and in fact, many of them did cooperate in murdering their fellow-Jews. But historical study has shown that a significant number of those employed in the Jewish Police and in the *Judenrats* acted commendably, despite being trapped between the hammer and the anvil. Dr. Isaiah Trunk writes:

> The chairman of the first Jewish Council of Lwow, Dr. Joseph Parnas, was arrested in October, 1941, and apparently killed shortly thereafter for refusing to comply with an order to deliver several thousand Jews, ostensibly for forced labor out of town. . .
>
> Numerous other Council members lost their lives endeavoring to help ghetto inhabitants. Some sought to alleviate the

misery of forced laborers or interceded on behalf of arrested Jews; others tried to have certain measures of persecution canceled or refused outright to comply with orders which endangered the lives of Jews. In this category belong Elisser and Lipe Mishelevski, one the chairman and the other a member of the Council of Kleck; also in this category was the second chairman of the Council at Wlodzimierz-Wolynski, the lawyer Dr. Pass. . . A member of the Council there, Symcha Bergman (according to another source, he was the police chief of this ghetto), was murdered together with his entire family during September 1942 because he did not round up the required number of Jews and, moreover, tried to set free those already arrested. . . In 1941 the Germans demanded that the chairman of the Council at Asndomierz (Lublin district), Leib Goldberg, deliver within a few hours a well-to-do Jew whom they accused of concealing personal property. Although Goldberg knew where the man had been hiding, he did not betray him. When the hidden person did not report at the appointed time, the German police shot Goldberg to death on the staircase of the Council building. Later on, SS men came to arrest the vice chairman of the Council, Apelbaum, for the same crime. Not finding him, they threatened to shoot twenty Jews. Apelbaum then reported to the police and was shot. (*Judenrat*, p. 437. And see there many additional stories; and on pp. 438 ff., incidents of *mesirus nefesh* on the part of ghetto policemen.)

Acts of awesome *mesirus nefesh* were performed by individuals trapped in the most extreme conditions. It is not within the scope of this work to cite all the extant accounts; entire books have already been written to chronicle them (*Ani Ma'amin*, by M. Eliav; *Bikedushah Uvigevurah*, by Y. Eibeschitz; and others). All the same, we shall cite a number of incidents:

The architect Greenberg was put in charge of a group of Jewish engineers who erected buildings in the Plashov camp. He was loved and admired by those imprisoned in the camp. He was also constantly beaten by the commander. "I don't remember ever seeing that man without bruises, without his head bandaged, or without wounds. That man — every single day — either dogs were set loose on him, or he got blows, a hundred lashes, or twenty-five, or just plain punches" (from the testimony of the judge Leon Valis in the Eichmann trial). In charge of many engineers and workers, he always took upon himself the blame for problems with their work, serving as a lightning rod for the tyranny of the camp commander. Greenberg more than once begged them to shoot him, but he did not kill himself. His wife and daughter, who were with him in the camp, were openly used by the commander as hostages to ensure his good behavior (cited by Sh. B. Beit-Tzvi, *Hatzionut Hapost-Ugandit. . .*, p. 446).

The Shotrim Legacy

THE LEGACY OF THE Jew is a proud one. When *Bnei Yisrael* were in Egypt, there also, their Jewish overseers (*shotrim*) were beaten by Pharaoh's officers because they did not fill the quota of bricks. In this merit, the *shotrim* later became the elders and judges of the people.

Other examples abound:

> It had been a bad day. On parade, an announcement had been made about the many actions that would, from then on, be regarded as sabotage and therefore punishable by immediate death by hanging. Among these were crimes such as cutting small strips from our old blankets (in order to improvise ankle supports) and very minor "thefts." A few days previously a semi-starved prisoner had broken into the potato store to steal a few pounds of potatoes. The theft had been discovered and some prisoners had recognized the "burglar." When the camp authorities heard about it they ordered that the guilty man be given up to them or the whole camp would starve for a day. Naturally, the 2500 men preferred to fast (Viktor Frankl, *Man's Search for Meaning*, p. 128).

> Buchnia, Galicia, the month of Av, 5703 (1943). This is the last ghetto in Galicia, but it, too, is being dismantled. The Jews already know the meaning of being shipped out. They hide in cellars, in bunkers, and among the goyim. Approxi-

mately two hundred Jews went into hiding this evening. About ten Jews work in the German factory and are legally permitted to reside in Buchnia. One of these is a respected householder from Cracow, Hirschel Zimmer, with his son. They volunteer to bake bread for the factory workers and supply bread to the hiding Jews. Without this, those in hiding would starve to death.

In this way, weeks go by, and they do their part. But suddenly, an S.S. man caught them carrying bread, and realized that the bread was intended for those in hiding. They caught them, tortured them horribly, and threatened them with death unless they revealed the Jews' hiding-place. The father and son encouraged each other not to reveal it, and went joyfully to their death.

These were the last words of Hirschel Zimmer as he was taken out to be executed in the presence of all the assembled "legal Jews": "Fortunate are you, my son; we are going to our death for saving Jews from starvation" (*Yoman Ghetto Varsha*, pp. 269-70).

One day I was lying on my cot in the children's hut in Auschwitz, and I saw the assistant commander of the hut walking with a thick rubber hose to beat someone. I jumped up and ran to see whom they were going to beat. They would give beatings for everything, and the number of blows was in accordance with the severity of the offense. On that day, the rubber hose came into use. Usually they would use a stick, which many times broke in the middle of the beating, and therefore they began to use a rubber hose, and I wanted to see how it worked. I might have to meet up with it myself someday.

The assistant commander of the hut went up to one of the cots. The boy there already knew, and was waiting for him. "Get down," the assistant commander told him. The boy bent over, and they began to beat him. We, a group of young men who were standing around, watched, each one counting the blows individually. The boy didn't cry or yell; he didn't even sigh. We were very amazed. . . There had already been more than twenty-five blows. Usually they would give twenty-five blows, and now it was already more than thirty. When the attacker passed forty blows, he turned the boy over and began to beat him on the legs and head. The boy didn't sigh, didn't cry — nothing! A boy of fourteen, and he didn't cry!

The soldier got very angry, finished the fifty blows, and left him. We picked him up. I remember one large red mark that he had on his forehead from one of the smashes of the rubber hose. We asked him why they had beat him. Then he answered: "It was worth it. I brought my friends a few *siddurim* (prayerbooks)." He added nothing more; he got up, climbed onto his cot, and sat there. (From the testimony of Zalman Kleinman in the Eichmann trial, cited in *Ani Ma'amin*, pp. 114-5.)

In Buna-Auschwitz, when we got up from our beds in the dark of the night, we barely managed to wash, and we were already rushed to backbreaking forced labor. The block officers and their assistants were already goading us with various and sundry decrees. And here, the prisoners were already lining up in long lines; not for bread and not for coffee, but to fulfill the *mitzvah* of putting on *tefillin*. Each one wants to be the first to perform the *mitzvah*. A special guard had been appointed, whose job was to make sure that no one left the *tefillin* on for more than the time necessary to say the first verse of the *Shema*; then he had to take them off immediately and give them to the next man. There were certain times when those individuals who were most exacting [about the performance of *mitzvos*] had *tefillin* hidden at their place of work, in order to fulfill the *mitzvah* of *tefillin* at the proper time, i.e., during daytime.

Likewise, we lit Channukah lights in the presence of hundreds of prisoners. We blew the *shofar* on the assembly ground of Buna-Auschwitz, surrounded by Gestapo guards, in the presence of many hundreds of Jews, at daybreak on Rosh Hashanah, 5705 (1945).

In the year 5704 (1944) we risked our lives to make a *sukkah* there. At the edge of the camp, between us and the S.S., near the quarters of the officers and guards, was a large storage area in which stood many rows of tall barrels. Between two rows there was enough space for a large, kosher *sukkah*. We set up a third wall, and put kosher *schach* on top before Sukkos. No one knew of its existence except a few chosen individuals who guarded the secret. On the first night of Sukkos we went there stealthily, made *Kiddush* over a slice of bread saved from the morning, and hastily ate a small measure (*kazayis*).

However, the place where the *sukkah* stood was surrounded by steel wire — for a prisoner to enter there was punishable by death. I had doubt whether I should recite the blessing for sitting in the *sukkah*, since it was dangerous to be there. [See *Shulchan Aruch, Orach Chaim* 640:4, where the *Rama* rules that such a *sukkah* is altogether invalid.] All the same, due to our love of the *mitzvah*, which had been done with *mesirus nefesh* — there had been no *sukkah* for several years — the blessings blurted forth from our mouths with heartfelt joy: ". . .Who sanctified us with His commandments and commanded us to dwell in the *sukkah*," and ". . .Who kept us alive, and preserved us, and caused us to reach this time." We were happy that we had merited to set up a *sukkah* from within the lion's mouth. Many men ate there, one going in as the other went out (R' Yehoshua Moshe Aharonson, in *Ani Ma'amin*, pp. 118-9).

On one of those days (winter, 5705/1945), as we stood in the darkness of night by the gate of the camp (Auschwitz), ready to go to work, one of the members of our group, a middle-aged Hungarian Jew, stood by me and said: "It is written in a verse, 'Hope in Hashem, be strong and fortify your heart, and hope in Hashem.' Sometimes a person finds himself in the type of situation where he might, God forbid, lose hope in Hashem. Hence, after the verse says, 'Hope in Hashem,' it repeats, 'Be strong and fortify your heart, and hope in Hashem.' Even in the worst times, one must strengthen oneself and hope in Hashem." This Jew was not trying to tell me a new interpretation of the verse. I knew that at that moment he was living that verse. The verse was keeping him alive. In just a few words he had expressed what he felt in his innermost self.

As time went on, I got to know him better, and learned that this Jew, whose name I have since forgotten, was a pure *tzaddik* in the full sense of the word. I personally witnessed a number of his righteous deeds, and still remember some of them.

One evening, when he came into our quarters, he went over to his cot and began to pray the evening prayer, quietly, without anyone noticing. Of course, while he prayed he left his hat on, although this violated the law of the camp, which stated, "Indoors, hats off." In the middle of his *Shemoneh Esreh* prayer, who should come in but the "elder of the block," a German prisoner wearing a green triangle — meaning that he had been convicted of criminal offenses, and by merit of this profession had earned his "honored" post.

When the guard saw that a Jew was standing there with his hat on, he yelled at him and ordered him to take it off. But the Jew didn't move or react in any way, and continued praying. All of us were stunned to see the courage of this Jew, who did not instantly obey the order of the person in charge of him; for despite the fact that the holders of these "honored" posts were also prisoners, they were feared no less than the S.S. men themselves. When the Jew finished his prayer, he took off his hat and went over to the "elder of the block," to explain his actions, saying that he had been praying, and our custom is to cover our heads when we pray. By a miracle, the wicked man's reaction was only curses, mockery, and arrogant ridicule.

Another incident made its way into my heart, and I have not forgotten it. One evening, everyone living in our room was ordered to be disinfected. . . After finishing our "bath," we had to wait to receive our clothes. That evening, apparently there was some problem with the disinfection of the clothes, for we waited for them a long time. In the end we were told that they would come later, and for the time being we should return to our room without clothes. Wearing only shoes and belts, we walked naked through the camp yard, which was covered with snow on that winter night. Every limb trembling, we entered our room. . . On the cot next to mine lay that Hungarian Jew. Like me, his whole body was shaking.

He called to me and asked me to come and lie down next

to him. It was very cold, and if we lay next to each other we might be somewhat warmer. I did as he asked, and after a few minutes he told me that he remembered Tractate *Beitzah*. I don't remember whether he knew the whole tractate, or only some passages, but when he lay down on his cot he would set fixed times for Torah study by reviewing, word by word, the passages he knew by heart. Now, too, he did not wish to miss his fixed time, and asked me to listen. With the melody of Talmud study, he began reciting the *daf* of Gemara, word for word.

It is of people like him that it is said: "Fortunate are you, O Israel. Who is like you?" (Sinai Adler, *Begei Tzalmavet*, pp. 36-8).

D.

Confronting the Final Choice

KIDDUSH HASHEM TOOK many forms during the Holocaust. Death could come quickly and without warning, and many were never confronted with the possibility of giving their lives for their faith. Often, the choice was not whether to die, but how to. Faced with the stark terror of **Reconciling** sudden death, there were those who accepted **Death** upon themselves the harshness of the Divine verdict with a serenity born of love and faith.

The historian and Holocaust survivor, Dr. Meir Dworzecki, writes:

> If the Germans did not give the Jews a choice between remaining faithful to their religion or giving it up, the Jews gave themselves the choice between going to their death in humiliation and despair, or going with inner calm; with pride, standing upright, without cowering before the murderers. Through signs which showed that they had not lost their dignity, those who were taken to their death exhibited one of the attributes of *Kiddush Hashem*. On the contrary, the Jews of many communities adopted the practice of going towards death wrapped in their *tallis*, with Torah scrolls in their arms and the melodies of prayer on their lips. This constituted a new kind of choice, which came into being during the Holocaust: the choice between dying in denial or dying in faith — another attribute of *Kiddush Hashem* during the Holocaust.
>
> In this manner of behavior there was a kind of tragic and exalted declaration of faithfulness — faithfulness to the belief of their fathers even on the threshold of an incomprehensible death. Those who went to their death this way were saying: It is true that we are being taken forcibly to die. But we go to death with joy and enthusiasm, not only because we have to die, but because we are ready to die.

R' Ephraim Oschry relates that on the eleventh of Tammuz, 5701 (1941), when the murderers broke into an assembly of *rabbanim* and *roshei yeshivos* in Kovno, R' Elchanan Wasserman told those gathered there: "We must remember that in truth we are going to be sanctifying the name of Hashem. . . we shall go with heads held high. . . we are now fulfilling the greatest of the *mitzvos*, *Kiddush Hashem*" (see E. Oschry, *Churban Lita*, New York, 5712/1952).

L. Feingold relates that R' Nechemiah Alter, a *posek* in Lodz, said at a gathering of *rabbis*: "It is not just in public that we are obligated to sanctify the Name. . . each individual should sanctify Hashem to the extent of his ability. Let us not lower ourselves before the *goyim*, and let us not obey their orders."[1]

R' DESSLER WRITES similarly regarding the destruction of the *beis midrash* of Kelm, Lithuania:

"Ashreinu" But how did they leave the world, those great men, mighty ones of the heart, searchers for the truth? I remember days long past, the nights of Simchas Torah at the Talmud Torah. The rabbis of the institution went out into the street and made a procession through the city, leaping and dancing with all their strength from joy, singing with all their might: "*Ashreinu* — Fortunate are we, how goodly is our portion. . ."

Some forty years passed. The time arrived for the fearsome destruction. The rabbi and their families gathered in *Beis Hatalmud* and poured out their hearts, asking for mercy from Him Who is full of mercy. But. . . the gates of mercy were locked . . .And at the gate. . . here were the murderers. . . They took every man and woman, even every child, into the street, making them run through the city, pressed and beaten incessantly. . . Where to? To the field of killing.

Who could imagine what those supremely holy ones did at that hour? They strengthened their hearts and fortified their spirits, firing their souls with tremendous joy over the *mitzvah* that had reached their hands: *Kiddush Hashem* through *mesi-*

---

1. (See L. Feingold, *Migei Heharigah*, in the newspaper *Hatzofeh*, 13 Kislev, 5706/1946; cited in the anthology, *Sho'at Yehudei Eiropah*, pp. 279-80.)

rus nefesh. Instead of crying and wailing, they leaped and danced with all their strength, singing with all their might that very same melody of joy: "*Ashreinu* — Fortunate are we, how goodly is our portion. . ." (Fortunate are we to be Jews, and fortunate are we that we have merited to die for being Jews. . .)

In this way they went with dancing and joyful enthusiasm that constantly increased. Rising upwards, upwards, with a holy stubbornness, until they reached the edge of the city. . . the field of killing. . . where. . . they gave up their lives to their Master, in attachment to Him, the joyful attachment to a *mitzvah* . . .

Deep are the ways of truth, exceedingly deep. Who could find them? Therefore the masses do not know them, but only the chosen few, people of truth. Many ask, puzzled: What good is there in these deaths? If they had died during a religious persecution, giving up their lives for the sanctification of His Name, that would be something. But those murderers did not ask about anyone's faith. They simply came to annihilate, kill, and destroy, believer and non-believer alike, to kill all because they were born Jewish. What point is there to that? Those killed were not even given the possibility of sanctifying His Name, blessed is He! And so, for what did they die? A major question. . .

But the people of truth knew the meaning. The trial was not one of religious persecution, and not to sanctify the Name of Heaven in the eyes of the peoples, but. . . hardest of all. . . a tremendous, unparalleled task. . . the trial was to determine who was sincere in his heart, who would sanctify Hashem within his own heart. Who would turn his heart *entirely* to Him, Blessed is He, without reserve, and genuinely rejoice in the fearsome sufferings of death. . . a complete rejoicing in the happiness of attachment to Hashem (*Michtav Me'Eliyahu*, part 3, pp. 347-8).

HERE TOO, ENTIRE books have been written chronicling incidents of this kind. One can not always choose whether to die. But

The Final Choice

the choice of *how* to die — the possibility of accepting the Divine judgment with serenity — this was a choice open to every individual. Tens of thousands of Jews in fact sanctified the great Name through this choice. Many recited the confession of sins (*vidui*). Others said the benediction, ". . .Who has sanctified us by His commandments and commanded us to sanctify Your Name in public," and uttered the *Shema*. There is even eye-witness testimony of a group of young men who, inside the gas chamber, danced fervently — joyously anticipating the great *mitzvah* of *Kiddush Hashem* that awaited. Their actions paralleled those of R' Akiva when he was taken by the Romans to be executed. The episode is described by *Chazal* in *Berachos* 61:

> It was time to recite the *Shema*, and they were combing his flesh with iron combs. He concentrated on lovingly accepting the yoke of heaven. His students said to him: "Rabbeinu — even to this extent?" He replied: "All my life I was pained over the verse, '. . .with all your soul,' meaning, 'even if He takes your soul.' I thought, 'When will I have the opportunity to fulfill it?' And now that the opportunity has come, shall I not fulfill it?'"

The actions we have cited were not the exceptional acts of one or two outstanding men, but typified entire communities.

Even the survivors, those who continued in the path of faith in the wake of shock and disaster — they too sanctified the Name of their heavenly Father. There were those whose spiritual world fell to ruin as a consequence of the Holocaust, and, as we stated earlier, this spiritual destruction was itself part of the devastation of the Holocaust. But many persevered, grief stricken from loss, but whole in faith: "And Aharon remained silent" (*Vayikra* 10:3). It is these men and women who express the inner essence of *Klal Yisrael*: for the faith of a "stiff-necked" people is not shattered by external disaster; it is only forged and strengthened.

In conditions of overwhelming strain, how one chooses to die — even how one chooses to live — becomes as significant a choice as the very decision to sacrifice one's life. *Kiddush Hashem* of this sort is a private one; its domain is within one's own heart. But an element of public *Kiddush Hashem* is contained herein as well, for even non-Jews were moved by the spiritual strength and courage of Jews during the Holocaust. A Nazi officer wrote the following in a report to his superiors:

One must admit that the Jews go to their death with great self-control. When they reach the place of execution, they stand very quietly, while the gypsies, under the same circumstances, incessantly wail, scream, and run around (quoted by Sh. B. Beit-Tzvi, *Hatzionut Hapost-Ugandit. . .*, p. 443).

A GERMAN ENGINEER, Herman Grabbe, who witnessed the massacre of the Jews of Dubno in the Ukraine, related:

The Dubno Massacre Without crying or tears these people undressed, stood in family groups together, kissed and said good-bye, and waited for a sign from another SS-man who stood by the trench and also held a whip in his hand. During the quarter of an hour that I stood near the lorries I heard no moaning or begging for mercy. I watched one family of some eight persons, a man and wife both of about fifty, with their children, about one, eight, and ten years old, as well as two grown-up daughters of twenty to twenty-four. An old woman with snow-white hair held the one-year-old child in her arm, sang to him and tickled him. The child chuckled with joy. The father and mother looked on with tears in their eyes. The father held a youngster of some ten years by the hand, and spoke quietly to him. The boy fought back his tears. The father pointed with his finger to heaven, stroked his head and seemed to be explaining something to him.

The SS-man at the trench called out something to his comrade. The latter detailed twenty persons and told them to go behind the mound of earth. The family of whom I spoke was among them. I remember exactly how a young woman, dark-haired and slim, pointed to herself and said "twenty-three years old" as she passed near me.

I went to the mound of earth and stood before the gigantic grave. People lay in it so closely packed one upon the other that only their heads could be seen. The trench was already three-quarters full. By my reckoning there were already about a thousand people lying in it. . .

The. . . people went down a few steps which had been dug in the wall of the trench, and scrambled over the heads of those who were lying there to the position the SS-man indicated.

There they lay down among the dead or wounded people; some stroked those who were still alive, and spoke quietly to them. Then I heard a succession of shots (ibid., p. 304, cited from *The Nurenburg Trials*).

To cynical eyes, this might be "sheep going to slaughter." But to any objective observer, this testimony constitutes one of the most shocking and moving accounts to emerge from the Holocaust. The spiritual bravery it recounts is the quiet legacy of the anonymous victims.

LET US CONCLUDE with the following:

The Last Ne'ilah

I have no words to adequately express what we felt that Friday, the eve of Shavuos, 5703 (1943). The Germans roused all the residents of the ghetto to assemble in the market square. The Nazi order said nothing of the purpose of this assembly, but we all knew what lay in store for us. A few days before Shavuos, the Gestapo murderers had suddenly arrested ten Jews, nearly all of them chassidim, and officially charged them with "economic sabotage" and smuggling food into the Ghetto. . . and since this time, too, ten victims had been chosen and the date of the action coincided with Shavuos, one's turbulent heart guessed that once again they would present before the eyes of the entire Ghetto a painful and horrifying spectacle, the hanging of ten Jews. And so it was. . .

The Jewish policemen who worked in the service of the Germans told, in strictest secrecy, about the amazing behavior of Shlomo Zelichovski in the tiny cell in which were placed all ten of the Jews sentenced to hanging. Shlomo Zelichovski, with his sweet voice, proposed to the ten Jews in the cell that they fast on the eve of their hanging and that he would pray with them the prayers of Yom Kippur. And all of them agreed. Thus was conducted a personal "Yom Kippur" of ten Jews condemned together in an isolation cell, and the prayers of Shlomo Zelichovski, when he reached the *Ne'ilah* service, so touched the heart that even the hard-bitten ghetto policemen, who were present in the prison yard, cried like babies. . .

The *Ne'ilah* service, however, did not end in the jail cell, for

Shlomo Zelichovski purposely left the conclusion of the prayer for the next day when they would go to the gallows. And so it was. All ten Jews, their hands tied behind their backs, were led this way through the streets of the ghetto, from the prison to the appointed place. Along the way, Shlomo Zelichovski raised his voice in a mighty, exalted singing of the prayer, *Ezkerah Elokim Ve'ehemayah* ("I shall remember, O God, and I shall moan"). The Jews stood straight and in a powerful, soulful voice accompanied him in the conclusion of the *Ne'ilah* prayer. They had almost reached the site of the gallows. Their heads were upright, their eyes raised heavenward, as they approached their final prayer.

Then, during these last preparations for the hanging, I too glanced into the smiling, radiant face of Shlomo Zelichovski. I was one among a pressed crowd of pained, humiliated Jews. And suddenly, a tiny wind of encouragement blew through that crowd which had been so despondent. The gallows had been set up in a straight row, one next to the other. Under each gallows was a bench to climb up on. The Nazi murderers did not hurry at all, for they didn't want to waste a minute of their "game." All the same, Shlomo Zelichovski, his mouth filled with song, annoyed them. "Enough?" the hangman next to him asked impatiently. And he, Shlomo Zelichovski, jumped up onto the bench in order to put his head into the noose.

Our breath was held for a few moments. A dreadful silence prevailed everywhere, and instantly the heavy silence was split by a flaming voice: "*Shema Yisrael*". . . It was the voice I knew well, the voice of Shlomo Zelichovski. Who could describe what took place in the hearts of those masses of Jews, those downcast onlookers, at that moment? We were raised up, exalted, we exclaimed without voices, wept without tears, straightened up without moving, and all of us cried out, "*Shema Yisrael*" in our innermost soul. Could anyone have the ability to describe that moment?. . .

I was then sixteen or seventeen. To this day, two fearless cries reverberate in my ears as I heard them from the mouths of those who were hanged. Even before Shlomo Zelichovski's roar of "*Shema Yisrael*" which electrified everyone, a great and fearsome shout had been heard: "Jews, avenge our blood!" At the time, I didn't know whose shout it was.

Afterwards, I found out that it had been the porter, a simple, pure Jew from among the masses. . .

Even then, the deep realization crystallized within me that in fact those two cries were connected; for that is the greatest possible vengeance. The Germans wanted above all to murder the Jewish soul. That is why they deliberately chose to attack and persecute the Jews on the eve of Shavuos, the festival of the giving of the Torah. This was their attempt to weaken our faith. And what did Shlomo Zelichovski prove to them? That they, the German hangmen, had no dominion whatsoever over the Jewish soul, and they had no power at all to uproot faith from the heart of the Jews (*Ani Ma'amin*, pp. 49-51, citing R' Moshe Prager, *Eileh She'lo Nichne'u*).

E.

In Conclusion

HEN ALL THE evidence has been gathered, we are led to conclude that the Jews of the Holocaust died, for the most part, not like "cowards," and not like "heroes"; not like sheep and not like lions; — but as human beings. They were mortals who found themselves in a situation utterly beyond their

The Fringe and the Essence control. A few broke under the strain, and cooperated with their murderers — at first under compulsion, later, sometimes willingly. Others — also a few — took up armed resistance. For the most part, such armed struggle was motivated more by the despairing hope of vengeance than considerations of survival. The activities of each of these groups represent the fringe, not the essence, of Jewish reaction to the Holocaust.

INDEED, MOST OF those who died cannot be described as "heroes" in the popular sense. Yet there is such a thing as inner

Spiritual Freedom heroism as well. Can one question the valor of those Jews who put the safety of their community before their longing for revenge? Can one doubt the bravery of those who, in spite of everything, never surrendered their will to live? The multitude of Jews who gave their lives to save their brothers — the scores who fulfilled the *mitzvos* of the Torah with love and *mesirus nefesh* — these were heroes too.

"Who is strong? One who controls his desires." The essence of heroism is the ability to maintain one's inner freedom in the face of external pressure. It is the ability to, despite everything, act in accordance with what one considers correct and desirable. We are repelled by the submissiveness of the term "like sheep to the slaughter" only because it implies behavior completely dictated by external circumstances. But quiet actions can come from strength too. Dr. Viktor Frankl, himself a concentration camp survivor, writes:

But what about human liberty? Is there no spiritual freedom in regard to behavior and reaction to any given surroundings? Is that theory true which would have us believe that man is no more than a product of many conditional and environmental factors — be they of a biological, psychological or sociological nature? Is man but an accidental product of these? Most important, do the prisoners' reactions to the singular world of the concentration camp prove that man cannot escape the influences of his surroundings? Does man have no choice of action in the face of such circumstances?

We can answer these questions from experience as well as on principle. The experiences of camp life show that man does have choice of action. There were enough examples, often of a heroic nature, which proved that apathy could be overcome, irritability suppressed. Man *can* preserve a vestige of spiritual freedom, of independence of mind, even in such terrible conditions of psychic and physical stress.

We who lived in concentration camps can remember the men who walked through the huts comforting others, giving away their last piece of bread. They may have been few in number, but they offer sufficient proof that everything can be taken from a man but one thing: the last of the human freedoms — to choose one's attitude in any given set of circumstances, to choose one's own way (*Man's Search for Meaning*, pp. 103-104).

As a "kingdom of *Kohanim* and a holy nation"(*Shemos* 19:6), *Klal Yisrael* is historically unique only through its sanctity. The Holocaust once again underscored this uniqueness. Consciously or unconsciously, deliberately or through the very events they experienced, the Jewish nation succeeded in sanctifying the name of their Creator. The holiness which their actions displayed both transcends and encompasses heroism.

"Why should the nations say, 'Where is their God?' " (*Tehillim* 115:2). At first glance, the Holocaust appears to have constituted a supreme desecration of God's Name. And yet, on an inner level, *Kiddush Hashem* persisted. The very challenge to the uniqueness of the Jewish nation highlighted the special quality of this people. The very confrontation between the Jew and his antithesis served to demonstrate that only through the Jewish People does the *Shechinah* (Divine Presence) dwell within our world. For the enemy did not seek only to change this people's religion; they did not wage war only against the more apparent *kedushah* (sanctity) of Torah and *mitzvos*. In their quest to assault the physical, emotional and spiritual being of the Jew, they attempted to annihilate all that the Jew stood for; all that his essence implied.

THE HOLOCAUST MUST be seen as an integral link in the chain of Jewish history. As early as the days of Mordechai and Esther,

An Eternal Antipathy there existed persecution which was not purely or explicitly motivated by religious hatred. Haman tried to annihilate all Jews alike, men, women, and children; young and old, regardless of their level of Torah observance. It is true that subsequent wars against the Jew were usually directed against his religion rather than his race. However, the Holocaust still does not escape the Jewish historical continuum, for the same essential anti-Semitism merely resurfaced in new form.

The irrational hatred, the eternal hatred against an eternal people — all was the same. The antipathy which took on religious garb in the Christian Middle Ages, in the twentieth century showed itself as it truly is. Anti-Semitism finally revealed itself as a blind hatred for all that the existence of the Jew implies. In the end, the war against the Jew became the rebellion against the moral responsibility and recognition of the Divine which his nationhood had brought to the world.

The Nazis plotted with special intensity against Torah-observant Jews and Torah scholars. The Germans made a conscious effort to attack the Jews on *Shabbos* and Jewish festivals. Such efforts were not inconsistent with the policy of racism, for hatred of the Jewish race is nothing other than hatred of the Jewish essence. The greater and more obvious the holiness of the Jew, the greater antipathy he arouses.

OUR RESPONSE TO the Holocaust must thus be not only to strengthen the physical existence of our people. We must actively

In the Holocaust's Wake sanctify this existence with *kedushah* as well. This, too, is made evident by the actions of Jews during the Holocaust — Jews who strove as much as possible to guard their Torah while caught in the very teeth of the enemy. Such has always been the way of those who gave their lives in sanctification of their Creator.

The question of "sheep to the slaughter" merely distracts attention from the pivotal issues of the Holocaust. Indeed, the Jew has been characterized by the Psalmist as having "been considered like sheep for the slaughter" (*Tehillim* 44:23). But this verse must be seen in its entirety: "For You we have been killed every day; we have been considered like sheep for the slaughter" — for You and for Your sake we were slaughtered like sheep. It is this fact which breathes a different soul into the Holocaust. The massacre is no longer a meaningless slaughter in a meaningless world, but a *Kiddush Hashem* of unfathomable proportions: the enthroning of our Creator as the hidden, but all-powerful, Sovereign over a world full of meaning.

Armed resistance is not the fundamental reaction to the Holocaust. Adopting the weapons used by murderers, attempting to exact "an eye for an eye," cannot be the only answer. In the wake of the Holocaust, the Jew must commit himself to thwart the essential plot of the Nazi enemy — the elimination of the name Israel from the world. If our adversary schemes to annihilate us, our only task is to ensure our eternal existence as a people. In the end, this is our most noble struggle.

The memory of six million beckons us to preserve their legacy. May it be His will that we rise to the obligation.

7

From the Eye of the Inferno: the Rescuers and the Rescued

A.

A Silent World

"Do not stand by your neighbor's blood." (*Vayikra* 19:16)

"Because of the oppression of your brother Yaakov,
you shall blanch with shame and be cut off forever.
On the day when you stood by,
on the day when foreigners plundered his wealth,
and aliens entered his gates and cast lots for Jerusalem
— you, too, are like one of them." (*Ovadiah* 1:10-11)

IN *WHILE SIX MILLION DIED*, Arthur D. Morse describes the apathy of the Roosevelt administration towards the plight of Europe's Jews. Other nations that escaped Nazi conquest were no less indifferent. The evidence points to the conclusion that the Germans viewed the world's

Political Apathy silence as tacit applause to their genocidal scheme. Goebbels, the Nazi propaganda minister, writes in his diary:

> The question of Jewish persecution in Europe is being given top priority by the English and the Americans. . . At bottom, however, I believe both the English and the Americans are happy that we are exterminating the Jewish riff-raff (*The Goebbels Diaries*, trans. Lochner, p. 241, entry of Dec. 13, 1942).

A few days later, this entry appears:

> The Jewish question is receiving a big play both in the enemy and in the neutral news services. The Swedes protest hypocritically against our treatment of Polish Jews, but are by no means willing to receive them in their country. The leading newspapers of Stockholm warn emphatically against having the ghetto Jews from Warsaw forced upon them (ibid., p. 249, entry of December 18, 1942).

THERE WERE MANY gentiles who actively rescued Jews and for this, we must be grateful. The list is a long one: Sweden, Britain,

Gentile Assistance Switzerland, and Spain absorbed thousands of refugees who fled various lands of German conquest. The Danes succeeded in saving nearly all of Denmark's Jews from the Nazis. While Italy was allied to Germany, the country's populace nevertheless foiled the official government policy, and successfully rescued the greater part of Italian Jewry. Although the total number of Norwegian Jews was very small, about half escaped with the help of the Norwegian underground. The United States established the Committee for War Refugees, which rescued tens of thousands. On a smaller scale, extraordinary individuals saved many Jews, often at great personal risk. The most famous among them was the Swedish diplomat Raoul Wallenburg, who single-handedly rescued thousands in Nazi-occupied Hungary. To him, and those like him, Jews around the world owe their enduring gratitude.

Unquestionably, there were gentile efforts to save Jews. The overall picture, however, is a grim one. For the most part, what was done came too little and too late. The American Committee for War Refugees was established towards the end of the war. By that time, the greater part of European Jews were no longer alive.

Other countries occasionally consented to absorb survivors, but took almost no steps to prevent the extermination of Jews.

The absorption effort which did exist was limited. Switzerland had no qualms about expelling thousands of Jewish refugees to Nazi-controlled territory. A few Allied nations agreed to accept a limited number of refugees, but for the most part, they locked their gates to Jews fleeing the Nazis. The British engaged in diplomatic activity to prevent the exit of Jews from Europe by any possible escape route. They sealed off *Eretz Yisrael*, and severely limited Jewish entry into other countries of the British Empire. Any Jew who had managed to get from Europe to *Eretz Yisrael* by "illegal" means was liable to arrest by British naval authorities.

BERNARD WASSERSTEIN CONDUCTED a comprehensive study of British policy towards the Jews of the Holocaust. His book,

British Policy *Britain and the Jews of Europe 1939-1945*, contains a number of noteworthy passages:

> There is little to celebrate in this account of British policy towards the Jews of Europe between 1939 and 1945. A few flashes of humanity by individuals lighten the general darkness. Churchill's attitude towards the Jews was one of sympathy and compassion. But the effectiveness of his interventions in favor of the Jews was repeatedly blunted by the actions of his subordinates. The generous impulses of a small number of officials and politicians stand out from the documents mainly by virtue of their isolation amidst an ocean of bureaucratic indifference and lack of concern. The overall record leaves a profoundly saddening impression.

> During the first two years of the war, when the German authorities bent their efforts to securing the exodus of Jews from the Reich and from Nazi-occupied territory, it was the British Government which took the lead in barring the escape routes from Europe against Jewish refugees. On the second day of the war an overcrowded hulk, carrying terrified refugees, including women and children, in flight from the terror of Britain's enemies, was fired on by British forces when those on board sought haven on British-held territory (in a country which Britain, under the different exigencies of a

previous war, had thought fit to declare their 'national home').
In January 1940 the Colonial Office considered it necessary,
in order to preserve British security in the Middle East, to seek
to prevent an American charity sending food to dying families
who had been marooned for months on the frozen Danube.
The Government of Palestine, in December 1940, after the
Patria explosion, was so anxious to get rid of the surviving
passengers from the *Atlantic* that it was not prepared to delay
their deportation for a matter of days in order to isolate typhoid
carriers: the result was an epidemic and many deaths. A few
days later, when the *Salvador* sank in the Sea of Marmara with
the loss of two hundred lives, the head of the Foreign Office
Refugee Department wrote that he considered the event an
'opportune disaster'. . . (pp. 345-346).

. . .It is worth remarking the frequent disparity between the
public professions of the British Government as to its concern
for the fate of Jewish refugees and the reality of British policy.
In public on 17 December 1942, Eden, in a memorable scene
in the House of Commons, read out the Allied declaration
condemning the Nazi persecutions of the Jews. In private on
31 December 1942, Eden presided over a meeting of the
Cabinet Committee on the Reception and Accommodation of
Jewish Refugees at which it was agreed that Britain could not
admit more than 1,000 to 2,000 further refugees. . .After 'ten
days of agreeable discussion' the British delegates reported to
London that 'so far as immediate relief to refugees is
concerned, the conference was able to achieve very little.' It is
hardly surprising that it was considered imprudent to publish
the final report of the conference . . .In December 1943, there
appeared a possibility of securing the departure of 70,000
Jews from Rumania. The Ambassador was informed that 'the
Foreign Office are concerned with the difficulties of disposing
of any considerable number of Jews should they be rescued
from enemy-occupied territory.'

. . .Among all the resistance movements of occupied
Europe that of the Jews stood almost alone in the near-total
absence of aid, whether in weapons, outside advisers, or
propaganda, from the Allies. . . Pleas to the Government to
relax the economic blockade of Axis Europe to permit some

food and medical relief to be sent to the ghettos and concentration camps met with little substantial success. The proposal for the bombardment of Auschwitz by the Allies, although favored by Churchill and Eden, was obstructed by officials in the Foreign Office and the Air Ministry (pp. 348-350).

There is, for example, a painful contrast between the niggardly quantities of food relief which the Ministry of Economic Warfare permitted to be sent to Jews in central and eastern Europe, and the wholesale operation by which the Allies supplied the entire food needs of the population of Axis-occupied Greece between 1942 and the end of the war. As against a total of 4,500 tons of foodstuffs which the International Red Cross was permitted to send to inmates of concentration camps between autumn 1943 and 1945, $40,000,000 worth of foodstuffs (comprising up to 35,000 tons per month) were permitted to go through the blockade to Greece. The huge disparity between those figures calls for explanation. . .

Whatever the merits of the Greek case, there is a striking incongruity between the solicitude shown towards the Greeks on the question of relief, and the *non possumus* attitude characteristic of British handling of proposals for the relief of Jews in occupied Europe. There is a similar dissonance between the welcome accorded to tens of thousands of Yugoslav and Greek refugees from Nazism in the Middle East after 1941 and the more chilly reception accorded to Jews. Even more remarkable is the contrast between the official preparations which were said to have been in hand in 1940 for the reception of up to 300,000 Dutch and Belgian refugees in Britain, and the consistent refusal of the Home Secretary to consider the admission to the United Kingdom of more than one or two thousand Jewish refugees (pp. 353-354).

THE CONCLUSION IS as clear as it is shocking. The world not only remained silent — it passively aided the murder of the Jews.

Ovadiah's Scorn One is reminded of Ovadiah's caustic prophecy to Esav, chastising him for his indifference to Yaakov in time of catastrophe. "You should not have stood at the exit-point to destroy his refugees; you should not have handed over his remnant on the day of disaster" (*Ovadiah* 1:14). The heirs of Esav, counted among the most advanced nations of the modern world, have in our day fully lived up to their progenitor's dubious legacy.

In his book, Wasserstein ventures an explanation for British apathy to the plight of the European Jew. He argues that the British did not view the Jews as a nation, and consequently did not see aid to the Jews as an integral part of the war effort. Winning the war took precedence over every other consideration, and thus rescue was given secondary priority. Wasserstein's thesis, however, does not seem sufficient. He himself writes, "Certainly there was a tinge of anti-Semitism in the words of some British officials and politicians. . . There is no doubt that anti-Semitism was in the air in Britain during the war. . ." (ibid., p. 351).

ANTI-SEMITISM HAS never been a logical phenomenon: The British were the only nation to have fought from beginning to end

Sinai's Name

against Nazi tyranny — yet they too appear to have succumbed to a subtle and insidious irrational hatred of the Jew. Our surprise is tempered only by recognition of a historical pattern: *Chazal* tell us that the mountain where the Torah was given was called Sinai, derivative from the word *sin'ah,* "hatred"— for there the hatred of the nations fell upon Israel. Anti-Semitism has always been an eternal hatred against the eternal people; an inexplicable antipathy to the fact of Jewish existence as a chosen people.

"It may be objected that if Britain's record on the Jewish question during the war was unimpressive, that of other countries was often far worse" (ibid., p. 357). Once again, current realities verify the isolation of a people whom a gentile prophet more than three thousand years ago called: "a people that dwells alone, not counted among the nations" (*Bamidbar* 23:9).

B.

The Jewish Rescue Efforts

Cruelty is common only among the idolaters,
as it is written, "They are cruel and will not be merciful"
(*Yirmeyahu* 50:42);
but all Israel, as well as those attached to them,
are like brothers, as it is written, "You are sons
of Hashem your God" (*Devarim* 14:1),
and if the brother does not have mercy
on the brother, who will have mercy upon him?
And to whom do the poor of Israel look —
to the gentiles, who hate and persecute them?
No, they look only to their brothers. . .
(*Rambam, Hilchos Matnos Ani'im* 10:2).

F THE GENTILE RESPONSE to the Jews' plight was less than spirited, what of the Jews themselves? Were Jewish rescue efforts from the Free World adequate or effective?

The answer is equivocal. On the one hand, there were those who were quite active in rescuing Jews from occupied Europe.

Jewish Aid Jews smuggled their brothers across borders, sent food, medicine and money, and urged national powers to participate in the rescue effort. Without American Jews' financial aid to Polish Jewry in the first year of the war, one can only speculate how many might have starved to death. Nearly all of the budget of the American War Refugee Board — $17 million out of $18 million — was donated by Jewish organizations, and were it not for the initiative of influential Jews, even the limited rescue activities of the allied nations would never have been launched.

While the war still raged, however, the Jews of Europe cried out that they had been abandoned; not only by the gentile nations, but by their brothers abroad. In letters to family in *Eretz Yisrael,* there are some vehement accusations leveled against the *Yishuv* , and against the Jewish public as a whole. Within *Eretz Yisrael* itself, a small group known as *Al Domi* ("Do Not Keep Silent") acted during the war years under the leadership of Prof. Fishel Shneurson. *Al Domi* strongly denounced what they saw as the general apathy of the *Yishuv* leadership towards the Jews of Europe. The argument advanced by *Al Domi*, that the *Yishuv*'s indifference to the fate of European Jewry led *Yishuv* leaders to suppress crucial information about the Holocaust, is still brought to bear in current debates on the issue.

IN 1981, A PRIVATE group of noted American Jews formed the Jewish-American Committee for Holocaust Research, commonly

Exaggerated Caution known as the Goldberg Commission. Their conclusions, published a few years later, created an uproar among the American Jewish community. Had United States Jewry put heavier pressure upon the Roosevelt Administration, they argued, the lives of tens of thousands would surely have been saved. In fact however, Jewish leaders fearful of anti-Semitic backlash exercised an exaggerated caution in the face of reports of the massacre of European Jewry. By and large, the Jewish Establishment refrained from publicly protesting the murder and in doing so, unwittingly reinforced the indifference of President Roosevelt.[1]

R' Joseph Dov Soloveitchik writes:

> To trust in man is idol worship. The *Aggadah* (*Sanhedrin* 7) quotes a folk saying: " 'The man I trusted clenched his fist and attacked me.' Shmuel told R' Yehudah: 'The same thing is written (*Tehillim* 41:10): 'Even the man who was at peace with me, whom I trusted, who used to eat my bread, raised his heel over me. . .' "
>
> Stinging confirmation of this viewpoint was given during

---

1. A short summary of this study was published in the newspaper *Maariv* , 20 Nissan, 5744/1984, p. 23.

the war years, when the president of the United States refused to bomb the railway tracks that led to the ovens of the extermination camps. The leaders of American Jewry accepted the transparent excuse of the State Department that this involvement might, supposedly, harm the war effort. Why didn't the Jews of America act like Mordechai the Jew in his time, who, when he heard of the decree, went out "into the city and raised a great and bitter alarm" (*Esther* 4:1)? Why didn't they hold mass demonstrations, tearing their garments as Mordechai did, to shake the complacency of the Jewish leadership and awaken the conscience of Christian America? If our reaction had been like Mordechai's, would President Roosevelt have acted with such hard-heartedness? Perhaps we are commanded to add another line to the *Al Chet* confession of Yom Kippur: "For the sin that we sinned when we ignored the outcry of our brothers, *Bnei Yisrael,* in Europe, when they were being slaughtered by a cruel hand."

It was, apparently, American Jewry's blind faith in the president, which blocked all effective action; a submissiveness bordering on idol worship. Had it not been for the idolization of that man, millions of Jews might have been saved. President Roosevelt was a great leader of America, but he was a great catastrophe for the Jews (J.D. Soloveitchik, *Machshevet HaRav,* ed. R' Avraham Besdin, pp. 52-53).

Elsewhere, R' Soloveitchik writes:

Let us be honest: At the time of the terrible Holocaust, when European Jewry was systematically exterminated in the gas chambers and the furnaces, the American Jewish community did not rise to the proper heights, did not act as would have befitted Jews who had a developed awareness of a shared fate, a shared suffering, and also a shared action — to take action. We did not properly feel the suffering of the nation, and did but little to save our unfortunate brothers. It is hard to know how much we might have accomplished if we had been more active. I myself think that we could have saved much. But there is no doubt that if we had properly felt the pain of our brothers, if we had raised a great outcry and shaken worlds, insisting that Roosevelt proclaim a sharp warning and protest, accompanied by deeds, we would have been able to considerably slow the process of mass murder.

We witnessed the most horrible tragedy of our history, and we remained silent. I shall not discuss the details now; it is an extremely painful episode. But all of us sinned through silence at the spectacle of the murder of millions. Are not all of us standing before the throne of judgment for the terrible sin of "Do not stand by your neighbor's blood"? Especially since the sin involves not only "your neighbor" but "your neighbors" — millions! When I say "we," I mean all of us — including myself — members of rabbinical federations and *baalei batim*; orthodox and non-observant; Jewish political federations of all kinds: "Your leaders, your tribes, your elders and your policemen — every man of Israel. . . from the woodchopper to the waterdrawer" (*Ish HaEmunah*, pp. 100-101).

IN *ERETZ YISRAEL,* the principal accusations of failure to rescue the Holocaust victims have been directed against the Zionist

Zionist Efforts

Movement. Fear of European anti-Semitism was the historical raison d'etre of the Zionist Movement; the Holocaust was its founders' worst nightmare. Yet Zionists in *Eretz Yisrael* were all but helpless to aid their European brothers. As long as the Nazis encouraged the exit of Jews from Europe, the Zionist establishment helped tens of thousands of the refugees to emigrate to *Eretz Yisrael*. But as the war began, the British White Paper locked Israel's gates, and Zionist rescue efforts came to a virtual standstill. In all, only a handful of *ma'apilim* ("illegal" immigrants) were successfully smuggled out of the Nazi inferno.

A comprehensive study of the action — and inaction — of the Zionist Movement during the Holocaust was compiled by Sh. B. Beit-Tzvi, a member of the Israeli Labor Movement. In his work, *Hatzionut Hapost-Ugandit Bemashber Hasho'ah* ("Post-Ugandan Zionism in the Crisis of the Holocaust"), the author concludes that for the most part, the story of the Zionist rescue effort is a distressing one:

> With the outbreak of the War, the rescue of Jews did not become a prime goal of the Zionist Movement or of the

Jewish *Yishuv* in *Eretz Yisrael*. In fact, this aim was given no priority at all in relation to the two main goals which Ben-Gurion declared at the outbreak of the War (to fight Hitler and to fight the White Paper). All during the Holocaust, even after the dimensions of the annihilation became publicized, the task of rescue never became a central activity of the Zionist Movement. It was not the "full-time" work of the top leaders (Dr. Weizmann, Berl Katzenelson). At most, at its high point, it was only the "part-time" occupation of other Zionist leaders, and was dealt with by marginal institutions of the Movement (p. 4).

Beit-Tzvi goes on to outline actions taken by the Zionist Movement which, in his opinion, actually prevented the rescue of Jews. A number of concrete possibilities arose which aimed to save Jews by bringing them to places of refuge outside *Eretz Yisrael*. Beit-Tzvi charges that Zionist leaders consistently battled these proposals and in so doing, adopted a stance which hardened the intransigent immigration policy of the British. The possibilities of emigration to other lands were not acted upon, and in time, they were forfeited.

The author points to other failures as well. In the waning months of the war, Eichmann conducted a lightning campaign in which, within an alarmingly short time, he annihilated half the Jewish population of Hungary. At this time, *Yishuv* leaders were reliably informed that twelve thousand Hungarian Jews were being sent to the gas chambers of Auschwitz daily. Beit-Tzvi argues that for several critical weeks, the Yishuv suppressed this information. According to the author, it is certain that if the Jews of Hungary had known that their shipment eastward meant annihilation, a large number would have escaped or taken refuge.

When in the end of June 1944, these shipments to the death camps at last became known in the West, the United States, Sweden, the Red Cross, and the Vatican protested the murder to Admiral Nicolas Horthy, the ruler of Hungary. Roosevelt informed Horthy that unless the deportation was immediately halted, the United States Air Force would target Budapest. After the Hungarian capital was in fact bombed, Horthy announced the cessation of the shipments, and the Jews of Budapest were saved. One can only speculate as to how many additional lives might have been spared had this information been made available earlier.

Beit-Tzvi pushes his argument further. Yitzchak Gruenbaum, the head of the *Yishuv*'s Rescue Committee, did not himself believe in the possibility of actual rescue. He vigorously opposed financing rescue activities from Zionist funds, so long as a specific fund for rescue had not been established. The author claims that in contacts with other nations, too, the importance of the rescue effort was downplayed. Zionist leaders for the most part accepted the gentile agenda, that top priority be given to the war with Germany, with all else being of no more than secondary importance.

Beit-Tzvi writes:

> In July, 1941, the Joint Boycott Council [set up by several Jewish organizations to enforce the British-declared boycott against Germany] stationed pickets at the offices of Agudath Israel in the United States. The reason for the extreme step had been Agudath Israel's refusal to halt shipment of food packages to the Jews of Nazi-occupied Poland. The Council had demanded a halt to the food shipments on the grounds that they violated the embargo which England had imposed on Nazi Germany. On these grounds, the Board had succeeded in stopping the food shipments of all other public organizations in the United States. Only Agudath Israel clung to its rebellious position. The man who had headed the project to stop the food shipments through persuasion and pressure was Dr. Joseph Tennenbaum, one of the leaders of the American Jewish Congress and the American Zionist Federation. . .
>
> In 1940, the Council had sent Agudath Israel a letter which demanded the halt of food shipments to Poland, since this action violated the agreement with the British embargo authorities. . . Dr. Tennenbaum explains: "At a time when the peoples of the world are spilling blood and tears and making innumerable sacrifices, we, the Jews, must not allow this kind of irresponsibility. . ."

Tennenbaum gives special emphasis to countering an argument put forth by a representative of Agudath Iisrael in a private conversation. England, the man had said, has no right to decide what is or is not in the interest of the Jews. To this Tennenbaum replies: "First, we are not dealing with a question of Jewish interests alone, but of world interests, to which the interests of the Jews must be harmonized or given up. Anything which hampers the military needs of Britain contradicts the essential interests of the Jews. As a people, or an organization, we must do nothing that would awaken even the suspicion that we constitute a little world of our own" (ibid., pp. 249-51).

A SIMILAR INCIDENT is related by R' Weissmandl, regarding the reply he received when he applied to the Joint Distribution **The Cost** Committee to help fund rescue efforts. Such **of Blood** action would have violated the monetary regulations of the Allies. Nathan Schwalb, director of the Hechalutz office in Switzerland, wrote the following reply, which R' Weissmandl, a man with a photographic memory, recorded after the war:

> Since an opportunity arose to get a letter through, he [Schwalb] writes to our people that they should always keep in mind the most pressing thing — the main thing which we should always keep before us. And that is, that sooner or later the Allied nations are going to win, and after the victory they will reapportion the world anew among the peoples, as they did at the end of the First World War. At that time, they opened before us the way to the first step [to the acquisition of *Eretz Yisrael*]. And now, as the end of the war approaches, we must do everything in our power to ensure that *Eretz Yisrael* will become the State of Israel. Important steps have already been taken in this matter.
>
> As for the cry of distress that has come from our country, we must know that all the peoples of the Allied nations have poured out great quantities of blood, and if we do not make sacrifices, how will we merit the right to approach the negotiating table when the time comes to apportion the lands after the war? Therefore, it is nonsense, and even imperti-

nence, to go to the gentiles, who are pouring out their blood, and ask them for permission to bring their money into the country of their enemies, in order to protect our blood. For only at the cost of blood will the Land become ours.

The above applies to the people as a whole. As for you, the members of the group, take a trip [a code word for leaving the Nazi-occupied countries], and to this end I have arranged money for you in a black manner by means of this messenger (*Min Hameitzar*, p. 92).

R' Weissmandl explains the letter's significance:

That is to say: "You, the members of the select group, fifteen or twenty people, 'take a trip' outside the land of Slovakia and save your own lives, and through the blood of the rest, through the blood of all the men and women, children, elderly, and suckling infants, the Land will become ours. If so, it is a crime to send money into the land of the enemy in order to save all those people's lives. But in order to provide a 'trip' for you, beloved friends, and to save your lives, I am arranging money for you through illegal means" (ibid., p. 93)

R' WEISSMANDL TELLS of other bitter failures. The greatest of these was the torpedoing of "Project Europe," a plan he proposed

Project Europe

together with other leaders of Slovakian Jewry, which aimed to ransom from the Nazis all the Jews remaining in Europe in 1943. It is now clear to historians that the German representative to these negotiations was Himmler himself, who was in charge of the genocide. There is no doubt that Himmler had authority to stop the killing at any moment. The amount demanded by the Nazis was approximately two million dollars — a paltry sum relative to the large budgets of the Jewish Agency and similar organizations. Nevertheless, the project failed — because the needed money was not sent on time. The first payment, $2,000,000, was raised by the Jews of Hungary, but neither the Jewish Agency nor other Jewish organizations agreed to supply the rest of the money. The retelling of this portentous failure is a major theme of R' Weissmandl's book. His account is confirmed by other witnesses.

The famous Kastner Affair had its roots in the same negotiations. The Nazis had occupied Hungary and began their decimation of the Jewish population. Dieter Wisleceny, the Nazi officer who had earlier been the contact with Rabbi Weissmandl in Slovakia, was sent by him to open negotiations with Hungarian Jewry as he had done with Slovakian Jewry. These ransom negotiations, too, were in the end stalled. Only a small number — Kastner's relatives, Zionist leaders, and other privileged individuals, totalling 1686 people — were transported to freedom by means of a special train sent from Budapest.

In their discussions with Kastner, the Nazis once again raised the proposition of trading money for lives. But while in the original "Project Europe" the funds were supposed to come from world Jewry, this time the Nazis requested that it come from the Allied Nations who were at war with them. Using a tactic designed to create division between the Soviet Union and the Western powers, the Germans asked the latter to supply them with trucks for the war against Russia on the eastern front. This was Joel Brand's famous mission — he was sent by Adolf Eichmann to secure the Jewish Agency's agreement to the proposed exchange of "trucks for blood."

As it stood, the proposal had no chance of success. We have already seen how indifferent the Allied Nations were towards the Jews, and when the plan became public knowledge, the Russians opposed it vehemently. In the opinion of Beit-Tzvi, the Brand mission was simply a deceptive tactic devised by Eichmann to gain time to carry out the liquidation of Hungarian Jewry. All the same, according to R' Weissmandl, if the proposition had been better publicized, and if the British government had been informed of it, it would have been possible to direct the dealings into an acceptable forum — negotiation between world Jewry and the Nazis, rather than between the Nazis and the Allies. But this opportunity elapsed also. Yoel Brand was arrested by the British, and interned for the duration of the war. His contacts with the leaders of the *yishuv* were fruitless, and he died with bitter enmity towards its leadership.[1]

The Historical Debate

IN ALL FAIRNESS, it must be said that historians are sharply divided in their views upon "Project Europe" and other rescue attempts mentioned above. There are reputable historians who assert that everything possible was done under the overwhelmingly difficult conditions which prevailed. The Nazi stranglehold was complete, they argue; concrete possibilities for rescue simply did not exist. If individuals acted irresponsibly, their actions were not typical of the community as a whole. If mistakes occurred, they were, by and large, only the innocent failings of human nature.

The debate over this issue will not be resolved in the present work. However, it is interesting to note the words of Prof. Yehudah Bauer, of the Hebrew University. Although he belongs to the school of historians who defend the leadership of the Yishuv, he is compelled to make this qualification:

> This does not mean that we must ignore the failures which can be pointed out in the actions of institutions and the Jewish public of that time. In the main, the topic here is the manner in which the Yishuv conducted its daily life . . . it is hard to claim that the public institutions provided a leading and guiding example for the public to follow in this matter. Moreover, the interest of the Yishuv, including all its institutions, was centered around itself: its political future, and also its internal political conflicts. The divisions and struggles within each of the various political parties took center stage.

---

1. As for Dr. Kastner, he was accused of collaborating with the Nazis in a pamphlet published by a Jew named Malkiel Gruenwald. Kastner, a government official (and Knesset candidate of the Mapai Party), later sued Gruenwald for libel. Gruenwald's defense attorney succeeded in convincing the court that Kastner had in fact carried his relationship with the Nazis beyond a point required by negotiations over Jewish lives. It was claimed that Kastner concealed from the Jews the fact that their shipment eastward meant certain death, even though he knew this to be true beyond reasonable doubt. Likewise, it was alleged that Kastner was not alone in the Zionist establishment, but that leading figures of the Yishuv approved his acts or at least knew about them and covered up for him. In the end, Kastner was murdered by a former agent of the Israeli Secret Service. After his death, the Supreme Court overturned the verdict of the district court and accepted the claims of the prosecution against Gruenwald.

The inability to cope psychologically with what was happening in Europe stands out strikingly. Even decades after the fact, it strikes a discordant note to see the front pages of the newspapers full of headlines about the doings of the political parties of the *Yishuv*, while the inside pages report the murder of the Jews of Europe (*Teguvot Be'et Hasho'ah*, p. 149).

AS FALLIBLE, MORTAL OBSERVERS, our task is not to judge; the Creator alone knows the intricate designs of man's heart. Ours

An Anomaly

is only to understand, to clarify how indifference could have prevailed among Jews while catastrophe devastated their brothers. *Chazal* wrote that our people is distinguished by its benevolence; that the Jew is by nature "merciful, bashful, and kind." That mark of character is the Jew's national heritage; how did it come to abandon him?

The Holocaust stands as an anomaly in the annals of Jewish response to tragedy. R' Nosson Nota of Hanover, in *Yeven Hametzulah*, writes the following concerning the Polish pogroms of 5408-09 (1648-49):

> Our brothers *Bnei Yisrael* in Constantinople ransomed them, as well as other captives from Poland — about ten thousand souls. They spent a great fortune on them, paying whatever was demanded. They fed and supported them until now, and also did other favors for them, beyond measure.
>
> The whole land of Turkey did the same; especially the community of Salonika, may God protect them, which ransomed multitudes of captives, as did the noble communities of Venice, Rome, and Livorno. And in the other communities of Italy tens of thousands of *zehuvim* were donated for the ransom of the captives, and the money was sent to the great community of Constantinople, may God defend them. May Hashem repay the good deeds they did for our brothers, the House of Israel, and guard them from all trouble and distress, until the coming of the Redeemer. . .
>
> In every country where those fleeing the sword set foot — Moravia, Austria, Bohemia, Germany, and Italy — [the Jews] did good to them, [providing] food, drink, lodging, clothing, and generous gifts to each one according to his

importance. They benefited them in other ways as well, especially in Germany, [where] they did more than their means allowed.

Despite primitive standards of communication and travel, Jews' reaction to the persecution of their brothers in other times was forthcoming. How then, did this change in our day?

"OUR NATION IS A NATION only by virtue of its Torah." With these words, R' Saadia Gaon pithily summarized the crux of

R' Saadia's Maxim

Jewish historical identity. The Jewish People share neither a land of birth, a language, nor a common racial basis, since converts are accepted without regard to racial origin. They are geographically scattered, as well as linguistically assimilated in their lands of dispersion. Throughout history, the Jews have had little to bind them but their Torah. In Yemen and Lithuania, Morocco and Russia, Iraq and England, Jews prayed the same prayers and celebrated the same holidays. A Polish Torah scholar could well debate the intricacies of a Talmudic passage with his Turkish contemporary. The *Shulchan Aruch* was written in *Eretz Yisrael*; *Rama*'s glosses on it, in Poland. Its later commentators hailed from every corner of the Diaspora. The Torah wove the strands of dispersed Jewish life into a living national unity.

THE SITUATION CHANGED radically with the advent of the Enlightenment. The granting of equal rights to Jews brought in its

Merging Identities

wake unprecedented assimilation. Masses of Jews ceased to believe in the special nature of their people as they sought to merge identities with their gentile neighbors. The Jew began to define himself as "German" or "Hungarian," rather than as an adherent to the faith of his ancestors. As Jews' perspectives upon their own identity changed, the inherent bond between them loosened. One who was in his own mind primarily "a German" could for the first time look with indifference upon the plight of his Polish brother.

R' Yissachar Shlomo Teichtal writes:

In the past two hundred years, the Jew has been given freedom in the kingdoms of Europe. They have made him equal to the other citizens of the land. He can enjoy their benefits like all their other inhabitants, can do whatever his heart desires, live wherever he wishes, and study their wisdom and their language. These rights provided the force for his final separation from his connection with the Jewish people, for this caused absorption and assimilation into the people among whom he dwelt.

This is the antithesis of the principle expressed in the verse (*Tehillim* 87:5): "Of Zion it will be said, 'this man and this man was born there,' " — meaning that the persons born there are completely distinguishable, by their spirit and by their behavior. From that time on, the connecting cord with the Jewish people in other countries was severed completely, and there was no equality among them.

Before the time when they [the Jews] were given their freedom, when they still dwelt in ghettos, there were not great differences among them. One can see this from the fact that communities in Germany, Hungary, Bohemia, and Moravia would take one of the Polish rabbis, and consider him fit to lead their congregation. Such is not the situation after the liberation that has been given to Israel. We no longer find that a Polish rabbi is qualified to be rabbi in Hungary, Germany, or Moravia, for these communities have become separate from one another; as distant from each other as east from west. All this is the result of assimilation among the gentiles.

This effect of assimilation has had its influence even upon the Jew who has held firm to Torah and *mitzvos*. We see and hear ourselves how in Germany, and even in Hungary, a Jew from Poland was considered almost inferior — *ein Polisher Jude* ("a Polish Jew"), and in Germany they were accustomed to call him, *ein ost Jude* ("an Eastern Jew"). This nickname was sufficient to accord him the lowest possible status. Even among perfectly God-fearing rabbis, standard-bearers of the Torah, it was possible to discern a certain disrespect in their hearts towards the Polish individual, almost as if the Polish Jew belonged to an alien people — not their own.

This is exactly what I spoke of before: the exile has turned the Jew into a *galus Yid*, an "exile Jew," as I defined it above. He is distinct and separated from the Jewish People as a whole. Wherever he settles, he lives a life of isolation; he breaks his natural connection to the people as a whole. He no longer lives the life of his people, nor feels his nation and his heritage. He is removed from all this, and no longer knows anything beyond the immediate circle of his environment. This is the true definition of a *galus Yid,* and this is what has brought us to our present situation (*Em Habanim S'meichah*, pp. 243-4).

Exile and the Observant Jew

R' TEICHTAL, EMPHASIZES repeatedly that he speaks not only of the completely assimilated Jew, but even of those who still adhere to the Torah. They, too, live in a prevailing atmosphere of assimilation, and cannot help but be influenced by it. He writes:

> We speak not of the common Jew, whose interest is centered only on his business and livelihood, and is lost within these concerns. He doesn't know — doesn't sense — that he is part of the general and eternal people, the Jewish people, or that he has any further obligation to *Klal Israel*.
>
> . . .But even among our brothers *Bnei Yisrael* who hold firm to Torah and *mitzvos* — learned, God-fearing, pious and devoted Jews — one can also see their isolation and separateness from the people as a whole. They have no [sense of] unity and connectedness with the whole nation, for their field of vision does not extend past the place where they are active.
>
> Take for example a typical chassid, devoted to his rebbe and to the other chassidim attached to the rebbe. His world revolves only around the limited circle in which he spends his time. This is his "*eruv*"— anything beyond this doesn't concern him. He doesn't consider the whole Israelite people, scattered and separated throughout the world. If he is asked to contribute to a matter that affects *Klal Israel*, only with the greatest difficulty is it possible to get a little something out of him. But in the circle of the world in which he spends his time, money means nothing to him; whatever he is asked for he

gives, and more.

Similarly, we could contemplate the faultlessly Orthodox man who, morning and evening, is never absent from the synagogue, and who is foremost among the participants in all sessions of the *chevrah Shas*, the Talmud study group. The circle of his world is the *chevrah Shas*, but beyond the boundaries of this group, he is aware of nothing. And he thinks that he fulfills his obligation and his destiny with regard to the Torah and the Israelite people by accepting responsibility for all his obligations to the *chevrah Shas* and its various activities. Beyond this he does not wish to know anything.

One can find many similar examples of the *galus Yid*. Is he not distinct and separated from the Jewish People as a whole? But this is all he has been used to since birth, all the time he has lived in the Diaspora: that he is attached only to those clods of earth upon which he dwells, and he does not peer beyond the circle of his surroundings. It is not surprising that he cannot warm his heart at a time of trouble for his fellow-Jew far from his own circle of residence, [a Jew] with whom he has had no connection until now (ibid., p. 243).

Likewise, R' Weissmandl, writes:

All the same, we did not give up hope that in just a few more days the money would come for all the needed things. In particular, we did not have strength to think how it could be possible that we would not receive money for the Polish refugees who were dying by the thousands from hunger and every kind of deprivation. . . We relied on logic: Here, where everyone lacks a source of livelihood, people give of their funds, the money upon which their lives depend, which they need for bread to eat and to save their lives; how much more so, will those overseas send large amounts of money, all that we ask and need. And certainly, clearly, they will do so without delay; for they are simply *gabbaim*, officials in charge of the funds of the Jewish People which they collect in synagogues in America and in other free countries; they, the *gabbaim*, are not giving of their own. On the contrary, they receive payment, or honor, or both, for distributing these funds.

How were we to know that there were two refutations of this logic: one, the refutation of the assimilated *west Yid* ("Western

Jew"); the other, the refutation of the nationalist "Zionist?"

How could it enter our minds that the *west Yid*, the man of the "Joint," would come and deny the essence of our logic by telling us outright that there is no "how much the more so" here, and nothing to get excited about? There is no blood here, no tears, only a scheme on the part of the *ost Jude* ("Eastern Jew") to swindle funds — all was lies and deception. This was only the well-known formula of the *schnorrer* (charity collector) from Poland, Lublin district, using scare-stories; and "we're not going to get upset by these fables. We're already familiar with the crooked, twisted road of the *ost Jude,* by which he extracts the reliable penny from the pocket of the naive, honest *west Jude.*"

And how could we dream that the nationalist Zionist, the Jewish Agency man, would come and say: "Certainly there is a 'how much the more so' here, but it doesn't apply to you people in the exile, not to your blood and not to your tears! There's something much more serious than that — building up the Land. Certainly there is a 'how much the more so' here, but it works the opposite way. Your blood is the easier side; shed it happily, for it is easy, and with it we shall purchase the more important side: 'For only at the cost of blood will the Land will be ours' " (*Min Hameitzar*, pp. 95-6).

R' Teichtal has indeed observed that apathy affected even the Torah-observant. But the facts are not one-dimensional. A highly disproportionate number of the activists who spearheaded Holocaust rescue efforts were Torah-observant. As noted earlier, the Rescue Committee of Agudath Israel in the United States was virtually the only organization which dared violate boycott regulations to send food to the starving Jews of Poland. The Rescue Committee also succeeded in raising sums of money which stood in dramatic contrast to the Committee's organizational strength. Later in the war, four hundred Orthodox rabbis demonstrated before the White House in protest against the American government's inaction.[1] This demonstration was one of

---

1. The reform rabbi, Stephen Wise, president of the Zionist Federation of America and friend of President Roosevelt, worked vigorously and successfully to prevent a meeting between the Orthodox rabbis and Roosevelt.

the early steps in the campaign that resulted in the establishment of the Committee for War Refugees.

The relatively greater involvement of Orthodox Jews in rescue efforts is not astounding. If the root of apathy is assimilation, it follows that the heart of the Torah-observant Jews pulsed more strongly with a sense of mutual responsibility. Nevertheless, one can not avoid R' Teichtal's observation that even the Torah-observant were not immune to the winds of indifference. R' Moshe Blau, the leader of Agudath Israel in *Eretz Yisrael*, wrote the following:

> We have also undergone an overwhelming decline in our level of morality and ability to feel the suffering of our brothers. Would it have been possible to imagine that *Bnei Yisrael,* the "dispersed lamb," would hear what was happening to their own flesh and blood, and go on with business as usual? Would it have been conceivable that after news like this, the masses of the House of Israel would continue their occupations and daily concerns, as if nothing had happened?
>
> Would it have been possible to imagine that at the moment when tens of thousands of brothers and sisters were drowning in their own blood, tortured with hellish torments, buried and burned alive — the descendants of the Jewish People would go on frequenting theaters and circuses, and would crowd amusement halls?
>
> To a terrible, unimaginable extent, the heart is blocked and unfeeling. How, then, shall we make ourselves worthy of heavenly mercy? And how can we speak to those who have distanced themselves from the roots of Israel? True, they lack the feeling of the unity of Israel, a feeling that flows from unification with the God of Israel. But what can we say to them, if even those who keep the faith of Israel were not shocked; if even Orthodox Jewry has remained almost silent on its pedestal, and does not shake the upper worlds with its prayers, does not pierce the heavens with its outcry?
>
> This apathy is part of the punishment with which the Jewish People is chastised in our day. It is as if, God forbid, the heavens will not give us the opportunity to repent, as if an iron partition has been placed between us and the sensitive, merciful Jewish heart (*Kisvei R' Moshe Blau*, pp. 219-220).

But if Torah-observant Jews lapsed in their sense of unity and concern, they were also more equipped to strengthen this concern. The above words appeared in an article intended to inspire *teshuvah*. Almost immediately after its publication, two days of fasting and prayer were declared throughout *Eretz Yisrael*.

IN THE END, IT MUST BE conceded that one can only say, "All Israel are brothers" if he also understands that "You are sons of

The All-Inclusive Man
Hashem your God" (*Devarim* 14:1). The thought is eloquently illustrated by *Meshech Chachmah*, in his commentary on *Parashas Va'eschanan*:

> "And there you will seek Hashem your God" (*Devarim* 4:29) — The principle is that the Jewish People as a whole are like one man, and each individual Jew is a limb of the all-inclusive man. But when is this true? When they cleave to the center — the source of true life, the Life of the worlds, Blessed is He. Then they are like rays radiating from a central point. Every ray is connected to every other because they originate from a common source, the true center — Hashem, Blessed is He.
>
> But when they sin, and become concealed from His Providence, then, since they are not attached to Him, Blessed is He, they also are separated from one another. . .

The forces which gave rise to indifference during the Holocaust still exist today. The fate of Soviet Jews, as well as those oppressed in other lands, to this day evades the day to day consciousness of the average Western Jew — Orthodox or not. Unfortunately, even many observant Jews neglect to reflect upon the *kedushah* (sanctity) that is of necessity the central pivot of their lives. Indifference to fellow Jews, in some degree or another, inevitably results. As was demonstrated fifty years ago, the ramifications of such indifference can be shattering.

"Don't imagine in your soul that in the palace of the king you can evade [the fate of] all Jews" (*Esther* 4:13). The ageless relevance of Mordechai's warning lives on.

C.

The Miracle of Survival

> If Esav comes upon the one camp and smites it,
> the remaining camp shall escape. . . *(Bereishis* 32:8).

THE SON OF A MAN who had spent several years in the death camps once told me of an argument his father had with a fellow survivor. The latter asked: "How can you still believe in Hashem and His Torah, after everything you witnessed?" The father, a simple Jew, replied: "And how could I not believe, after everything I went through? Is it not an obvious miracle that I survived?"

AS MUCH AS it applies to the individual, the father's answer applies to the Jewish People as a whole. Once again we have seen **An Eternal Nation** the ancient axiom proven: The enemies of Israel can never destroy our name; the Jewish People, His eternal nation. In the words of the Prophets: "So said Hashem, Who placed the sun to illumine by day, and established the laws of the moon and stars to shine by night; Who churns the sea so that its waves roar, Hashem of Hosts is His name: 'Just as these laws will not depart from before Me, so says Hashem, also the seed of Israel will not cease to be a nation before Me, all the days'" *(Yirmeyahu* 31:34-35). "For I, Hashem, do not change. And you, the sons of Yaakov, do not come to an end" *(Malachi* 3:6).

The *Yaavetz* writes in the introduction to his *Siddur*:

> How can it be that one who denies Divine Providence does not stand in shame when he studies the uniqueness of our status in the world? We are a nation long exiled, a "dispersed lamb" from early times. After all the sorrows and changes we have endured for two thousand years, there is no nation as

persecuted as we are. Many and mighty are those who rose to annihilate and destroy us, yet they could not overcome us. What can the clever philosopher reply to this — that the hand of chance caused all these things? By my life, when I contemplate these wonders, they seem to me greater than all the miracles that Hashem, Blessed is He, did for our forefathers in Egypt and in the wilderness!

A hundred years prior to the Holocaust, the greater part of the Jewish People was concentrated in Europe. If, God forbid, the Holocaust had occurred then, it is doubtful whether any significant remnant would have survived. During this century, waves of Jewish emigration swept to the United States and other countries in the Western Hemisphere, South Africa, and later *Eretz Yisrael* as well. The hand of Hashem seems apparent, quietly ensuring that the Jewish People would survive their loss.

Chazal seem to have anticipated such Providence. Our sages taught: "If Esav comes upon the one camp and smites it' — this refers to our brothers in the south; 'the remaining camp will escape' — this refers to our brothers in the Diaspora." (*Bereishis Rabbah, parashah* 76). *Ramban* comments on the same passage:

> For Yaakov knows that his descendants will never fall entirely into the hand of Esav; therefore, at least one camp will be saved. This also hints that the sons of Esav will not decree upon us to wipe out our name. Instead, they will do evil to part of our people in some of their lands. In one country, one of their kings passes an evil decree against our property or our persons, while another king, in his land, takes pity, providing a haven for the refugees.

THE HAND OF PROVIDENCE seems evidenced by the unfolding of the war itself — indeed, by the very fact that in the end, the enemy was destroyed. Dr. Aharon Barth writes:

Winds of War – the Hand of Heaven

> Short-sighted observers do not understand that with purely human powers alone, the enemies of Germany would have suffered complete defeat. Anyone who did not witness this during the war years can read Churchill's memoirs, and his eyes will be opened. When

France fell, after Holland was already occupied by the Germans, England lay open before the enemy. In the opinion of the British chiefs of staff at the time, there was no realistic chance that a concentrated German attack could be resisted. And the Germans were always aggressive in war, quick to decide and swift to execute. But this time they hesitated time after time, until the opportunity passed and England managed to arm herself.

In the Middle East, a handful of troops, almost unarmed, stood in the way of the enemy. If an isolationist, rather than Roosevelt, had occupied the White House at the time, who knows how the world would look today? Last but not least, Hitler could have kept his pact with Russia peacefully for another year or two. If he had, he would have broken his enemies one by one. Instead of doing so, he attacked the giant, and thereby brought unity between his eastern and western opponents during those decisive years.

Human beings put themselves at the disposal of a specific Divine goal. The Holy One, Blessed is He, uses them, and this cooperation leads to the accomplishment of the Divine aim. Churchill himself understood this. In volume 3 of his memoirs, chapter 15, he writes the following, concerning [his] unexpected success:

"Certainly it was unexpected, but again I felt — forgive me for saying so — that I was serving as the instrument, albeit unworthy, of the plan of Providence" (*Doreinu Mul She'elot Hanetzach*, Jerusalem, 5714/1954, pp. 94-95).

Dr. Barth writes further:

An American officer, Peter V. Reind, published the account of one episode in a book called *Pipeline to Battle*: On July 4, 1942, the last important fortification which had defended Alexandria, as well as Egypt and the road to Israel, fell. A fierce battle erupted between Rommel's forces and the British. As in previous battles, there was great danger that the forces of the Satan would win. But suddenly the Germans threw up their hands and surrendered. No one understood what happened, until the riddle was solved. The German forces had advanced up to the British water pipes. Thirsty from the burning desert heat, they had broken open the pipes and drunk copiously. As they swallowed gulp after gulp, they realized they were drinking sea water; for the pipes were new, and in order to test them without wasting drinking-water, the British had filled them with salt water. This scorching drink broke the strength of the German division and put an end to the battle. The officer who relates the incident says that this was the decisive battle in the defense of Alexandria, of Egypt, and of the road to *Eretz Yisrael*. Even if we do not accept his evaluation, who could fail to see this "coincidence" as a miracle from heaven, the finger of God? (ibid., p. 107).

In other theaters of combat, battles were resolved no less unexpectedly. The confrontations at El Alamein in Africa and Stalingrad in Russia are universally recognized as decisive land battles in the war. The German defeats in each of these conflicts were hailed as "miraculous" by the astonished world that witnessed them.

The rescue of individuals was no less miraculous. Let the reader question almost any Holocaust survivor, and he will hear a story so laden with hairsbreadth coincidence that the orchestration of events can hardly be denied. Noteworthy is R' Moshe Prager's account of the miraculous escapes of the *Admorim* of Gur and Belz.

ALSO DESERVING OF the reader's attention is R' Elchanan Yosef Hertzman's retelling of the miraculous escape of the Mir Yeshivah

The Shanghai Saga

to Shanghai, China. The saving of the Mir meant the rescue not only of its students, but of scores of other Torah scholars as well.

As such, the event was one of import for all of *Klal Israel*. R' Hertzman writes:

> We read in the Book of *Daniel* (9:14): "Hashem hastened the evil and brought it upon us, for Hashem our God is righteous (*tzaddik*)."
>
> *Chazal* comment (*Gittin* 88) that this refers to the Babylonian Exile. When Hashem brought about this exile, He took care — even at the time of evil — to ensure that the destruction and captivity would not cause Israel to forget the Torah.

Likewise, at the time of the destruction of the Second Temple, Rabban Yochanan ben Zakkai requested of the Emperor Vespasian: "Give me Yavneh and its sages" (*Gittin* 55). After the Destruction [of the Temple], it was from them that the Torah spread throughout the world.

The same can be said of European Jewry in the years 5700-5705 (1940-1945). The Holy One, Blessed is He, in His mercy preserved the majority of the *roshei yeshivos*, and thousands of their students. From them, Torah was disseminated throughout the world after the war. Most were rescued through Vilna, as will be related below.

On the eighth of Elul, 5699 (1939), only nine days before the outbreak of the World War, Hashem brought about the signing of the Ribbentrop-Molotov Pact between Germany and the Soviet Union. . .

This pact was odd from every vantage point. First of all, bitter hatred prevailed between the two signing nations. Each had declared the destruction of the other as its ideal. . . Also because of the timing: At the very moment that the Russians were engaged in serious negotiations with France and Britain concerning a mutual defense pact, they suddenly announced that an agreement had been signed with Germany. . .

After the war, it was discovered that the published agreement (guaranteeing that neither side would attack the other during the next ten years) contained a secret appendix. . . amazingly, there was also a clause regarding the city of Vilna. Both sides recognized the right of Lithuania to this city. The clause constitutes a "miracle within a miracle"— for we are dealing here with the greatest satanic murderers the world has ever known. In the midst of their plunder and division of states, they "recognized" that Lithuania — one of the very states they robbed — had a right to the city of Vilna. Such were the wonders of Providence in bringing about the rescue of the *roshei yeshivos* and their students. . .

It had been agreed in advance that on a certain day, the Lithuanian army would enter Vilna and receive control of the city. [But] on the prescribed day, not a single Lithuanian soldier was to be seen in the town. A few days passed, and still there was no sign of the entrance of the Lithuanian army.

The suspicion began to grow that the whole Vilna affair was nothing more than a trap for "traitors" concocted by the Russians.

When this suspicion was expressed to R' Chaim Ozer Grodzinsky, of Vilna, he replied: "Don't worry; not all the yeshivos that are on their way to Vilna to be saved have arrived yet. This is the reason for the delay."

And so it was. Day by day, more groups of yeshivah students arrived in the city. When the stream of *bnei yeshivos* entering into the city had ceased — only then did the Lithuanian army enter. . .

By Hashem's grace, among the jumbled groups of war refugees arriving in Vilna there were also *admorim*, *rabbanim*, and *bnei yeshivos* from German-held territory. An organized group of students came from the Lubavitch yeshivah of Otvotzk. . . a few students from various yeshivos in Western Poland also arrived. The *rav* of Brisk, R' Yitzchok Zev Soloveitchik, . . . gave his wonderful lectures, full of life and profundity, to an elite group from the Vilna yeshivos, numbering about fifty or sixty. . . The Admor of Modzitz, R' Shaul Yedidyah Elazar Taub, through special *hashgachah* also reached Vilna to strengthen downcast hearts and help with the rescue. . . in Vilna masses of the refugees partook of physical and spiritual nourishment at his *tisch*, and they packed his *beis midrash* from wall to wall. His wonderful melodies uplifted harassed and broken hearts, implanting joy and encouragement. . . a few days after the Russian annexation, the *Admor*, with the aid of heaven, received an exit visa to the United States. . . the rest of his household reached the United States afterwards, with the other refugees, through Japan. . .

During the winter months, when it was possible to leave Lithuania by sea, hundreds of Jews set sail for *Eretz Yisrael*. Among them was the Gaon of Ponivezh, R' Yosef Shlomo Kahaneman. . .

During this period, only a short time before the establishment of the Communist government in Lithuania, the consul of Japan arrived unexpectedly in Kovno and opened an office. The consul's name was Sugihara. This was a great peculiarity, for there had never been a Japanese consulate in Kovno, even in the best of times. And precisely now, when the area was already clearly on the verge of desolation — i.e. Russian annexation — a Japanese consul made his appearance.

At first, the consul had nothing to do; only when Jewish refugees began streaming to his office to get visas to Japan, he had his hands full. The consul remained in Kovno until around Elul, by which time he had stretched the limits of the possible in the numbers of visas he distributed — through astonishing means. And then he left Lithuania. Everyone saw with their own eyes the wonders of Divine Providence. . .

As soon as Russia annexed Lithuania, the order was given to immediately close the consular offices in Kovno. In spite of this order, the Japanese consul continued giving transit visas for another three weeks, as long as he remained in the city. His office was small, and within two or three days he could have packed his belongings and left. Yet, for some reason, his preparations for departure took some three weeks, and during that time he continued giving visas to the multitudes who requested them. All those who had been late, or who had hesitated to apply for a visa before the Russian annexation, now hastened to do so (*Nes Hahatzalah*, pp. 33-60).

In his account of the story, Prof. Bauer adds that Sugihara distributed visas without authorization from his superiors:

On the twentieth of August, an urgent message arrived from Tokyo: "Do not apportion any more visas." But Sempo Sugihara continued disbursing them, apparently no less than three thousand. Two thousand four hundred Jews reached Japan by means of these documents. After the war, the democratic government of Japan brought Sempo Sugihara to trial for violating the orders of the wartime Japanese government. He was dismissed from the diplomatic service (*Teguvot B'eit Hasho'ah*, p. 63).

R' Hertzman continues:

It is difficult to know what motivated his self-sacrifice in the cause of saving Jews from Russia. But [in his actions] we see before our eyes the working of Divine Providence. The Holy

One, Blessed is He, sent a courageous and very daring Japanese consul, and inspired him with a fierce desire to save the *bnei yeshivos*.

R' Hertzman tells of the Yeshivah's amazing journey to Japan through the Soviet Union, and of the thinly veiled miracles they experienced during their exile in Shanghai. In the scope of the present work it is not possible to quote the account in its entirety. We shall, however, cite a passage from the letter of approbation of the Mir Yeshivah's *mashgiach*, R' Yechezkel Levinstein, who led the Yeshivah during the period.

> The Holy One, Blessed is He, provided good counsel and fortunate circumstances in our journey from Mir to Vilna, and afterwards from Vilna to Kaidan-Lithuania. After that came great wonders of Divine Providence regarding [travel] permits. The central miracle, beyond understanding, is that the Russians gave us permission to travel wherever we wished. This stands in total contrast to their nature and to their laws. Even more, they honored us, considering us tourists. They reversed their law and procedure; instead of sending such "criminals" to Siberia, they did them favors; not being able themselves to explain these actions. This exemplifies what is written (*Mishlei* 21:1): "Like streams of water, the heart of a king is in the hand of Hashem; He directs it wherever He desires" (ibid., p. 6).

Not only was the Yeshivah saved, but the students drew spiritual strength from their years of wandering. Through perseverance in times of hardship, their potential inner stature as Torah leaders was nurtured. It seems no wonder that, both in *Eretz Yisrael* and in the United States, an outstanding number of the present generation's preeminent Torah personalities were among the "exiles of Shanghai."

D.

The Survivors

PPROXIMATELY FIFTEEN YEARS ago, a survey was conducted among Holocaust survivors in *Eretz Yisrael*. Its purpose was to determine whether the religious convictions of those who endured the Holocaust were strengthened or weakened as a result of their ordeals. The results were published in Reeve Robert Brenner's *The Faith and Doubt of Holocaust Survivors* (New York, 1980).

In the work, Brenner writes that most of those interviewed had not changed their positions because of the Holocaust. For the most part, those who were previously observant continued to keep Torah and *mitzvos*, and those who were non-observant persisted in their way of life too. Surprisingly, however, a significant minority of those interviewed indicated that, in the aftermath of their dreadful experience, they felt compelled to return to Judaism. Some explained their response in terms of gratitude for the miracles that had saved them. Others replied that their experience simply confirmed to them that there was no way to avoid Jewish destiny — that assimilation among the gentiles was ultimately impossible.

ACCORDING TO BRENNER'S survey, one of every four survivors who changed his religious position made the choice to become an

The Significant Minority observant Jew. Although this group represents a minority, the number is statistically deceiving. The author quotes a survivor of Bergen-Belsen who later became a teacher in Tel-Aviv:

> I and a number of survivors I know have become observant and good religious Jews because of the Holocaust. And it seems singularly impressive to me, the number of Jewish survivors who had formerly been non-observant and because

of the Holocaust became observant. I expected in advance that many observant Jews would give it all up, and in a way I don't blame them at all. The number of observant Jews who became non-observant is important, of course. But to me, far more striking and important are those who became observant, even if the number is smaller. It is connected with the idea of polarization and radicalization and of giving things up. For example, if a concert pianist undergoes a traumatic experience which may cause him to give up the piano and become a non-musician like the average man on the street, it is not terribly astonishing. It is rather expected and happens all the time. But when the average man on the street undergoes a traumatic experience and will feel the need to push for a direction to express his feelings by polarization, and by some extreme act, he doesn't suddenly decide to devote his life to becoming a concert pianist. That's not how he becomes polarized. He can go in many directions and express his feelings in many different ways. . .

Bu the non-observant Jew, were he to be traumatized and polarized, there's no earthly reason to expect that he'd become observant. He's just as likely to become political: a socialist, for example, or a humanist or anarchist. Or a vegetarian for that matter. Or what have you. Or if his particular reaction must be a religious one, he could even become a "believing Jew" but not necessarily an observant Jew. Or he can convert out of Judaism altogether. He could make a religious decision and become a Christian.

So the Jews who become observant, even if fewer in number, tell us far more about Judaism and about Jews than the other Jews who gave everything up (*The Faith and Doubt of Holocaust Survivors*, pp. 68-9).

ONE SURVIVOR OF THE Buchenwald concentration camp relates that the glimmering of faith was awakened within him when he

The Renaissance of Commitment

saw a group of Jews going to their death. They were singing and reciting the *Shema*. He concludes:

From the time I arrived in the camps and became religious, I was able to be less and less afraid of the oncoming death even though death peered at me constantly around every corner. My newly found faith supported me. And it still does to this day (ibid., p. 120).

It was not only those who survived the camps who became *baalei teshuvah*, changing their way of life to become Torah-observant; the same phenomenon occurred in the camps themselves. Heightening of religious sensitivity was not limited to previously assimilated Jews. Among Jews who had already been Torah-observant as well, there was at times, also a renaissance of spiritual commitment:

> Before the Holocaust, I was a simple observant Jew. Today I'm an observant Jew, but very complex, not at all simple. Due to the Holocaust, I can now say that every single religious practice I keep — and I keep most — is because of what I have undergone and witnessed and experienced during those terrible years. I observe the *mitzvot* now because of the Holocaust, specifically because of the Holocaust. I have now a clear reason in my mind and very deep motives for practicing Judaism — whereas before it was not as clear. Besides everything else, it's my revenge against Hitler and the Nazis.. it is spitting on their graves. My way of getting even is by practicing my religion, with fervor and enthusiasm. Serving God and the Jewish people and carrying on my father's, my grandfather's and ancestors' traditions. (ibid., pp. 58-9).

Even among those who did not completely return, the tribulations of concentration camp life often prompted thoughts of *teshuvah*. Dr. Viktor Frankl writes:

> In general there was also a "cultural hibernation" in the camp. There were two exceptions to this: politics and religion. . .
>
> The religious interest of the prisoners, as far and as soon as it developed, was the most sincere imaginable. The depth and vigor of religious belief often surprised and moved a new arrival. Most impressive in this connection were improvised prayers or services in the corner of a hut, or in the darkness of the locked cattle truck in which we were brought back from a distant work site, tired, hungry and

frozen in our ragged clothing (*Man's Search for Meaning,*
pp. 53,54).

"Be A Jew"

IT IS A HISTORICAL fact that, in the aftermath of their
experience, many Holocaust survivors grew to admire the Zionist
movement. The most obvious catalyst of this
response was a practical one; the overwhelm-
ing majority of survivors had lost their place in the Diaspora. Some
tried to return to their homes and previous way of life, but quickly
discovered this to be impossible. The *gestalt* of Jewish European
life had changed unalterably, and besides, stolen possessions and
property were almost never returned. In Poland *after* the war, an
actual pogrom was conducted against the few surviving Jews, and
this event did much to speed the exit of the Jewish remnant there.
For these reasons alone, many sought to come to *Eretz Yisrael*.

However, beyond this, it would seem that for a number of
survivors, the Holocaust was sobering proof that there is no escape
from Judaism; that assimilation is an exercise in folly. The
response drawn from this realization, however, differed by
degrees. Some returned to the complete Judaism of the 613
mitzvos. Others joined the Zionist cause, which for them
symbolized the concept of distinct Jewish nationhood. Hence,
whether their choice of Zionism was correct or mistaken is not the
issue. The essential point is that most who survived sensed, with
an authenticity of feeling drawn from the very depths of the Jewish
soul, that the Holocaust proclaimed a Divine call — "Be a Jew!"
For a few, this intuition led to complete *teshuvah*, while for others,
only to an awakening of Jewish national feeling. But the essential
response was the same. At its core, it was the natural response to
the Holocaust.

Recovery

A NUMBER OF Holocaust survivors were physically or psychologically impaired from their ordeals in the camps. Some twenty years
ago, the government of Norway agreed to pay
compensation to its citizens who had sustained
such injuries during the Holocaust. At the time, Dr. Leo Eitinger
conducted a survey among Jewish and non-Jewish Norwegian

survivors. His conclusions, published in *Confronting the Holocaust* (p. 196), are of interest.

Dr. Eitinger notes that recovery patterns of Jewish and non-Jewish survivors differed markedly. He observes that the physical conditions of concentration camps where Jews were held were more loathsome than those of other camps. Whereas gentiles were kept in labor camps where the goal was not eventual extermination, Jews were consigned to actual death camps. Hence, the recovery rate of Jewish survivors from the physical abuse they had suffered was much slower than that of non-Jewish survivors. He notes, however, that the psychological and social rehabilitation of Jews after the war was far more complete than that of gentiles. Presumably, this is because of the feeling of brotherhood and mutual aid among Jews. It also provides another confirmation of *Chazal's* statement (*Beitzah* 25): "Israel is the most fierce nation" — the intention being to spiritual fierceness and courage. Dr. Eitinger writes:

> The group of people who were able to mobilize the most adequate coping mechanism were those who, for one reason or another, could retain their personality and system of values more or less intact even under conditions of nearly complete social anarchy. Those who were most fortunate in this respect were the persons who, thanks to their profession, could both show and practice interest in others, who could retain their values inside the camp at the same level as outside the camp. The few fortunate ones were some doctors, nurses, even social workers and priests, as described by Kral [Betreisinstadt] in Terezin. They were more preoccupied with the problems of their fellow prisoners than with their own, and came through their trials in better mental condition than the average inmate of the camp. Only a tiny minority, however, had this good fortune.

It is interesting to compare these conclusions with those of the *Admor* of Piastchene:

> In "a time of trouble for Yaakov," sins are atoned for. Nevertheless, it is painful that one becomes more habituated to be aware of himself, for all day long he is immersed in

himself. . . Is it possible that people should beat him and he should not feel his body's pain? . . .All day long he must worry about his life, dangling by a thread, and about his pains and sufferings — he again sinks into self-absorption. . .

Now, in order to awaken Heavenly mercy upon Israel, and to mollify the harsh judgments, we must kindle within ourselves a feeling of mercy towards our fellow Jews. We must give them all we can. . . the very pity for Israel that we arouse within ourselves has an effect in heaven (*Esh Kodesh*, p. 103).

In transcending one's self, one gives life meaning even in the most wretched of circumstances. The one who genuinely cares for his fellow not only improves his personal psychological state thereby, he awakens the empathy of heaven towards his own plight as well.

Preserving Values — the Struggle

IN HIS BOOK, *The Survivor* (New York, 1976), Prof. Terrence Des Pres details the results of a comprehensive psychological study of concentration camp survivors. Des Pres writes:

In *Night*, Elie Wiesel records two moments of advice, two prescriptions for survival in the concentration camps. The first came from an "old" prisoner speaking to the new arrivals:

We are all brothers, and we are all suffering the same fate. The same smoke floats over all our heads. Help one another. It is the only way to survive.

The second was an anonymous inmate's comment:

Listen to me, boy. Don't forget that you're in a concentration camp. Here, every man has to fight for himself and not think of anyone else. Even of his father. Here, there are no fathers, no brothers, no friends. Everyone lives and dies for himself alone.

Help one another. Every man for himself. The conflict is classic, and nowhere more starkly stressed than in the concentration camp ordeal. For as soon as survivors wake to the reality of their predicament they must choose. They must decide which view will govern their behavior and their perception of camp life as a whole. In extremity the claims of self-interest seem sounder, more logical; and the second prescription —help only thyself — dominates the description of events in Wiesel's books: men fight among themselves, fathers contend with sons to the death. The rule of war was total, or so he implies. Yet Wiesel did not abandon his father, and the prisoner who gave advice was, after all, a man living in Auschwitz.

There is a contradiction in Wiesel's view of the camps, a contradiction which occurs so often in reports by survivors that it amounts to a double vision at the heart of their testimony. In *The Holocaust Kingdom*, Alexander Donat describes Maidanek as a world in which "the doomed devoured each other," but he includes another kind of evidence as well, for instance his near death from a beating he received for refusing to beat others, and the help he was given, when he was desperately in need of time to recover, by someone who found him a clerking job. . .

Reports by survivors regularly include small deeds of courage and resistance, of help and mutual care; but in the larger picture, the image of viciousness and death grows to such enormous intensity that all else — any sign of elementary humanness — pales to insignificance. And surely this is understandable. The element of chance was so pervasive, the moments of salvation so unexpected, that the power of human encounters seemed slight and difficult to make sense of. Shock was another factor; what impressed survivors most indelibly was death, suffering, terror, all on a scale of magnitude and monstrosity not to be faced without lasting trauma. Primarily, however, survivors stress the negative side of camp existence because their accounts are governed by an obsessive need to "tell the world" of the terrible things they have seen. This determines not only the type of material they select to record, but also the emphasis they give it. As a witness, the survivor aims above all to convey the otherness of the camps, their specific inhumanity (pp. 97-99).

DES PRES GOES ON to outline the wide gamut of mutual aid activities undertaken by Jews in the ghettos and the camps. The

The Need for Help – The Need to Help German regulations were designed to make life impossible. Jewish survival depended principally upon "illegal" activities such as smuggling food, or "organizing" items necessary for life in the camps. All these ventures became possible only through the cooperation of a broad network of people.

Some helped their friends by performing various administrative functions in the camps. Outwardly, they cooperated with the Nazis, but in fact, they saved lives. In Buchenwald, the underground gradually took over all the functions entrusted to prisoners in the camp. Prisoners working in the camp office supplied their fellow inmates with advance reports on "selections," and sometimes forged lists of those condemned to death.

Empathy was spontaneous too. Simple prisoners helped each other in moments of crisis. People gave portions of their own meager ration of bread to others. The ill were condemned to death; yet, sick prisoners were carried by others to the line-ups so as to conceal their illness. Thousands of weak, frozen prisoners were often forced to stand erect for long hours; to falter meant immediate death. In these ominous line-ups, there were those who would have collapsed were it not for the help of those standing beside them. Des Pres concludes (p. 136) "The survivor's experience is evidence that the need *to* help is as basic as the need *for* help."

DES PRES' STUDY CONCLUDES with an ironic twist: it was precisely the "lone wolves" who had the most difficulty surviving in

Physical Strength – Spiritual Resolve the camps. The many who sacrificed for one another gained by their actions the psychological strength and existential resolve necessary to survive. Apparently, an inner identity links the laws governing human survival with the moral imperatives of reaching out to others. Indeed, all were given by one Shepherd.

Prof. Eitinger, in his study cited above, confirms that those who became alienated from their value systems — those who felt that there was no longer someone or something to live for — were more easily crushed. He too, concludes that psychological fortitude was at least as important a component as physical strength in the struggle for survival.

Dr. Viktor Frankl writes along similar lines:

> In spite of all the enforced physical and mental primitiveness of the life in a concentration camp, it was possible for spiritual life to deepen. Sensitive people who were used to a rich intellectual life may have suffered much pain (they were often of a delicate constitution), but the damage to their inner selves was less. They were able to retreat from their terrible surroundings to a life of inner riches and spiritual freedom. Only in this way can one explain the apparent paradox that some prisoners of a less hardy make-up often seemed to survive camp life better than did those of a robust nature (*Man's Search for Meaning* pp. 56-57).

"A man's spirit supports his illness, but if the spirit is crippled, who will bear it up?" (*Mishlei* 18:14). The findings of Frankl, Eitinger, and Des Pres attest to what Judaism has long ago known to be true. One's physical being is animated only by his spirit — for in the end, only the soul is the essence of the man.

Dr. Frankl, himself not an observant Jew, concludes his book with a profoundly personal account of liberation from the camp:

> The crowning experience of all, for the homecoming man, is the wonderful feeling that, after all he has suffered, there is nothing he need fear any more — except his God (ibid., p. 148).

He continues:

> One day, a few days after the liberation, I walked through the country past flowering meadows, for miles and miles, toward the market town near the camp. Larks rose to the sky and I could hear their joyous song. There was no one to be seen for miles around; there was nothing but the wide earth and sky and the larks' jubilation and the freedom of space. I stopped, looked around, and up to the sky — and then I went down on

my knees. At that moment there was very little I knew of myself or of the world — I had but one sentence in mind — always the same: "I called to the Lord from my narrow prison and He answered me in the freedom of space" (*Tehillim* 118:5).

How long I knelt there and repeated this sentence memory can no longer recall. But I know that on that day, in that hour, my new life started. Step by step I progressed, until I again became a human being (ibid., p. 141-142).

❦ ❦ ❦

We too, have survived the Holocaust. In Nazi government offices, plans were found for the extermination of American Jewry. *Eretz Yisrael* was saved from German conquest only by a miracle. Hashem not only redeemed our brethren who were rescued from the concentration camps. He also redeemed us.

The duty thus falls upon us to sense our interconnection with the Jewish people as a whole. In witnessing the demise of European Jewry with relative complacency, apathy was once our greatest failing. Only through palpable recognition of the bond which binds Jew to Jew shall we succeed in escaping the numbing solitude of indifference.

8

Remember!

Remember what Amalek did to you.
(Devarim 25:17)

ECADES HAVE COME and gone. The specter of Nazi Germany is static and lifeless, frozen safely in the past. Judaism blossoms anew in other lands. As the last of the memorials is solemnly erected, we stand tempted to turn the page of history. The future beckons; but the obligation to remember the Holocaust compels us.

Many Holocaust survivors feel a profound need to tell what they experienced. Even while in the ghettos and camps, Jews wrote journals and collected documentary evidence, determined to preserve the reality of what would later seem a fleeting nightmare. Such efforts were destined to bear fruit: The Warsaw Ghetto's "*Oneg Shabbos*" group, led by Dr. Ringelblum, succeeded in gathering volumes of material documenting ghetto life. The greater part of this material was preserved and is now in our possession.

The goal of telling the world of the horror was often so powerful that it sometimes became the reason for life itself:

I felt I was witness to a disaster and charged with the sacred mission of carrying the Ghetto's history through the flames and barbed wire until such time as I could hurl it into the face of the world. It seemed to me that this sense of mission would give me the strength to endure everything (*The Survivor*, p. 31).

In the waning months of the war, the last prisoners of Treblinka organized an uprising. To liberate the camp was beyond their dreams — the fighters sought only to ensure that one or more survivors would escape to tell the world of Treblinka. Preparations for the revolt were painstaking, and continued for weeks. The prisoners well understood that most would perish in the struggle, but carried out their plan nonetheless. As documented by Des Pres, the rebels of Treblinka were not alone; their sentiments, if not their actions, were echoed by thousands of Jews throughout the Holocaust.

A feeling so all-encompassing must necessarily be rooted in the innermost soul. To witness injustice on such an enormous scale and then remain silent is to approach indifference. But to remember is to protest, and the sensitive soul cannot help but to protest with all his being. There are times when anger is a positive reaction too.

There are pragmatic reasons to remember the Holocaust as well. Even after the awesome destruction of European Jewry, anti-Semitism continues to be a powerful force. Only public revulsion at the Holocaust can help prevent its recurrence.

During the First World War, the Turks decimated the Armenians, murdering some one million human beings. The carnage was quickly forgotten. It is told that when Hitler was planning the annihilation of the Jews, his advisers objected that the world would not stand by in silence. The Nazi leader replied: "When all is said and done, who speaks today of the massacre of the Armenians?" (ibid., p. 48). We cannot allow such calculations to be made again.

"Let me become wise from my enemies" (*Tehillim* 119:98). Contemporary anti-Semitic groups invest great efforts to prove that the Holocaust never happened. This in itself shows how important it is that the Holocaust continue to trouble the world's conscience. The pangs of conscience were among the main reasons why we were given independent nationhood, and they continue to exert an influence to this day.

But there are other reasons why we must not forget. We are obligated to remember the Holocaust just as we are required to identify with all Jewish history. *Ahavas Yisrael* — loving and identifying with the Jewish People — is a concept whose application is not confined to those Jews who are alive with us today. On Tisha B'Av we mourn not only for the Temple, but lament the massacres of 5408-9 (1648-9) and 4856 (1096) also. As for the Holocaust — not even a full generation has passed since its occurrence; survivors of the concentration camps and ghettos are still among us. Had Hitler succeeded, we too would not be alive today. Even one who is indifferent towards history in general cannot help but take to heart events which directly affect him.

Unfortunately, the reality is that the Holocaust is already being quietly forgotten. R' Michoel Dov Ber Weissmandl writes the following in his introduction to his *Min Hameitzar*:

> Thirteen years have passed since the completion of the destruction. Silence has descended upon the world, and there is no one to raise an alarm. The wicked are successful in their attempt to gloss over in silence the murder they committed. They have even succeeded in erasing its memory from the heart of the Jewish People themselves.
>
> This is no simple forgetfulness, but a profound, devious neglect, one bought with a penny of ransom money. [The reference is to German reparations to Holocaust survivors.] And this forgetfulness grows stronger day by day. It will be no wonder if, while we still live, our sons and grandsons deny everything before our faces when we grow old. They may say, "Perhaps they accidentally killed a thousand Jews during the tragic course of the war, and this foolish old man has got thousands confused with millions, and adults confused with infants, and accident confused with deliberate murder."
>
> And yet — what can we do? Cry murder and lament all day long? How could it be so? And is it possible for people of flesh and blood to compress within their limited speech the

enormity of the murderers' wickedness, or the profundity of the injustice done to the murdered nation?

Just as their trial is reserved for the great day of judgment, and is beyond any punishment that can be meted out by flesh and blood, so too, their lament is reserved for a prophet — as the lamentation over the earlier Destruction of Israel was reserved for the prophet Yirmeyahu, may peace be upon him. Undoubtedly their lamentation is reserved for the book of the *Mashiach*. . .

During the war years, when news of the murder's dimensions reached *Eretz Yisrael*, *rabbanim* declared a day of public fasting and prayer for the Jews of Europe. However, an annual day of remembrance was not at that time established. The Chief Rabbinate later proclaimed the tenth of *Teves* as a day on which *Kaddish* would be recited for Holocaust victims whose day of death or burial was unknown. This, however, is not a day of Holocaust remembrance *per se*.

Concurrently, the legislature of the State of Israel established a "Remembrance Day for the Holocaust and Heroism" on the twenty-seventh of Nissan. Such a proposal, put forward by a secular law-making body, carried no halachic force. For several reasons, the motion aroused a degree of resentment among the religious public. For one, the *Halachah* explicitly prohibits lamentation during the month of Nissan. Secondly, the day of commemoration, chosen to coincide with the anniversary of the Warsaw Ghetto uprising, was felt to place an exaggerated emphasis on "heroism" over "Holocaust."

Yet, no halachic day of remembrance or fasting has been established instead. Why?

Immediately after the Holocaust, the *Chazon Ish* wrote the following:

> Matters of *halachah* are fixed according to the Torah. The main principles are found in the Written Torah, with the explanation given by the Oral Torah. A prophet is not allowed to give any new law, unless a basis is found for it in the Torah. And just as the removal of a *mitzvah* constitutes a deviation from the Torah, so does the addition of a *mitzvah*.

On this basis, one must consult a halachic authority to determine whether we are obligated to observe seven days of mourning for the dreadful catastrophes that have come upon us. If we are so obligated, we do not need anyone's approval. If we are exempt, then we have already been commanded to act accordingly, for this exemption comes from the Torah, and "to obey is better than to sacrifice" (I *Shmuel* 15:23). . .

Likewise, the establishment of a fast day for all future generations is included in the category of Rabbinic enactments. Those fast days which we observe have come down to us from the time when there was still prophecy. How could we — a generation whose best recourse is silence — be so brazen as to consider establishing things for all future generations? (*Kovetz Igros Chazon Ish*, Part 1, *siman* 97).

Pe'er Hador quotes R' Binyamin Mendelson who tells of a conversation he had with the *Chazon Ish*. The latter said:

The catastrophes that have happened now were beyond the course of nature. . . Some believe, following their subjective personal understanding, that an eternal fast day should be established. . . Only the prophets were capable of establishing fast days. . . It is not within our power to institute laws.

R' Mendelson asked: "Why did the *Taz* [author of *Turei Zahav*, a commentary on *Shulchan Aruch*] institute a fast on the twentieth of Sivan in commemoration of the massacres of 5408-9 (1648-9), which certainly did not reach the dimensions of the catastrophes of our day?" The *Chazon Ish* replied:

First of all, this is not explicitly written by the *Taz*. . . Second, we are not on the level of the *Taz*. . . Generations which will follow us will be better than our generation, and we do not have the ability to institute laws for them. . . (*Pe'er Hador*, Part 3, pp. 124-5; and see the notes there).

In analyzing the *Chazon Ish*'s argument, we shall discover three essential points:

First: The scholars of our generation are not empowered to enact eternal laws.

Second: The purpose of the fast days which have been

established is to inspire *teshuvah* (repentance); the fast itself is not the essence. When the people of Yeshayahu's generation asked Hashem, "Why have we fasted and You have not seen, afflicted our souls and You have not acknowledged?" the Prophet answered: "Even on the day of your fast you seek your needs, demanding payment from your debtors. You fast to argue and fight, to hit with wicked fists. You do not fast as the day requires, to make your voice heard in heaven. . . .Rather, this is the fast that I favor: Untie the bonds of wickedness; disband the groups who pervert justice and set free the oppressed; sever every dishonest judgment. Rather, slice your bread for the hungry, and bring home the downcast poor; when you see the naked, clothe him — do not ignore your own flesh" (*Yeshayahu* 58:3-7). Although the *Chazon Ish* does not state the point outright, his opinion would seem to be that in our generation, there is little chance that such a fast would be fulfilled properly. If so, it is preferable to avoid its establishment.

The third point concerns the words "The generations which will follow us will be better than our generation." His intention would seem to be that complete *teshuvah* and redemption are to be expected in the near future, and this will render an "eternal" fast day superfluous.[1]

The institution of a new law of this sort is impossible without the near unanimous agreement of the great Torah scholars of the generation. The opposition of such Torah giants as the *Chazon Ish* essentially annulled the possibility of establishing a halachically binding day of remembrance for the Holocaust.

Other suggestions of appropriate ways to mourn the Holocaust have been put forth. One proposal has suggested that one or more special *kinos* be added to the lamentations recited on Tisha B'Av. Recently a booklet of such *kinos* was published, containing lamentations composed by such notable *rabbanim* and *admorim* as R' Shmuel Wosner (author of responsa *Shevet HaLevi*), the *Admor* of Bobov, and R' Shimon Schwab. A number of great

---

1. Not all the sages of the generation agreed with the *Chazon Ish* on this point. See responsa *Sridei Esh*, Part 2, p. 53.

Torah authorities have agreed that these *kinos* ought to be recited in the framework of the Tisha B'Av service.

But this suggestion, too, has aroused opposition. R' Eliezer Menachem Shach (Rosh Yeshivah of Ponivezh and author of *Avi Ezri*) vehemently opposed additions to the *Kinos*. He argued that any change in the format of prayer would set a dangerous precedent, lending a false sense of legitimacy to wholesale Reform emendations of the service. Indeed, other Torah authorities who approved the recital of special *kinos* gave qualified support: They stipulated that the extra *kinos* should not be an integral part of those recited by the congregation. Rather, they should be said by each worshiper individually and voluntarily, so as not to constitute a substantive addition to the service.

From the above it is evident that, on the one hand, all agree to the principle that it is desirable to commemorate the Holocaust. The Jewish People have always remembered the significant events of their history. Yet, there has been no consensus upon fixed public enactments to this effect. Our generation has had to guard against the corruptive forces of so-called "reform," and the Torah leadership has been keenly sensitive to the danger of providing a semblance of precedent for non-halachic change.

The reservations expressed towards proposals of Holocaust commemorations, however, apply only to the institution of new public enactments. From the individual's angle, it remains clear that every person is bound to personally remember the Holocaust, and to mourn for the sanctified ones who were murdered. We are duty-bound to perpetuate the memory of the deceased, and to study the implications of the catastrophe. It is related that R' Eliahu Lopian would encourage his students to read Holocaust literature on Tisha B'Av, to palpably feel the contemporary weight of the Destruction and exile. We hope that the present work, too, will contribute in this direction.

A.

Great Is Vengeance

O nations, sing the praises of His people,
for He will avenge the blood of His servants
and take vengeance upon His enemies.
(Devarim 32:43)

Great is vengeance, which was placed between
two letters [two Names of the Holy One, Blessed is He],
as it is said *(Tehillim* 94:1),
קֵל נְקָמוֹת ה׳, "God of vengeance is Hashem."
(Berachos 33)

REVENGE. THE THIRST for it is the immediate corollary to remembering the Holocaust. Yet at first glance, vengeance of this kind is pointless. No amount of retribution will revive the dead. Furthermore, vengefulness is apparently forbidden by the Torah: "You shall not take vengeance upon, nor bear a grudge against, the members of your people" *(Vayikra* 19:18). However, we also find verses which seem to praise the concept of revenge against the enemies of Israel. Indeed, the *Gemara* states: "Great is vengeance, which was placed between two letters" *(Berachos* 33). Apparently, there are times when retribution is appropriate too.

WHY IS REVENGE, a quality generally considered undesirable, lauded when it is directed towards the enemies of Israel? The

Why Revenge? reason is apparent: In seeking to destroy the Jewish people, our enemies engage in active rebellion against the kingship of heaven. Their actions thus express a concealment of Divine Providence. Vengeance against the enemy, then, constitutes a revelation of

Providence and a restoration of Hashem's sovereignty. Therefore (*Tehillim* 58:11): "The *tzaddik* shall rejoice when he sees vengeance; he will wash his feet in the blood of the wicked." For through this vengeance, "people will say: 'the *tzaddik* is rewarded; there is a God Who judges the earth' " (ibid., v. 12).

THE THIRST FOR revenge upon the perpetrators of the Holocaust is deep. Even those long ago assimilated, Jewish in name only, felt

Historical Justice

a certain satisfaction when Eichmann was condemned to death. Had he died a natural death, the heart's inborn sense of justice would not have been sated.

For similar reasons, many feel consoled in the knowledge that, as a consequence of the Second World War, Germany suffered a decline in her international status. Part of her territory was annexed to Communist Poland, and as a result some nine million Germans were expelled from their homes. For two generations her remaining land was divided into two states, and a significant part of her population found itself under the harsh yoke of Communist rule. A non-religious Holocaust survivor comments:

> I do not believe in metaphysical historical justice. But we have daily evidence that crime has in it the seeds of forthcoming punishment, and that unpunished crime boomerangs on the criminals.
>
> Item: When the fighting Warsaw Ghetto begged for arms from the alert and combat-ready "Aryan" Warsaw, icy silence was the answer. What moral right of protest had this very same Warsaw less than a year and a half later when it begged for help from the Red Army across the river, obtaining in answer a similarly "political" silence?
>
> Item: What moral right of protest do the Germans have against the Berlin wall, they who invented this disgrace? Germany from wall to wall — this certainly has its irony (*The Geography of Hell*, an article in *Out of the Whirlwind*, p. 66).

While there are those who have similar feelings regarding the suffering of Eastern Europe's populations under Communism, others point out that the retribution against those responsible for the Holocaust is far from complete. West Germany is today one of the wealthiest nations in the world. A number of the Holocaust's most notorious murderers, Dr. Mengele, Martin Bormann and others, were never brought to justice. Of the other thousands of Nazi criminals, many were never tried in earthly courts. Of the few who were, most received relatively lenient sentences. The giant cartels which exploited Jewish slave laborers were never required to pay compensation.

It is not within our power to fully understand why the wicked elude the clutches of earthly justice. Whether in reference to the Holocaust specifically or to history generally, the intricate workings of the Divine shall always escape the mortal grasp. We can only be assured that "He certainly will not acquit" (*Shemos* 34:7) — if nothing else, in the ultimate accounting those who committed injustice will not go unpunished. In discussing retribution upon Germany, however, we may perhaps be permitted one speculative thought:

The *Gemara* (*Bava Basra* 4) states that Nevuchadnetzar's punishment for destroying the First Temple was delayed because he gave charity (*tzedakah*) to the Jewish poor. Perhaps in our day, too, the punishment of the wicked has been postponed for similar reasons — possibly because of the compensation paid to Holocaust victims.[1]

MANY TORAH LEADERS were opposed to accepting German reparations. R' Yitzchak Meir Levin, leader of Agudath Israel,

The Implication of Forgiveness

argued at the time that any compensation agreement would be "*viedergutmachen*" — an implication of forgiveness. Others countered that reparations were simply a legitimate return of stolen Jewish property. Whatever the motivation, however, the payment of compensation has had its practical effects: It has influenced masses of world Jewry to once again accept the German people with admiration, or at least with indifference. The State of Israel currently maintains diplomatic relations with Germany, and many Jews do business with

---

1. See also *Midrash Esther Rabbah, parashah* 1, para. 1.

Germans, or innocuously tour Deutschland as if nothing was ever amiss. As mentioned earlier, R' Weissmandl associated forgetfulness of the Holocaust with the acceptance of "a penny of ransom money":

> Woe to the son who refused to take his father's name, who closed his ears to his screaming blood while he was murdered, and who even commanded his brothers to cause the *mitzvah* of his death to be forgotten from among his people. And by the law of the orphan [this son] accepted [his father's] inheritance from the hand of the murderer, ransom money, and with the father's strength, and with his fortune, and with his blood-payment, he turned his own inheritance, too, to ashes (*Kinah* on the Holocaust, printed at the end of *Min Hameitzar*).

THERE WERE THOSE who argued that Jewish leaders ought to enact a *cherem*, a ban, upon Germany — that no Jewish foot be

Cherem allowed to tread its soil. Such action is not unprecedented in Jewish history: It is told that the Jews expelled from Spain in 1492 placed a similar ban on that country. According to one tradition, the popular Jewish name Toledano means, "Toledo — no!" i.e. "we shall not return to the city of Toledo." The historical reality of *cherem* against lands of persecution is confirmed by the Pinkas [Record Book] of the Council of the Four Lands (ed. Y. Halperin, pp. 79-80): "After the persecutions of the year 5409 (1649), which were part of the massacres of Chmelnicki, a ban was enacted throughout the whole land of Lithuania, Poland, and Turkey not to dwell in the land of the Ukraine." It is not entirely clear, however, whether these two bans (following the disasters of 1492 and 1648-9) were ever actually effected.

In the halachic realm, the sages of our generation have tended to rule that no *cherem* of a strictly legal sense exists upon Germany. (See responsa *Tzitz Eliezer*, part 5, *siman* 17, and responsa *Kol Mevasser*, Part 1, *siman* 13.) However, even if no actual prohibition is involved, one cannot help but view with distaste the maintenance of convivial relations with our brothers' murderers.

B.

History's Pawns — Free Will and Providence

THE HOLOCAUST HAS served to re-ignite an age-old philosophical quandary. Believing Jews trust that history lies in God's hands, that Providence guides events both great and small. Thus, no matter what the ultimate reasons for the destruction of European Jewry, one thing remains clear: the Nazis were nothing but the pawns of Divine Providence. Apparently, the agents of history's global designs cannot help but carry out destiny. If the Nazis seemingly acted without free will, the question then becomes, why ought they be punished?

IT IS ONLY THE context of this question that is new. The essential problem has been posed by Jewish thinkers throughout the ages.

An Ancient Quandary In his discussion of the Jewish nation's first exile in Egypt, *Rambam* writes:

> It is written in the Torah (*Bereishis* 15:13): "They [*Bnei Yisrael*] will serve them, and they [a foreign nation] will afflict them." If so, Hashem decreed upon the Egyptians that they must do evil... why then, did He punish them?" (*Hilchos Teshuvah* 6:5).

The answers offered by the Torah's commentators vary. *Rambam* himself states:

> The same [principle of free will] applies to the Egyptians. Among those Egyptians who victimized Israel, any particular individual had the option of refraining from doing harm if he so wished. For the decree was not upon any given person, but was to inform [Avraham] that eventually his descendants would be enslaved in a foreign land (ibid.)

IN OTHER WORDS, God had decreed that on a national level, Israel would be enslaved in Egypt. On an individual level however,

The Nation and the Individual

free will still reigned: Each particular Egyptian retained the choice of whether to take part in the injustice. As applied to the Holocaust, *Rambam's* understanding of the Egyptian scenario provides a near-perfect analogy. No individual German, Ukrainian, or Pole found himself compelled to take part in the slaughter of the Jews. All who did thus bear full responsibility for their crimes.

Other approaches exist as well. *Ramban*, in his commentary to *Bereishis* 15:13, writes:

> Know and understand: If on Rosh Hashanah a man is signed and sealed to be killed, this does not excuse the bandit who murders him, simply because he carried out what was decreed to happen to this man. He [the victim] was a wicked man who died for his sin; but the murderer must pay the price for his blood.

RAMBAN CONTENDS THAT intent is the determining factor. Had Pharaoh intended to fulfill Hashem's decree in his enslavement of

A Question of Intent

Bnei Yisrael, he would not have been punished for doing so. But such was not his objective. *Ramban* declares:

> For he intended to sin, and it was a sin for him. Likewise, the verse says of Sancheriv [leader of Ashur]: "Ho, Ashur, the rod of My wrath, and My anger is a staff in his hand. I will send him upon a sycophantic nation [Israel], and upon a people who have angered Me I shall command him." Then it goes on to say: "But this [to act as My agent] is not what he [Ashur] imagined, nor did his heart think this; rather, annihilation was in his heart" (*Yeshayahu* 10:5-7). Therefore He punished him in the end.

Even when a given situation is pre-determined, *Ramban* points out that one's thoughts, if not his actions, always remain fully within his control. At all times, one freely chooses whether to act with evil intent or with the desire to fulfill Hashem's wishes. Upon the basis of this choice, reward and punishment are fittingly bestowed.

Ramban also advances other arguments to justify the punishment of the Egyptians:[1]

> . . .[they] added more evil, for they cast [Jewish] sons into the river, embittered their lives, and planned to eradicate their name. . . and it is clear that throwing their sons into the river is not included within [God's decree], "they will serve them, and they will afflict them." Rather, this was an attempt to uproot them totally.

Ramban finds support for his position in *Zechariah* (1:14-15): "I shall punish zealously on behalf of Jerusalem and Zion, with great zeal; and I am angered greatly against the placid nations; for I was mildly angry [at Israel], and they aided the evil" [i.e., they added to it]. In this too, Nazi Germany remains culpable. If the Germans were pawns of Divine Providence, they were still given no license to exceed their charge. In reveling in sadism, the Nazis brought upon themselves the ultimate weight of responsibility for their actions.[2]

---

1. Also see *Raavad* in his glosses on *Rambam*, *loc. cit*.

2. For a more detailed treatment of this topic, see *Michtav Me'Eliyahu*, Part 4, pp. 93-98.

C.

Writing the Historical Record

THE HOLOCAUST OCCURRED half a century ago. Books have been written, testimony has been gathered, photographs have been preserved. Yet, for all this, there is no single, unequivocal account of the Holocaust. Historians bring subjectivity as well as scholarship to their work,

Scholarship and Subjectivity and each views events through the prism of his world view. As the *Chazon Ish* warns, the historical record is by no means immune to inaccuracy:

> History books accumulate many falsehoods. Indeed, people by nature do not hate inaccuracy; many love and court it. Hence the sage must carefully sift through the stories he reads, accepting truth and discarding falsehoods (*Sefer Chazon Ish, Emunah Uvitachon* 1:8).

PRESENTLY, NEO-NAZI GROUPS across the globe deny the very existence of a Holocaust. The destruction of European Jewry is

The Fantastic Lie touted as a Jewish myth, foisted upon the world to wrest reparations from Germany, or to enlist support for the Zionist cause. Proponents of this fantastic lie even include university professors. It recently became known that a French university student earned his doctorate in history by writing a dissertation which "proved" that the Holocaust never took place. Only after a storm of public protest was the university's decision to grant the doctorate canceled.

The relative success of neo-Nazi groups seems odd. How is it possible to spread effectively such an outrageous and easily refuted lie? The truth is, of course, that the phenomenon of the "big lie" has convinced masses before. As a propaganda technique, it was perfected by Goebbels, and was used with devastating success during the Holocaust itself. Even in hindsight, the fact of genocide remains an almost incomprehensible reality.

R' Yaakov Yisrael Kanievsky — the "Steipler"— writes the following:

> One might ask: How is it possible that totally worthless claims — nonsensical inventions — could be accepted by thousands and millions, among them talented and educated people?
>
> Know that the force of education and propaganda is extremely powerful. Not suddenly are nonsensical lies accepted, but in gradual stages. . .
>
> At first, this type of thing is taught to the children of a given region by means of entertainment appropriate and interesting to a child's imagination. Little by little, [the lies] are spread from region to region and from country to country, being taught in the form of children's stories. The children grow up, and the thing is already implanted in their hearts as absolute truth. Afterwards, this is used as a proof: The claim must be true and correct, they argue; otherwise, how could so many thousands and tens of thousands of people agree upon it. . .?
>
> Here is [an] example: About thirty years ago in Germany, a certain worthless person arose, a completely wicked man. Together with other worthless and irresponsible people, he founded a party called the Nazis. They claimed that the cursed Germans were a superior race, and that the Jews were a contemptible people which must be eradicated from the world. Within the space of ten years, he changed the consciousness and thought processes of tens of thousands and millions of people, both in his country and outside it. They believed that all this was absolutely true and just, and . . .annihilated millions of Jews with all kinds of tortures and sufferings. They committed these atrocities with pleasure and complete equanimity. Finally, Hashem mercifully left a remainder of the House of Israel, and that wicked man became entangled in war with other states and met his end. So, Hashem, may all Your enemies be destroyed.
>
> Now, Germany for a number of generations had been an extremely cultured nation; its government [had been] fair to

every person. Yet within a period of some ten years they turned into the most terrible and fearsome destroyers, believing with complete faith that the opinions of [Hitler] were correct and just beyond all question. The majority of the educated and the intellectuals were also swept along by this, eagerly taking part in the wickedness. All this was the fruit of evil and constant propaganda, day after day (*Chayei Olam*, pp. 36-37).

The Nazis themselves understood that to succeed they must hide their scheme of extermination from the world. The process of genocide was carried out in complete secrecy. Later in the war, the Nazis even sought to conceal all trace of the death camps. To this end, they exhumed thousands of bodies and ground them to dust, so that no evidence of the murder would remain.

THERE IS NO SHORTAGE of methods available to distort the historical record. Another contemporary propaganda technique **A Second** actually emphasizes the crimes of the Nazis, but **Method** ignores that these crimes were directed against the Jews as a religious/racial group, and not just as human beings. Their history texts read, for example, that a given amount of "Polish citizens" or "Soviet citizens" were murdered, as if to imply that the slaughter of Polish communities for opposing the Nazi regime is equivalent to the murder of Jews for being Jews.

This latter method has been used particularly by Communist historians, whose ideology dictates that there is no such thing as a "Jewish nation" *per se*. It is true, of course, that during the Second World War, Stalin tried to enlist support from American Jews by stressing the Jewish factor in the war; to this end, he established a "Jewish Anti-Fascist Committee." Later, however, every effort was made to blur the Jewish aspect of the war.

Communist historians also gloss over the fact that the Soviets signed a pact with the Nazis, and only joined the war against Germany after they were themselves attacked by Hitler. Similarly, Communist propaganda makes no mention of the direct participation of the Russians in the Holocaust, the aid given by many

Ukrainians in the murder of Jews, or of the thousands of Jews who fled into the forests of Poland, only to be killed by partisan units under the command of the Soviet military.

The lies of omission do not stop here. Communist historians have not acknowledged that the Nazi propaganda techniques, organizational schemes, and methods of terror were borrowed from the Soviet repertoire. Neither is it officially recorded that Stalin was himself responsible for the murder of millions, many of whom were Jews. According to Stalin's daughter, who later defected to the West, the dictator had at the end of his life plotted nothing less than a second Holocaust: the deportation of all Soviet Jews to Siberia. The "Doctors' Trial," staged in Stalin's later years, charged twenty doctors, most of them Jews, with attempting to poison the Communist leader. The trial was intended as a prelude for the eventual slaughter of Russian Jewry; the dictator, however, died before the scheme could be put into effect.

OTHERS BLUR THE Holocaust's uniqueness by comparing it with current phenomena. The attempt is made to draw parallels **Trivializing the Holocaust** between contemporary military conflicts and the Germans' systematic murder of an entire continent's civilian Jewish population. Some Jews also fall victim to this minimization of the Holocaust, drawing flimsy analogies between anti-Arab sentiment in the State of Israel to Nazi anti-Semitism. Whether or not incitement against Arabs is justified, it cannot be denied that the sentiments which cause it derive principally from a very real national security dilemma. Such discrepancies, though, are all too often ignored.

But it is not only gentile historians who trivialize the implications of the Holocaust. To a lesser, but ultimately no less dangerous extent, Jews are guilty as well. As noted in Chapter 6, Jewish historians, seeking to minimize the prominence of the Old World "exile Jew," place exaggerated emphasis on Jewish armed resistance to the Nazis. Beit-Tzvi, in his *Hatzionut Hapost-Ugandit Bemashber Hasho'ah,* discusses this historical short-sightedness in detail. He shows, for example, that the Warsaw Ghetto Uprising, valorous as it may have been, lasted, in active form, for no more than four days:

> What happened after this is commonly termed by establishment Holocaust historians: "defense of bunkers." However, these bunkers were merely hideouts. Their occupants did not "defend" them; they simply hid in them. To reach them, the enemy did not have to overcome opposition, but just had to discover where they were located. Once the "bunkers" were discovered, their fate was sealed.

The number of S.S. men killed during the "Uprising" was only sixteen. However, in the extensive literature which has grown up around the Warsaw Ghetto Uprising, the rebellion is seen as lasting several weeks, being conducted from inside "bunkers," and resulting in the death of dozens or hundreds of German soldiers.

Misrepresentation of the Holocaust is also propagated in the tacit claim that Holocaust victims were at least partly to blame for their own fate, for they "went like sheep to the slaughter," or "cooperated" with their murderers. These accusations have been leveled by such respected figures as Hanna Arendt, Raul Hilberg, and Bruno Bettelheim. The historical inaccuracy of these claims has already been demonstrated.[1]

In this author's opinion, Jewish acquiescence to the "sheep to the slaughter" claim forms a silent acceptance of age-old gentile stereotypes. The anti-Semite has long touted the supposed cowardice or dishonesty of the Jews. Likewise, Christians have believed for centuries that the Jewish People is condemned by its very nature to submission and humiliation. It is disturbing to see the fallacies of gentile perspectives so readily accepted by contemporary Jews.

From the distortion which Holocaust history has suffered in this half century, a need beckons for the composition of an accurate historical record, a record devoid of partisan sentiment. Such a history cannot be tainted by ulterior motive; it must seek only to

---

1. See above, Chapter 6, and see Dr. Yaakov Robinson's book, *He'Akov Lemishor*, refuting the claims of Hanna Arendt.

preserve the memory of our nation's bitter tragedy. Inevitably, the story it conveys will be a shocking one. It will tell of spiritual heroism and moral frailty, of the triumphs and failures of both Jew and gentile. The story will not be easy to recount, nor will it be painless to hear. But it must be told. We dare not forget or close our eyes to its message.

This volume is part of
THE ARTSCROLL SERIES®
an ongoing project of
translations, commentaries and expositions
on Scripture, Mishnah, Talmud, liturgy,
history, the classic Rabbinic writings,
biographies, and thought.

For a brochure of current publications
visit your local Hebrew bookseller
or contact the publisher:

Mesorah Publications, ltd

4401 Second Avenue
Brooklyn, New York 11232
(718) 921-9000